Expect a Miracle

Understanding and Living with Autism

2nd edition.

First edition formerly called, Expect a Miracle:

A Mother/Son Asperger Journey of Determination and Triumph

SANDY PETROVIC
AND
DAVID PETROVIC

Forewords by

Beth Anne Martin, Ph.D

and

Mary Jo O'Neill, M.Ed.

I

Your First Source for Practical Solutions for Autism Spectrum and Related Disorders

Exceptional Resources For Extraordinary Minds

AAPC PUBLISHING
PO Box 861116
Shawnee, KS 66216

Local Phone (913) 897-1004 Fax (913) 728-6090
www.aapcpublishing.com

Published July 2020 by AAPC Publishing

1st edition published November 2014 by Infinity Publishing.

Names: Petrovic, Sandy, author. | Petrovic, David, 1993- author. | Martin, Beth Anne, writer of
                   foreword. | O'Neill, Mary Jo, writer of foreword.

Title: Expect a miracle : understanding and living with autism / Sandy Petrovic and David Petrovic ;
              forewords by Beth Anne Martin, Ph.D. and Mary Jo O'Neill, M.Ed.

Description: 2nd edition. | Shawnee, KS : AAPC Publishing, [2020] | "First edition formerly called,
                        Expect a miracle: a mother/son Asperger journey of determination and triumph."--Title
                        page. | "1st edition published November 2014 by Infinity Publishing"--Title page verso.

Identifiers: ISBN: 978-1942197492 (paperback) | 978-1942197508 (ebook)

Subjects: LCSH: Asperger's syndrome--Patients--Biography. | Asperger's syndrome in adolescence--
                  Patients--Biography. | Autism spectrum disorders--Patients--Biography. | Autism in
                  adolescence--Patients--Biography. | Autistic youth--Biography. | Mothers of autistic children
                  --Biography. | Mother and child. | LCGFT: Biographies.

Classification: LCC: RJ506.A9 P48 2020 | DDC: 618.92/858832--dc23

THIS BOOK IS DEDICATED...

to Frank, with love—our husband, father, and rock. He provided the impetus to start the book and the support and encouragement to finish it.

to all our Guardian Angels who selflessly gave their time, talents, and support—starting with Steve and Craig, who joined us on our family journey.

to all people who have given David a chance.

to all people who are misunderstood.

Table of Contents

Acknowledgements

We would like to recognize and thank the following individuals for their contributions to the creation of this book:

Dr. Beth Anne Martin: a huge thank you for your unwavering guidance, support, and consultation—with this book and with David's needs. Beyond your valued foreword and critique of the manuscript, you changed our lives and inspired hope.

Mary Jo O'Neill: thank you so much for writing your foreword, evaluating the manuscript, and enthusiastically supporting this project. More significantly, thanks for your caring and astute interventions early on in Dave's education—and for giving him the cherished gift of theater.

Mark Avsec: thank you for your guidance, expertise, and generous gift of time—and for your belief in this endeavor.

Betty Kozan: thanks for your friendship and immeasurable support over the past twenty-seven years while you lived this journey with us! I am also grateful for your candid and helpful review of the manuscript and for your encouragement throughout this effort.

Kathryn Brock: thank you for your respected critique and suggestions for the first edition manuscript.

Don Trask: thank you for handcrafting the stained-glass art piece that inspired us over the years.

Danna Avsec: thank you for your marketing expertise and faith in our message.

Natanya Fleming: thank you for your editing and suggestions for the last two chapters.

Ellie Vayo: thank you for the photograph featured on our back cover, as well as for the family photo concluding our book (www.ellievayophotography.net)

Ruth Prystash: thank you for your expertise in the final editing of the second edition two ending chapters. Your recommendations and insight inspired additions that enhanced our messages.

Erin Yilmaz (marketing specialist at AAPC Publishing): our heartfelt thanks for going "above and beyond" to keep this project moving forward. Your support, advocacy, and expanded roles were key to this publication every step of the way! Thank you for your efficiency, warm professionalism, and valued communication.

Genuine thanks to **Kelly Stefanek** and **Steve Cavolo** for their mentorship and friendship. Their guidance in David becoming an educator made all the difference.

SPECIAL thanks to principals **Barbara Doering** and **Friederike Wintersteller:** champions who believed in me and embraced the teacher and person that I am.

and most importantly...

Frank Petrovic: thank you for your patience, sacrifice, and steadfast support (of all kinds!) in seeing this project to fruition. You made it happen!

Forewords

"I'm always going to have struggles, but with hard work, determination, and the support of others (as well as faith), instead of having a life I have no control over, I can have the life I've always dreamed of!"

Meet David Petrovic: a teacher, an inspirational speaker, a son, a brother, a friend, an actor, a young man diagnosed with Asperger's Syndrome (now categorized as Autism Spectrum Disorder). David's outlook may not have always been this upbeat, but his journey is one that will inspire and give hope to anyone whose life has been touched by a disability. *Expect a Miracle*, co-written by David and his mother, Sandy, offers a unique perspective and an intimate view into the lives of the Petrovic family. In the midst of two thriving careers and raising three healthy and active boys, their stable and predictable routine began to change as Sandy and her husband, Frank, noticed developmental differences and behavior challenges in David that they had not experienced with their two older boys. With some trepidation and a lot of resolve, Sandy headed straight down the path of assessment, treatment, and education, ultimately blazing her own trail to understanding, support, and advocacy for her son.

As a pediatric psychologist, I am often fortunate to be admitted into the lives of struggling but motivated families. While parents come to me for answers and expertise, I am frequently humbled by what I learn from them about commitment, acceptance, courage, and, most importantly, hope. I began working with the Petrovics when David was six and one-half years old. Bright-eyed, with a huge smile, and frequently in motion, David had his own brand of creativity and persistence! What another parent may have labeled noncompliance or stubbornness, Sandy and Frank accepted as unique features of David's Asperger's, to be shaped—not tamed. Never in denial when specific challenges hampered David's functioning, they chose to meet those challenges head on with honesty and collaboration, and always in a manner that aimed to preserve David's dignity.

The ultimate joy in working with the Petrovics over a ten-year span was to watch the unfolding of an active, dependent, and socially challenged little boy into a driven, mature, and social young man who is now carving an independent path for himself. Over hundreds of hours of teaching, modeling, and "social interpreting" for David, his parents have slowly but surely passed him the baton of self-advocacy. And he is off and running! Perhaps even more importantly, neither Sandy and Frank nor David has ever looked for a cure for his Asperger's Syndrome; rather, they have cultivated an acceptance of who he is, Asperger's and all, and promoted his courage to tell the rest of the world.

In David's own words,

" I can confidently say that I was/am living a life that I would not trade for any dollar figure or to be any other person. I am now comfortable in my own skin. I am comfortable with who I am."

— Beth Anne Martin, Ph.D.
Clinical Child Psychologist
Clinical Assistant Professor

When I first met David all those years ago, I was struck by the ability he had to impact those around him. At the age of seven, he had an infectious energy which pulled you into his orbit and invited you to stay. Everything from his facial expressions to his dramatic walk to his advanced vocabulary was supremely unique. In his wake, he trailed a pathway filled with light, curiosity, and intrigue. I did not hesitate in supporting David as he walked down his path, and I am honored today to not only write this foreword but to count David and his parents as true friends and allies in our collective journey.

The Petrovic family was introduced to me in the fall of 2000 when I was teaching a class of first graders with a variety of learning disabilities in a small, independent school. My class size was also small, and the one-on-one attention enabled me to truly understand David's learning style and connect with his parents.

Because of this environment, recognizing David's struggles with learning – and more importantly, recognizing his strengths – was straightforward. I was able to dig deep within the learning process and bring David's true talents to light. And teaching David was a thrill.

As a teacher, helping students learn and discover their strengths and talents was incredibly rewarding. However, I equally enjoyed the opportunity to connect with their parents. I took a sincere interest in learning about the dynamics of each family I served: how the house was managed, how the family worked together as a unit, and where they might have felt disconnected or unsupported in their journey. I made it my mission to help parents understand, appreciate, and support their child's unique learning style and journey in life.

I loved to sit with moms and dads and hear about their experiences with educating their unique children: what methods of delivery worked, which teaching techniques flopped, and – at the end of the day – how these parents just wanted their child to have the same opportunity to learn as any child in any school setting. Some parents were told that their child would NEVER read, or graduate from high school, or live independently. To my frustration and dismay, these types of "death sentences" were all too often rendered independent of any testing, screening, or formal assessment.

What I wanted these parents to know, above all else, was that it is never too late to change the footprint of a child's educational path. Together we would shed tears while mapping out a plan to cast light and hope upon their child's educational journey. Every one of these meetings was unique; however, all of our tears came from the same well. My goal was to give parents the proper tools, dogged determination, and eternal optimism to carry their children through school and beyond. Most of these parents were highly educated. They were accountants, bankers, doctors, and attorneys. But they were not educated in learning disabilities. Once mom and dad squatted down low enough to sit in their child's seat, the real learning began.

Sandy is a parent who took head-on the challenge to understand her son's path – filtered not through her own hopeful eyes, but through David's. Sandy, as much as David, became my student, and watching her journey unfold was truly a joy. She read, reviewed, and immersed herself in the learning process. She had an innate ability to recognize the difference between fact and fiction, and she understood how to advocate for her son while setting aside her own ego and interests. David's mother took a look down an unknown and unexpected pathway and turned herself into an expert. Where others saw roadblocks and dead-ends, Sandy found detours and unexpected walkways leading through uncharted, yet exciting, territory.

Reading this book, you will find yourself learning and reflecting on your own path in life. When you finish the last page, my hope is that you walk away with strength—restored, refreshed, and able to visualize your travels in a new light. Let *your* guardian angels carry you through your journey as you create your own pathway full of color, texture, and depth. After all, everyone's path has pavement, but not every journey is paved with such richness and complexity. Celebrate the uniqueness of your own path – as David and Sandy have celebrated theirs.

— Mary Jo O'Neill, M.Ed.
Licensed Intervention Specialist
Special Education Advocate

CHAPTER ONE

Why?

We are not scientists, psychologists, or education specialists. We are simply a devoted mother/son team who embraced this "trial and error" journey years ago with a relentless determination and tenacity that has not waned. Simultaneous with the realization that David had differences and special needs, I began my search for knowledge, for resources, and mostly—for hope. I was desperate for a guaranteed pathway of intervention and the assurance that my little boy would fulfill his potential and find happiness.

There was no such recipe or absolute promise.

What we did discover along the way, however, were countless guardian angels, both lay and professional, who added their support and special gifts to the therapies, programs, and resources we utilized. This combination, along with dedication and hard work, resulted in a truly miraculous and inspirational outcome. Challenges still exist, as they do for everyone, but David has exceeded every dream I dared to dream—and continues to amaze us daily with his steadfast determination to achieve his own dreams. The intentions and motivation for this book are numerous. First and foremost, we would like to provide the hope for others that we sought ourselves. Congruent with the claims of experts, our personal testimonials will exemplify that many skills and behaviors deficient in persons with Asperger's Syndrome* CAN be learned. We will show that self-fulfillment and happiness CAN be obtained. The diversity of Asperger's Syndrome is concurrently fascinating yet challenging. As emphasized by Drs. Klin and Volkmar, its presentation varies between persons, and therapies must vary accordingly (2). Because of this, though paramount to David's success, the interventions expounded upon in this book will not be relevant or effective for all. I defer specific therapy and education strategies to the writings and treatment of the experts, but we hope that *our* thoughts and experiences might provide additional insights or new ideas for the reader.

In my opinion, what *can* universally apply is this: with intervention, perseverance, support, optimism, and much advocacy, persons with Asperger's Syndrome (AS) can reach their potentials and thrive. Central to this premise is my passionate belief (and probably the belief of many educators and therapists, as well!) that families must work WITH the schools and service providers rather than simply leaving the education and therapy up to the professionals. Based on our own personal experiences, additional components essential for success are the fostering of good self-esteem in the individual with AS, preparation for change, and a continual sprinkling of humor. (Yes, the latter *can* be learned!)

Everyone has strengths, and everyone has weaknesses. It must be remembered that even typicals** have social skills flaws—no one is perfect, and *everyone* has gifts to contribute to the good of all. In addition, it might not be realized that not all the characteristics of autism are negative: there are some commendable and amazing features that are, in fact, coveted and treasured.

The previous statement provides me with the perfect segue to another purpose we have in writing this book. **Different** does *not* equal **inferior.** We hope to stimulate an epiphany of understanding and tolerance for those who are perhaps unknowingly prejudiced towards individuals with differences, with autism being one of them. We implore these parties to rethink their assumption of superiority and to give relationships a chance! Go beyond superficial idiosyncrasies to explore and connect with the person within—you may never experience more talent, sincerity, loyalty, or unconditional love. So much has been written about individuals with AS having problems with understanding the ways and perspectives of the mainstream. **This is my attempt to address the reverse.** We aim to educate and inspire the "typical" world's understanding, appreciation, and acceptance of those with AS/autism.

Autism expert Tony Attwood has likened people with Asperger's to those of another "culture" in describing their difficulties with others who are encountered (167). I love this comparison, for I do see many parallels that exist between these populations. As the saying goes, when in Rome, do as the Romans do. However, this is pretty overwhelming to do for your entire life—especially if one is alone and possesses rudimentary skills or unclear understanding. As is often said on return from a vacation, "It feels so good to be home!" But realistically speaking, even if the language is ultimately learned and the land and culture become better navigated, my son will always be a visitor. Attwood states that "special interests" can enable "order and consistency" and the chance "to relax in the security of routine" (among other benefits) (93-94). Thus, back to our analogy, perhaps David's chosen and beloved topics allow him that sought-after *home* relief and familiarity.

It's time you visit David's country. Things are not wrong there—they are, just simply, different! Perhaps you may then appreciate why persons with autism behave as they do in the "typical" world. Furthermore, you may then learn what can be done to help them function there more effectively without compromising the uniqueness of who they are. Dual citizenship IS possible! In this era of increased cultural sensitivity, let us include Asperger's Syndrome/autism!

In keeping with our travel theme, I am reminded of an incredibly insightful piece which I read early on in our journey and many times since. I share it with you now, for it is incomparable in its powerful and brilliant analogies:

Welcome To Holland

by Emily Perl Kingsley © 1987

I am often asked to describe the experience of raising a child with a disability – to try to help people who have not shared that unique experience to understand it, to imagine how it would feel. It's like this......

When you're going to have a baby, it's like planning a fabulous vacation trip – to Italy. You buy a bunch of guidebooks and make your wonderful plans. The Coliseum. The Michelangelo David. The gondolas in Venice. You may learn some handy phrases in Italian. It's all very exciting.

After months of eager anticipation, the day finally arrives. You pack your bags and off you go. Several hours later, the plane lands. The flight attendant comes in and says, "Welcome to Holland."

"Holland?!?" you say. "What do you mean Holland?? I signed up for Italy! I'm supposed to be in Italy. All my life I've dreamed of going to Italy."

But there's been a change in the flight plan. They've landed in Holland and there you must stay.

The important thing is that they haven't taken you to a horrible, disgusting, filthy place, full of pestilence, famine and disease. It's just a different place.

So you must go out and buy new guide books. And you must learn a whole new language. And you will meet a whole new group of people you would never have met.

It's just a different place. It's slower-paced than Italy, less flashy than Italy. But after you've been there for a while and you catch your breath, you look around....and you begin to notice Holland has windmills....and Holland has tulips. Holland even has Rembrandts.

But everyone you know is busy coming and going from Italy...and they're all bragging about what a wonderful time they had there. And for the rest of your life, you will say "Yes, that's where I was supposed to go. That's what I had planned."

And the pain of that will never, ever, ever, *ever* go away...because the loss of that dream is a very very significant loss.

But...if you spend your life mourning the fact that you didn't get to Italy, you may never be free to enjoy the very special, the very lovely things... about Holland.

I am still touched every time I read this poignant and thought-provoking interpretation, and I thank Ms. Kingsley for the comfort and perspective this piece has provided me over the years. Continuing with this frame of reference, I must say that, for our situation, my husband and I let go of "Italy" long ago. We have refreshingly found that nothing is taken for granted in Holland, and every victory there is so much sweeter and appreciated. As parents, our lives have been greatly enriched by our special detour around Italy, and we can't imagine life any other way. We have experienced unsurpassed joy and pride because of it and have been humbled by our journey.

Finally, it is my hope that this book may serve as an "orientation manual" to enable David's significant others (both present and future) to understand him as I do and to interact with him accordingly. As he approaches the developmental stage in his life when romantic and committed relationships begin to form, I am concerned that misunderstandings, unknowns, or idiosyncrasies could jeopardize their quality. The same holds true for the world of employment. Perhaps this book will facilitate communication of subtleties in order to minimize exasperation and maximize opportunities for his success and fulfillment on all levels.

Though each person with autism is distinct, we hope that there are select anecdotes in this book that resonate with every reader. Our hope is that others may benefit from our experiences. Following each chapter, the "lessons we learned" are a summary of personal convictions and conclusions. They are a subjective culmination of what I have surmised on David's unique life journey. In later chapters, many come from David himself. Some lessons were gleaned the hard way: they were learned from my mistakes or missed opportunities. Others took root from the people, strategies, and occurrences which positively impacted David's still-evolving success. Surely, readers will not unanimously agree with all of my decisions, deductions, or tactics, but I hope additional avenues for help or improved quality of life may be illuminated nonetheless.

NOTES

*Asperger's Disorder was identified as a diagnosis in the American Psychiatric Association's *Diagnostic and Statistical Manual of Mental Disorders, Fourth Edition* (DSM-IV™) in 1994 (75, 77). Alternate names I have commonly seen substituted are Asperger Disorder, Asperger Syndrome, Asperger's Syndrome, Aspergers, and Asperger's. For the purposes of this book, we will mainly utilize Asperger's Syndrome (AS) or Asperger's, per personal preference. **See the next chapter for the changes imposed by the DSM-5™.**

**Simply for ease in writing, I occasionally refer to individuals without AS/autism as "typicals," shortened from "neurotypical," as frequently seen in other works. I intend no offense with this categorization and hope none is taken.

In order to protect privacy and retain anonymity, names and places have been changed or omitted except for family, David's childhood psychologist, and his first-grade teacher.

The authors share their ideas and experiences with readers, but they take no responsibility for outcomes. The contents of this book do not replace medical or professional intervention.

~Sandy Petrovic

Hello! My name is David Petrovic. Now, like my mother said, we are not any kind of Ph.D. experts, but we do have some insight based on our experiences. I am writing this book because I want it to be a beacon of hope for typicals, families, and exceptionals alike. There are three principles that I've learned in my life that I want to get across in this book:

1. Don't settle for a life that people expect you to live because you have a disability. Go for the life that you "want" and don't let anyone or anything get in the way of you living that life; I didn't.

2. I am a person with an exceptionality (key word: PERSON). People with disabilities aren't mutants or other worldly species; we're just what we are: people! The one rule I've used in my life is the Golden Rule: Treat others the way you want to be treated. Simply, you're nice to someone, you get it back, and vice versa. At school, the office, and social events, don't be too quick to judge someone based on what you see on the outside. Take a chance to actually have a conversation starter. You may be surprised by what you learn.

3. **Everything happens for a reason!** It is my ULTIMATE belief that everything we go through in life has a certain purpose. Whether positive or negative, the experiences that life has to offer make up who we are as people.

Throughout this book, you will be getting the perspectives of both the mother and the son. My mom's views will be in regular print and mine will follow in italics.

CHAPTER TWO

Asperger's Syndrome:

What It Is and How We Approached It

What is Asperger's Syndrome? I reply to this loaded question during very confusing times, and the answer is not as simple or straightforward as one would expect. It seems that there has always been controversy surrounding Asperger's placement and relationship in the autism world. Throughout our journey, Asperger's was consistently considered an autism spectrum disorder. However, disagreement surrounded whether it existed on the less severe extreme of the autism continuum *or* as a divergent subset with unique qualities unto itself.

Compounding the confusion, classification was recently revised by the American Psychiatric Association. In May of 2013, the *Diagnostic and Statistical Manual of Mental Disorders, Fifth Edition* (commonly referred to as the DSM-5™) was published. In this updated version, the "diagnosis" of Asperger's Disorder was *eliminated* from the "neurodevelopmental disorders," and it was replaced by the broader diagnosis of autism spectrum disorder (DSM-5™ 31-32, 51). I will leave associated explanations up to the field professionals, but for the purposes of **this** book, besides speaking of autism, we often continue to refer to David as having Asperger's Syndrome or a variant of that phrase—for this is the designation he grew up with and incorporated into his identity.

Furthermore, I will proceed to describe the predominant characteristics of what was once labeled Asperger's Disorder, for I need readers to gain familiarity with the specific differences and challenges David embodied. This will provide a foundation for understanding the remaining chapters. I also seek to explain some of the common nomenclature of this field so that unfamiliar persons can appreciate the lingo utilized in practice, in the literature, and in select pages that follow. I have lived this Asperger journey for over twenty years and have worked as a registered nurse for much longer than that; therefore, the scientific, medical, and therapeutic vocabularies of these two adopted cultures have been assimilated into my own natural expression and writing. I will thus attempt to educate and clarify via explanations and examples—the same as I would personally desire from *my* chosen resources on computers or football— and the same as I have always done for David.

The following is not intended to be a comprehensive discussion. From what I have read, attended, and lived, this is my understanding of potential components of the syndrome historically described as Asperger's:

Asperger's Syndrome impacts a multitude of functions and capabilities. Some are readily apparent, and others are not obvious at all. For David, both the seen and unseen differences contributed to others' frequent misunderstandings and false presumptions regarding his true self. Despite typically possessing standard or better smarts, individuals with AS are often challenged with daily functioning due to the multifaceted issues expounded upon below. Summarizing the complexities in a word, this population is often described as quirky, odd, or eccentric.

Communication and socialization can be extremely problematic because of Asperger differences. Since these two categories share many components which overlap, I will address them together. Speech usually develops within normal time frames but may be awkward and inept in practice. Many people with AS aspire to relate with others but struggle with the mysteries of appropriate content and procedure. They seem oblivious to the regulations and decorum governing interactions (known as social rules); this differs from "typicals" who appear to innately know such information and skills.

Appropriate communication is further complicated by other common deficits. Those with AS are often challenged regarding the nonverbal aspects of language; they may not notice or decipher it in others, and they might not demonstrate or utilize it in self-expression. This group overlooks supplementary clues provided by others' gestures, mannerisms, tone of voice, or facial expressions. The resulting lost information interferes with the Asperger receipt of correct messages and adds to the likelihood of their improper responses.

Individuals with AS often see the world only from their own perspective and may assume that everyone else does, as well. Challenged in recognizing others' differing viewpoints and emotions, the affected person might not comprehend other people's situations or anticipate their responses. Hence, exhibiting sympathy or compassion may also be compromised. Furthermore, proper control and expression of their own feelings may be troublesome for those with AS.

Persons with Asperger's may not catch the meaning or suggestion beyond spoken words; they understand what is verbalized but may miss the real intended message. This literal quality negatively impacts the interpretation of many language forms; the understanding of popular colloquial expressions, cynicism, fibs, or wittiness may all elude grasp. The person cannot "read between the lines" (this widely-used phrase in itself exemplifies one such puzzling remark) and may appear deficient in common sense. Considering all the above, no wonder talking or mingling with other people can be stressful.

Several idiosyncrasies may be noticed when observing and listening to an individual with Asperger's. As suggested above, facial expressions, gestures, and so-called body language may be scarce or hardly varied. The person might exhibit an odd or blank stare or an unsuitable expression that seems out of place. He or she might not look a speaker in the eye. Speech may appear excessively proper, and the voice may have a unique quality or sound; there might also be an unusual lilt or pace, an unvaried rhythm or tone, and inappropriate loudness for the location or circumstance. David occasionally speaks with a unique accent and has been questioned regarding his region of origin.

When individuals with AS do talk to others, it is often about select matters which consume them. This concentrated and fanatical attention to chosen topics is a key component of Asperger's Syndrome. The special interest, as it is commonly referred to, may or may not change over time; its passionate study creates a proficiency that enables the person with AS to spout an ongoing litany of information—often to the listener's dismay. The individual may expound indefinitely, seemingly clueless to the other's reactions or cues. In addition, the person may talk in monologue fashion instead of conversing via a back-and-forth exchange. All the above can combine to challenge friendships and inclusion.

Those with AS are likely to perform and follow routines, as they have come to be called. Many sources go a step further and refer to some of these as rituals. Dr. Tony Attwood writes that habitual ways and behaviors may serve to achieve "order" and maintain sameness, thereby preventing the unbearable alternatives of ambiguity and confusion. A set "routine" eliminates chances for newness or alteration; it results in expectedness and can additionally help to decrease or deal with angst (99-101). Psychologist Teresa Bolick states that these practices, along with the "preoccupations" discussed in the preceding paragraph, allow the teen a little "predictability and control" in the midst of variability and bewilderment; consequently, she also concludes that "anxiety" may lessen as a result of "routines" (102).

Common examples of such behaviors include following precise routes to a destination or arranging items in a specific manner based on some criteria. For David, talking to himself with repeated recitation provided satisfaction, comfort, and relief, per his account. He would often say the same lines over and over again. David delighted in accruing and displaying complete collections, be they of toy figures in a series, juvenile books teaching various foreign languages (none of which he ever read), or later, assorted theater playbills. In a final personal example, David closed his bedroom and closet doors every night before he could wind down and sleep. Deviation from his routines and practices, or change of any type, was very stressful for David; he usually responded with resistance.

In addition to social and communication quandaries, individuals with Asperger's Syndrome often exhibit alterations in what the medical community calls sensorimotor issues. As this compound name suggests, differences may exist in this population's discernment of the signals taken into the body as well as in their movements and muscular responses. Speaking first of the five senses, some may appear underactive while others are potentially heightened; some stimuli seem barely noticed while others are magnified or cause apparent suffering. The diverse sensory experiences and responses of those with Asperger's may thus vary significantly from that which is typical or expected. Certain input may be desired and needed by the individual (like a firm hug or spinning around) or, in contrast, dreaded and not tolerated (such as feeling a tag in the shirt). Personal examples of these variations and their ramifications will be presented in the chapters that follow.

Shifting to motion considerations, three descriptions have been widely utilized to summarize the physical movements of persons with Asperger's: awkward, clumsy, and inadequately coordinated. This extends to certain bodily positions assumed by those with AS as well as to their performance of activities. Relative to peers, lags frequently exist in the age at which key physical abilities commence. Quite noticeably, the Asperger walk might incorporate an unusual spring or stiffness in the gait. Impairments may exist in movements or activities that utilize either large or small muscles, which the medical community respectively refers to as gross and fine motor skills. Exemplifying each, David experienced difficulties with bike riding and pencil grasping. Attwood discusses several other facets of movement that may also be impacted, with "balance," "manual dexterity," and "rhythm" among them (105-08).

Team sport participation can be a challenge on several different levels considering the vast variety of physical, processing, and social/communication issues potentially involved. Try to imagine other aspects of life that might also be complicated or impacted by the simultaneous occurrences of Asperger difficulties. Contemplate living with the added factors discussed in this chapter. Per Dr. Bolick, the day-to-day multifaceted strain can "lead to frank anxiety or depressive disorders" in "some" teens having Asperger's (128). This, then, must also be addressed.

These are just a sampling of the pervasive needs requiring attention in Asperger's Syndrome. Though no cure is available, there exists a wide range of therapeutic options to address many of these issues. Utilizing a mix of approaches and the specialized intercession of multiple types of professionals, a person with AS can take control over his or her challenges and lead an enjoyable life, which we aim to show. Additionally important and exemplified, our family dynamics and gratification improved as David's quality of life became better: we all benefited from our efforts and his progress.

Dr. McAfee describes the variation that exists in the AS characteristics exhibited from case to case, and she exemplifies differences in the intensity and impairment that may be experienced for each. Two people with Asperger's can thus be quite dissimilar based on their "unique" combinations (xxviii). Herein lies the challenge, for according to Drs. Klin and Volkmar, therapies must be equally diverse and customized to match the "needs and strengths" of each particular situation; this requires very complete and careful appraisal rather than stereotypic conjectures based merely on the given "diagnosis" (2). In addition, other practicalities and realities must be considered when formulating the plans, such as family resources and logistics.

Importantly, as I discovered, needs evolve over time relative to the person's growth, development, and changing life experiences; therefore, evaluation, planning, and intervention must also be ongoing and adapt to keep pace. In our experience, it is never finished: we continually search and strive to improve David's functioning on every possible level. But as the years have passed, I must also stress that many of his incredible assets and strengths have become apparent and helpful. This is the perfect transition to speak of the flip side of Asperger's...

Not all is negative! Persons with Asperger's are often gifted with extraordinary talents, which are more numerous than will be mentioned. Attwood discusses the astonishing "memory" that some people with AS exhibit. This may be of "photographic" type, or it may be the impressive ability to "recall" either an assortment of amassed details or early and remote past occurrences (116). Attwood describes the "visual style of thinking" that seems to chiefly take place in individuals with Asperger's: that is, the occurrence of "thoughts primarily or solely in the form of images" (125). This might explain their recollections or creative perspective and may contribute to their innovation (Attwood 116, 125–27).

Many renowned individuals with AS have greatly impacted the "science and art" worlds as well as academia and other fields (Attwood 126–27). On a less dramatic and more practical level, a person's dedication, focus, and knowledge regarding a favored topic could develop into a successful field of work. In David's life, his prowess provided avenues for gaining the esteem and recognition of others, and it also led to his personal fulfillment, as we will exemplify in the chapters ahead.

Bolick suggests that in viewing things differently, with thoughts free from the usual "social" confines, people with Asperger's might solve problems in ways that others have not considered. Exceptional artistry could also stem from this mindset. Furthermore, she describes the compliance and work ethic of those with AS as desirable attributes in the job or school setting (13). Clearly, Asperger qualities are advantageous in many ways, and they need to be more widely recognized and appreciated.

This concludes my brief overview in the hope that I've provided a basic frame of reference for the chapters that follow. I refer you to other official sources for additional information, diagnostic criteria, and causality. Strategies and methods for intervention are also abundant in the literature, and I urge their study. A multidisciplinary (educators, therapists, and specialists from several professions) approach was coordinated for David; we were blessed and privileged to learn and transform through the expertise of a stellar and still-evolving team.

Tactics that I adopted were influenced by countless experiences. Many were taught by our teachers and therapists, and some were gleaned from attended presentations or written sources. Sometimes, instead of providing new techniques or ideas, the writings of experts served to reinforce and validate what I had already thought, tried, or discovered. Various strategies were learned and applied from my own professional nurse training and practice, for I regularly utilized the following techniques as part of my skill repertoire during patient education: 1) requesting return demonstrations and/or explanations, 2) capitalizing on teachable moments, and 3) clarifying unplanned incidental learning. Some of my interventions were modeled from effective professionals working with us, and others came from trial and error, instinct, or input from David himself. Programs were discovered through research, networking (at seminars or with fellow parents), or simply by making phone inquiries.

This book describes our experiences as they unfolded in real time, and I thus cite some older, beneficial works which we read and used during David's varied life stages. Strategies mentioned are not all-inclusive; we definitely did not utilize every possible option, and additional alternatives certainly now exist. Still, David's customized combination was evidently good chemistry for *his* issues, and we invite you into our lives to witness "the before and after."

CHAPTER THREE

Infancy and the Toddler Years

D avid lit up this world in 1993; he was the product of a high-risk pregnancy and a delivery with additional maternal problems. He was born healthy, however, and displayed no perceptible deviation from normal. The youngest of three, he had two brothers; Steve was ten years old and Craig was seven. In addition, he was blessed with a loving and supportive father, Frank, as well as the most stable of family situations.

David's first year was wonderful and normal. There were no obvious developmental delays, and his socialization seemed typical. Early in the second year, however, problems began to emerge. While crawling and walking were age appropriate, he would not navigate on grassy surfaces if his skin would directly touch grass. He began to babble a little but used only three true words in his entire second year: mama, ball, and dada. He repeated certain sounds over and over (ah, ah, ah) and would occasionally thrust out his tongue. Play was not typical, and it was difficult to find toys that held his interest in the intended manner. Acknowledging that all children are different, we assumed that his emerging tantrums and extreme reactions were simply early and exaggerated manifestations of the "terrible twos." But in witnessing the behavior and development of his neighborhood peers, it soon became evident that we had a problem beyond the negativism of toddlerhood.

As the weeks progressed, David's language skills seemed frozen at the limit just described. And as he passed his second birthday, the more distressing issue was his escalation of screaming and aggressive behavior. Basic needs became a struggle to provide and eye contact regressed. He fought feeding, bathing, clothing, and diapering. I could not wear my glasses, pierced earrings, or any other items that he might rip from my body. It was usually a physical struggle to safely place and restrain David in a feeding chair, stroller, or car seat. On a milder scale and on many occasions, I felt much like Ann Sullivan battling over Helen Keller's dining skills in the 1962 film *The Miracle Worker*. It was exhausting, challenging, and stressful, especially in combination with other family and career responsibilities.

A benefit of their age differences, I was fortunate to have Steve or Craig available to keep a willing, safe eye on David while I hurriedly cooked or performed other domesticities. Otherwise, I would have accomplished little during his waking hours. Sensitive to his brothers' needs, appreciating their cooperation, and determined to prevent any bitterness, I tried not to over utilize their assistance. I resolved occasional desperation for more chore time by hiring neighborhood girls to occupy David while I simultaneously remained home. This enabled freedom to fully concentrate on desired tasks without interruption—a luxury well worth the cost!

We curtailed David's trips to church, stores, and social outings unless absolutely necessary, for they often ended in disruption and social embarrassment. David did not respond well in strange places or to attempted interactions by unfamiliar persons. My husband and I took turns to run errands separately, and we utilized the services of my supportive parents or extraordinary sitters to enable adult outings and activities with Steve and Craig. We joke, now, about how many of our acquaintances commented that they never knew we had a third child. However, to survive and thrive, such were the strategies we employed for the next few years; they helped us to cope, refresh, and continue the normal, necessary functions of a close nuclear family. Everyone's needs and desires were thus met, including David's. None of us could afford burnout or resentment, and we each contributed to make it all work.

Loving and peaceful times still existed, however. David was not always resistant to hugs or closeness, but when near my face, he often inappropriately attempted to suck on my chin or nose. David's comprehension of language spoken to him seemed age appropriate. We could still read to him, and he watched TV or favorite videos; he demonstrated understanding of this input and could correctly mimic some animal sounds when requested to do so (such as, "What does a cow say?"). But his consonant sounds remained extremely limited, and his verbalizations were basically meaningless babbling.

There were no new words; instead, he began to develop his own system of gestures to communicate. And he began certain ritualistic behaviors: he repeatedly opened and closed doors and lined up toys rather than playing with them.

Our lives changed dramatically at David's two-year pediatric examination. I carried him into the clinic, with his back arched, as he screamed and swatted at me. This had become our usual mode of transport, for he wouldn't cooperate by walking on his own. He fought throughout the nurse's attempt to gather preliminary information. Weighing him was impossible, as was much of anything else. Our physician could not examine him grossly, much less check his ears. Appearing exasperated, she ended the visit abruptly and said she was referring us to a multidisciplinary team, for we had "a problem." She recommended that David be evaluated by an audiologist, a speech therapist, and a pediatric psychologist. I was taken aback by the way in which she delivered her suspected diagnosis, but I was not surprised, nor in denial, at the message. Instead, I left the clinic in the same way I arrived—walking through the crowded waiting room carrying my screaming, combative son amid stares and disapproving glances from those who obviously thought that my child needed the discipline they could better provide. The only difference was that this time I had tears of frustration streaming down my face and a resolve to get him the help he needed as well as a new pediatrician who was more patient with my difficult toddler. I succeeded at both.

I immediately scheduled the necessary appointments, and David was thankfully found to have normal hearing. We then proceeded to the speech and language evaluation with the hope of gaining insight into his verbal delay and unusual, aggressive behaviors. As Frank carried our screaming toddler down the hall, with me trailing nervously on his heels, little did we know that we would soon meet the incredible woman who would change our lives and family dynamics forevermore. David finally calmed down as Frank cuddled him on his lap and drew for him on the trusty magic slate we took everywhere— David loved to watch the images repeatedly disappear when the top sheet was lifted. Eventually, the speech pathologist, Mary, was able to minimally interact with David without his resistance. Per cursory evaluation, we were informed that our two-year, eight-month-old toddler possessed communication skills similar to a twelve-month-old child, and a language disorder with several deficiencies was diagnosed.

Speech therapy sessions were scheduled twice a week, and a referral to the psychologist ensued to assess for the suspected existence of a wider-ranging developmental disorder. In addition, Mary recommended that David be enrolled in a special education school in the upcoming fall, for he would be three years of age by then. We were blessed to live in a community possessing an excellent public preschool early-intervention program, and we were thrilled with the prospect of this additional opportunity. While Mary confirmed our deepest fears, she also provided hope and guidance. Though it was the hardest day of our parenthood to date, Frank and I were never more unified in our resolve to regroup and conquer. And so we began on the long journey of therapeutic services...

Twice weekly, David and I made the trip to the hospital for speech therapy. Getting there was quite stressful in itself: the feeding, dressing, and transfers in and out of the car seat and stroller created many ideal conditions for resistance and tantrums. David was already too heavy for me to carry him long distances, especially with his needed paraphernalia in tow. I often survived the hike from the hospital garage to the impending appointment by half running through the halls in a most unique fashion: I would tip the stroller backwards on its hind wheels to balance the screaming, writhing child who was relentlessly trying to escape his belted confines. Thankfully, as the trek became more routine for him, the Petrovics became less and less disruptive to the surrounding hospital business—unless of course someone else pushed the elevator button to light up our floor before David got that chance. This frequent scenario then created another meltdown situation!

In the two months following our initial speech therapy appointment, David made substantial improvements in appropriate communication; as he became better able to express himself, he appeared less frustrated and was a bit more tolerant. At the pediatric psychology evaluation which finally transpired, a diagnosis for Pervasive Developmental Disorder (PDD) could not yet be stated with certainty, for it was too soon to distinguish this disorder from problems related to his language impairment. The psychologist concurred with our plans to continue speech therapy and seek specialized schooling. She further advised us to return the following year for reevaluation of David's status. Additional improvements in his communication eventually allowed for adequate assessment, confirming a diagnosis of PDD. It was further specified at a later date.

Mary was amazing in her interactions with David. She had a demeanor that calmed him immediately, and the journey back to the car was always so much easier than the harried journey in—especially with the hope I carried away from each session's progress and learned skills. Using bottled soap bubbles, which he loved, Mary reinforced each consonant sound by blowing bubbles for him. David initially remained on my lap, but he then sat independently while I faded off to a corner in the room. Finally, in time, I left him alone for therapy altogether and watched via a one-way mirror in the adjoining room. This was a glorious thirty minutes in which I could relax with a coffee and study Mary's approach. She worked on obvious issues that would impact his classroom success, such as staying seated when appropriate and improving eye-to-eye contact. In addition, she began years of intervention teaching David desirable behaviors necessary for socialization and reciprocal (give-and-take) play. Simultaneously, she targeted negative behaviors that were counterproductive to these goals. And of greatest immediate significance, Mary applied her art, science, and incredible talent to first teach David words, then joint phrases of understandable speech, and finally more comprehensive language skills. Frank and I were thus relieved of our justifiable fears that we might need sign language to fully communicate with him. Visits were eventually increased to one-hour sessions and continued for approximately four years.

Time has dulled my memory of tactics Mary used, and of course I am not trained in her field, but I tried to adopt some of the successful strategies I witnessed to continue David's progress at home and build on *my* intervention methods. I attempted to imitate her calm and simple manner of speaking. I copied her ingenious use of bubbles and tried to reinforce positive behavior utilizing them. We lived near a lake and beach, and I soon learned that he was equally intrigued with throwing stones into the water. So on warm summer days, while other toddlers played with each other, David and I were often found isolated on the beach; we would throw or skip stones in the lake following his successful repetition of a consonant sound or word. The peace of the sunshine and water usually brought laughter and cooperation. This provided an opportunity to bond, have fun, and deepen our loving relationship—wonderfully contrary to our frequent oppositional interactions.

David could tolerate the feeling of sand under his feet, but not grass, as previously stated. There were other tactile issues, as well. As he neared the age of three, he better endured bathing and dressing, but upper-body clothing had to be soft and could *not* be tight around his neck. Most importantly, all tags needed to be removed. He did not participate in dressing himself, for fine motor challenges existed. Quite frankly, we didn't encourage it. We were still focused on simply getting clothes on his body without a struggle; we didn't yet care about his independence. Washing hair, brushing teeth, and clipping nails continued to distress him and usually required the assistance of a second person.

Haircuts presented a major challenge. As if keeping still while wearing a tightly secured cape wasn't bad enough, the sensation of "pinchy" hair falling like needles on David's skin was unbearable to him. This was followed by intolerable itching during a ride home strapped in the car seat; a bath would then follow (also disliked) in the attempt to bring relief. Thankfully, my hairdresser understood the circumstances. I secured my writhing son in my lap for cuts and scheduled appointments for times when her shop wasn't busy. His poor behavior with this task escalated before it improved, which will be later described.

David did not like the feel of gelatin or squishy clay in his hands and had a very limited range of foods he would eat because of aversions to certain textures and tastes. He would eat soft and spicier options, but the temperature of food had to be moderate (he *still* lets hot items cool), and carbonation was out of the question. He used a tongue-thrusting motion to mash the food between his tongue and roof of his mouth, in addition to chewing, and this smacking motion caused eating sounds that were (and are) louder than usual.

Transitions continued to be difficult for David to handle. These included adjustments of clothing to match the seasons. As the weather warmed and long-sleeved shirts changed to short ones, he would scream and try to stretch his sleeves longer. Eventually, these issues resolved themselves and just had to be endured. Providing a choice of acceptable clothing gave him some control, but this also increased the time it took to dress him. I discovered early on that fifteen to thirty minutes had to be added on to the estimated time of each activity in order to prevent the added stress of being rushed or late. This would eventually allow him the necessary time to make choices and increase his independence and sense of self; personally, the added buffer afforded me the luxury of patience. This combination prevented situations from escalating out of control, which often occurred when David was pressured to hurry. Therefore, the investment of extra time was well worth the gains, but considering the preparations and travel involved, simply going to speech therapy would occupy most of the morning. Thankfully, he came to love going, for it presented an opportunity to play and experience positive interaction.

David's socialization with peers was minimal, for tantrums, limited speech, and his tendency to hit alienated him. I became his predominant playmate during that time and tried to exemplify appropriate play and acceptable behavior to him. Frank and I welcomed the prospect of a structured preschool environment and a multidisciplinary team to help improve both David's skills and our ability to interact more effectively with him. We juggled to additionally meet the needs of two other active sons and to be there emotionally, physically, and academically for them, as well as for David (and each other). A registered nurse, I worked on weekends and/or evenings to minimize the need for babysitting; David's routine care thus reaped the benefits of continuity from knowing parents. Hired sitters were greatly valued but were utilized to cover social outings rather than everyday needs (except for the brief interval between my evening-shift start and Frank's arrival home). Frank also gave 200% around his challenging career and other time demands. And so, with love and cooperation, it was all coming together. We had a plan and a professional team. And we looked forward to the next stage in our lives: the oldest starting high school and the youngest, with every prospect to improve, entering preschool.

I don't remember much from my toddler years, but what I do recall I'd like to share with you. I do remember always lining up my toys instead of playing with them; in a way, I was organizing them and "admiring" them. When I would go outside and play on the grass, I remember the prickly feeling against my skin that always bugged me a great deal. (To this day, I still can't lie in grass for more than five seconds.) And haircuts, like my mom said, did not go so well: the hair would be falling on my body and getting into the openings of my clothes. Yep, that would be something that would put my "autism level," as I called it, into full overdrive! All I could say about the haircuts was that I enjoyed the baths even more—not!!

Caregiver lessons I learned:

- If you suspect a problem or deficit, seek professional evaluation and immediate intervention. Do not adopt a "wait and see" philosophy. You cannot get that critical time back!

- Plan every task with the child for at least fifteen minutes longer than the estimated need. Inadequate time increases stress and decreases opportunities for positive outcomes.

- Find good sitters and a social outlet so that YOU can recharge, fulfill personal goals, and stay well-rounded. If *your* needs are not met, you cannot be as effective in helping others meet theirs.

CHAPTER FOUR

The Preschool and Kindergarten Years

The first day of preschool finally arrived. I was apprehensive because David was oppositional with strange adults and new situations, but my dominant emotion was hope. Recess was in progress when we entered the school, and the staff encouraged David to play while they observed him. Soon frustrated, he screamed and lay on the ground, thrashing about. Required to transition, share, or stop an activity that he enjoyed, this was his typical behavior (and was sometimes punctuated by hitting others). My eagerness for a good first impression was squelched by a dose of reality in about fifteen minutes.

The program was incredible. There were only seven students in David's class, so each received excellent attention. They were taught by a teacher and an assistant and received services from several other on-site specialists. A multidisciplinary evaluation (performed by the school's psychologist, occupational therapist, special education teacher, and speech therapist) ensued over several days and incorporated my input; David's customized plan of care was thereby developed.

David's vocabulary had grown to ten words, and he sometimes linked two together. Since his speech still lagged significantly behind the norm, he often expanded his communication with self-created motions that were akin to pantomime. Luckily, his understanding of spoken language appeared to be quite strong. Though delays were not then evident in gross motor skills, David had deficits in several other areas. He could not hold scissors in a workable manner, and he clutched writing tools with his entire hand, impeding their use. These were two of many altered abilities which stemmed from fine motor problems. He also exhibited sensory deviations.

Play consisted of David systematically lining up toys rather than properly using them. Since his next sibling was seven years his senior and never competed with his wants, David had no experience with sharing; he would get angry with peers when they desired toys and objects that he also wanted. David became upset if children didn't cooperate with activities *exactly* in the manner he intended. He was not flexible and could not comprehend that others might have *their own* ideas—he could not see life from their perspective. He was easily frustrated, often uncooperative, and wanted what he wanted without delay. David would hit, scream, and tantrum if crossed; he was slow to recover, and it was difficult to distract him away from his distress. Quite frankly, even the mere approach of someone unfamiliar could trigger his resistance. The deficits also included last chapter's issues and extended way beyond these examples—but you get the picture! Life with David was often a struggle—nothing was simple.

There was much work to be done. The plan addressed multiple needs using various approaches: 1) obviously, the structured class experience, 2) speech and language therapy to increase communication and social skills, 3) occupational therapy to improve fine motor skills, and 4) behavior therapy addressed throughout. In addition, speech therapy with Mary would continue in order to augment these efforts.

Once comfortable with these new people, David willingly separated from me to go to school. I helped in class whenever possible to witness his progress and interactions with peers and other authority figures. I also sought to learn and model the behavior management techniques which the staff utilized, for dealing with David's outbursts was still extremely challenging at home. I read to educate myself on every aspect of PDD (and eventually AS): books, magazines, and internet sources. I attended seminars and continued an ongoing quest for information, escalating efforts at each developmental stage. This vastly increased my understanding of David and therefore improved effective interactions with him. It also better enabled me to guide him and seek appropriate programs and resources for him.

As David's communication improved, so too did his tantrums. I believe that he was more frustrated by the inability to express himself than by the information or need he wished to convey. Recognizing that many of his outbursts were additionally caused by his deficits and underdeveloped skills, Frank and I chose to exclude him from optional situations that he couldn't yet handle— why invite the inevitable stress of a restaurant? While we realized, through our professional team, that much of his behavior was due to his developmental disorder, we also realized that he was a bright child who often just wanted his way, like any typical peer. Beyond the situations that we had learned required therapeutic solutions instead of disciplinary action (such as his extreme reactions to sensory challenges), there were other instances where we felt that discipline was indeed necessary to stop unacceptable behaviors (he could not be permitted to hit, for example). Frank and I sought to differentiate one from the other; we didn't want his challenges to be an excuse for him to act out uncontrollably at whim.

We looked to many experts (via print and on our intervention team) for guidance in how to handle discipline, when appropriate. This was in addition to efforts already underway to improve David's social skills and deficits. Frank and I chose to physically remove David when he behaved unacceptably; we verbalized our expectation to him in a simple statement, so that he understood the behavior change desired ("no hitting"). We utilized a safe, monitored, and short "time out" for certain predetermined situations. David soon recognized that the microwave timer signified the end of his time out, IF he quieted and cooperated. For extreme scenarios occurring in public places, we often improvised this time out. For example, I would hold him or seat him with me in an isolated corner of the mall, or I would remove him from the playground to stand by me next to a tree. In either case, I would ignore him until he quieted (regardless of others' stares). If these measures proved unsuccessful, we often left altogether and headed home.

Frank and I added other related strategies over time to fit specific situations, such as briefly confiscating an ill-used toy or object while providing a short reason as to why. On the flip side, we praised and rewarded him for successes and good behavior. David began to learn our rules and started to understand that there would be consequences for unacceptable behavior. Importantly, Frank and I shared the same philosophy and techniques; we always supported each other's measures and worked together as a team. We would not be played one against the other. If we set a limit, we enforced it—no empty threats.

Effort and consistency went a long way to restore a more restful home environment and improve our family dynamics. Over the next few years, with professional intervention and further language and skill acquisition, David's behavior improved. He began to learn alternate forms of expression and ways to problem solve that were acceptable and effective (such as using his words). In the future—as his exposure, skills, and age/maturity progressed—I would scrutinize his undesirable social responses; David and I would discuss consequences of his behavior along with alternatives that could have been tried. Each interaction was utilized as a learning experience to improve. The same was done for *positive* social interactions to reinforce his responses and help him apply them to other potential situations.

Throughout David's upbringing, my husband and I have often commented that we were "on his case" more than occurred with our typical children; we sought to maximally redirect him and teach him appropriate social responses. Special education focused intensely on his behavior, as well. In the end, we find David to be more polite, socially appropriate, even-tempered, and receptive than many of his typical peers! The quality of his social skills training, both professional and incidental, was enviable. Most children should be so lucky!

While certain behaviors and characteristics improved during the preschool years, others worsened or emerged. Sensory issues became more intense. David further limited his food choices based on texture, odor, and temperature. He ate the same breakfast and lunch for years and would not try new options. As he began to feed himself, he would eat all of one food group completely before moving on to the next. He still had an aversion to the fizz of carbonation, and to this day, he will not drink soda pop— not a bad thing! Loud noises and bright lights increasingly bothered him. His sense of smell was heightened, and his cooperation with haircuts greatly declined.

Along with the feel of prickly hair as it landed, David was overwhelmed by the scraping, vibration, and buzzing sound of the clippers. Scissors were also problematic, so they did not provide a viable substitution. He became so combative and disruptive to business that we moved a chair into the salon parking lot. I eventually could not handle the chore independently; Frank accompanied me to restrain David while the hairdresser worked as rapidly as possible on the frenzied, moving target. With everyone spent, physically and emotionally, we still had to endure the screaming ride home before the pinching remnants could be bathed away. Covered with sweat and hair himself, Frank often wondered how he would manage this task in the future. We pictured him trying to tightly hold the arms of a strong, resistant, and tall adolescent sitting on his lap—not a pretty thought!

Fortunately, before snowy weather precluded parking-lot cuts, we heard about a child-focused salon forty-five minutes away. David's behavior initially required traditional services in a back room. Thankfully, the hairdressers were skilled and fast in working with disgruntled, squirming children. It was still an ordeal, but eventually David improved and became intrigued by the salon proper. He unexpectedly agreed to try it.

The stylist tied a colorful kid cape loosely around David's neck. The lesser of two evils, the wrap was an option he preferred over trimmed hair falling on his unprotected body. David sat on a carousel-type seat for the duration of the cut, and he was distracted with other fun activities and surroundings; consequently, it worked! He demanded that his shirt be immediately removed afterward. A prompt baby powder application to his neck and torso eased the "pinchies," as he called them, until he got home to bathe. David earned a little reward from the treasure chest following his cooperation, and this served to reinforce his good behavior. He refused to don a jacket over his hair-covered skin; we accepted that compromise and I whisked him into the vehicle that Frank had warmed. After securing David in his car seat, we praised him profusely and presented his favorite edible treat. This made the long ride home more tolerable and sidetracked David from his discomfort. He became so controllable that haircuts eventually returned to a one-parent task that even I could manage. David was ultimately transitioned to a stylist located five minutes away, but the immediate shower is still part of his current routine.

Dental appointments were equally dreaded. More loathsome than pain, David detested the sound and pressure of the drill, the whining of high-pitched tools, the spray of cold water and air, the feel and sound of scaling, and hugely, the multifaceted misery created by suction. Tipped backward in the elevated chair, he stared directly into the glaring spotlight; combined with medicinal smells and the distress I described from equipment, a horrifying experience was created. Despite the pleasant dental services of close family friends, a temporary move to a pediatric specialist forty minutes away was necessary until David's fear subsided and his tolerance improved. Though visits were still an ordeal that required our initial assistance, the new office staff was skilled in working with frantic young patients. Following enough familiarity and desensitizing, David was able to resume care at our family dental practice in about two years. He recently revealed to me that scaling still bothers him, but he has learned to endure it (along with worse procedures!) without evidence of distress.

Mary reassessed David's speech and language as he neared completion of his first preschool year (four months before his fourth birthday). This occurred following almost fifty sessions with her, in addition to the services received at school. Five formal tests were administered that each focused on a different facet of language. His scores were considerably diverse; while some verged on normalcy, others were substantially subpar. Though his vocabulary and word combinations had increased, he still occasionally used his senseless, homemade vernacular and often echoed back the words of others. Bottom line, his overall language disability was assessed as moderate to severe. How disheartening that even with all the effort and progress that were made that year, David's impairment remained significant! In fact, *more* needs were discovered; comprehension and language processing were now added to the growing list of issues requiring intervention—and he still had many other unrelated developmental challenges to conquer. Obviously, we had a long road before us.

Despite these grim results, David seemed quite able to understand simple commands or questions in everyday life, and at times, he even shocked us with signs of high intelligence. I clearly recall a day when he was arranging magnetic letters on the refrigerator. I commented that the letter he was holding was called a "P." He got angry and threw it down. As it landed, I realized that it was actually an "R," but one appendage had not been visible because of his hold. I corrected myself that it was an "R," and he calmed. This indicated his understanding, and I wondered if, in fact, he knew the names of the other letters, as well. Sure enough, as I called out other letters one by one, he was able to choose each correlating magnet. I was stunned. We had been reading alphabet books to him, and he watched *Sesame Street*, a children's educational TV show, but we never tested his comprehension. We thus continued working with him on colors, numbers, letter sounds, and other concepts via books, toys, and computer software, just as one would do with any "typical" preschool child. Once speech significantly improved, we noticed other unusual behaviors and characteristics. David frequently repeated words and phrases over and over, especially those from his favorite television programs and videos. He became fixated on fairy tales: "Snow White" initially, which was followed by the "Three Little Pigs." He wanted to hear the stories, look at the books, watch the videos, and line up the toy figures continually—he didn't use the toys to recreate the stories or have the characters interact in meaningful ways, however.

On rare occasions, David exhibited strange hand movements when stressed or excited, known as hand flapping. These were replaced by other behaviors as he aged. He would open and close two particular doors in our house repeatedly. As they weren't necessary for privacy issues, the quirk was so annoying and potentially dangerous that Frank removed them from their hinges. Removing nonessential problem triggers always made life easier.

As David progressed through the second preschool year in the same program, we worked further on social skills and purposeful play—both in class and at home. I tried to explain, demonstrate, and engage him in imaginative play with dinosaurs, cars, or any other toy he showed interest in. One couldn't take for granted that he knew *how* creatures and people interacted; many of these "rules" and roles needed to be learned, as the experts in our life attested. And the family was recruited to help with this omnipresent challenge.

Steve, my oldest son, was highly committed to succeed with his challenging high school demands. Between hours of intense study, combined with extracurricular activities and a weekend job, his free time was minimal; availability for David's needs understandably declined— with total parental support and pride. Ten years David's senior and in a totally different life stage, Steve needed to focus on his own goals and future, though he still supported David and contributed whenever possible.

It was our middle son, Craig, ever present during David's formative years, who was his patient mentor and friend. Young enough to relate to David, but old enough to guide him, Craig's popularity gained David entrance into neighborhood socialization and activities. Together, we tried to teach David simple games, such as baseball, so that he could understand and participate in activities at the neighborhood pool and beach club. Craig's friends welcomed David and were accustomed to having him among them—then and for years to come. David also began supervised interactions with his own peers, both at the pool and via playdates. We would monitor his behavior and teach, reinforce, or remove him, dictated by his responses. He still displayed tantrums on the playground, but he also received a few coveted invitations to neighbors' birthday parties. His social circle and experience were broadening.

David continued to exhibit inappropriate behavior and obvious delays when he faced new challenges, but progress and the beginnings of reciprocal interactions gave us hope and enjoyment. He learned to ride a large-wheeled tricycle and loved the rhythmic movement of the swings. Swinging at the park or riding in the toddler seats on our bike backs became fun and wonderful stress busters amidst all his training—so fun that he accepted wearing the safety helmet as a condition to go riding. Of note was David's new tendency to "growl" and scowl in order to voice frustration or disapproval. This continued for a few years. His smile often looked forced and plastic when captured in photos, and his eyes were rather vacant and without a hint of emotion. He would retract the corners of his mouth, but his eyes and remaining face didn't reflect the joy of a true smile. Ironically, his senior high school picture was the most natural and handsome of my three sons. It was so heartwarming and rewarding to put David's earlier and later photos side by side for a visual of how far he had come!

Two incredible events transpired that year which foreshadowed gifts and talents that were to emerge as central to David's future. The first little miracle was the Christmas concert performed by the preschool classes. Somehow, the incredible teachers were able to assemble fifteen special-needs children into lined formation and KEEP them in place! The tots surprisingly kept the red Rudolph noses taped to their own noses, and they SANG! To follow directions and stay focused as a group was amazing enough in itself, but to actually sing, when some could not acceptably speak fifteen months prior, was miraculous to me.

David loved performing, and he looked comfortable, happy, and like he belonged. As the tears welled in my eyes, I looked to my left and saw my father with the biggest smile I had ever seen. He later shared that of the countless school events he had attended for his five grandchildren over the years, this was the best. It would also be his last—and is a cherished memory for me. I often think about how much he would have enjoyed witnessing other hallmark victories over the course of David's life, but in my heart, I truly believe he has been orchestrating them from heaven. I believe that he is part of the miracle, sending us both guardian angels and enlightenment for discovered paths and opportunities.

(He has likely joined forces with Frank's parents: a divine, interceding team—three grandparents strong!)

The second shocking event occurred while we were driving home from a theater. David was repeating phrases as he always did in the car, but Frank and I suddenly recognized *this* recitation as a verbatim section of the movie we had *just* seen. I asked David if he had been watching previews of it on TV, but this he denied; he simply remembered the dialogue. His memorization skills were astounding—for information he was interested in, I must add. Unfortunately, it did not later translate into the sciences or areas he disliked, but it was a skill that would certainly offset his difficulties with abstract knowledge attainment to balance out his grades in the future. And it surely came in handy for learning the songs and scripts in the many theater roles he would eventually undertake. We always marveled that in twenty minutes he would emerge from his room stating that he had his part "down," and he always did. Furthermore, during rehearsals, he could frequently be seen mouthing the words of the other actors. After hearing the run-through only a couple times, David would know everyone's part, often before they did themselves. We always joked that he could be an emergency understudy for the entire cast! In addition, when he got it, he got it. He often flawlessly recites passages of material memorized or heard years ago. This is one of the advantageous exceptionalities of his presentation of Asperger's, and one he truly seems to enjoy and utilize.

We had decided at David's birth, prior to any knowledge of the developmental challenges yet to come, that we would hold him back a year from starting Kindergarten.

With a late summer birthday and experience with two other boys having summer/fall births, there was never any alternative considered. The issue now became which track to take. At five years of age, he was eligible to continue at his current preschool for another year, but we were also interested in the "typical" prekindergarten (pre-K) that Craig had attended. The latter setting would expose him to an intellectually advanced and faster-paced curriculum, a larger class size, and an opportunity to start practicing social skills in a structured "typical" world. We were drawn by the challenge but also needed the continued therapies, social training, and individualization of the special-needs preschool program. Per my request to both institutions, David was approved to attend the pre-K afternoon sessions and *still* continue at the preschool in the mornings. If it was too much for him on certain days, he would skip the morning sessions (of which he missed only six all year). This was a beautiful marriage of services to match needs, and though hectic, it was perfect for him. I learned the value of researching options and then advocating for deviations to customize his experiences. It worked on multiple occasions to streamline efforts and maximally attain all our goals.

David advanced in both programs. I assisted at every party and field trip possible at the pre-K in order to assess his interactions and development firsthand, and I corresponded with the teachers frequently. He easily blended with the group, and though he often needed redirection, prompting, or extra assistance with work, he *did* keep up academically. He was fairly independent and did not disrupt the class, but he did have some social challenges there. He was able to model some of the typical behaviors, but ironically, we found that this was not always desirable!

David readily bonded with one child in particular, and I became quick friends with this classmate's mother. We often planned "kid" outings and hosted playdates at our homes. I noticed, however, that despite playing *beside* each other, the two children usually didn't play *together*. Rather than interacting with each other, they would each do their own thing in their own way—both preferring this. They were similar in other atypical ways, as well, and ironically, but not surprisingly, this other child was also later diagnosed with Asperger's. A support system to each other on many levels, our families' association was maintained throughout the elementary school years.

As David's time in the special preschool was ending, the team who worked with him for half his life performed a final assessment of his strengths, weaknesses, and continued needs. Intellectually, he was performing well in the classroom and was able to learn the presented curriculum. His speech was nicely progressing, but certain behaviors were still problematic and required sustained intervention. David frequently talked aloud to himself to get through assignments or challenges, and he emphatically declined assistance that was needed. The volume of his voice was often excessive, and he would complain, verbalize angrily, or "growl" when frustrated, stressed, or of a different opinion. On a good note, David was learning to vocalize what bothered him.

Change and transition remained the ultimate hurdles. Though he still reacted in the manner just described, David was at least improving in his responses. The special school prepared him for changing scenarios using three major methods. First, each day's itinerary was presented in pictorial form at the beginning of the day. This provided an advanced visual of the planned agenda. Second, staff engaged in explanations and discussions *prior* to change in order to increase David's understanding and anticipation. And third, teachers periodically announced the time remaining until expected changes would occur. ("Ten minutes until it's time to go home.") We continued to utilize some of these borrowed techniques at home; they assisted David to adjust to variations.

David improved in playing with others, but he still struggled with negotiation. Accepting help, correction, or input (even from peers) continued to be hard for him. Of significance, David did not respond well to teasing, sarcasm, or the laughter of others—which he often presumed was aimed at him. This would haunt him in adolescence as will soon be described. David continued in his performance of inappropriate, pointless, and sometimes lengthy recitations (often memorized excerpts of favorite tapes and programs). When conversing, he usually didn't stay on topic or alternate exchanges. Despite intervention, David's speaking voice had not attained proper rhythm, speed, or volume, and he wasn't consistent with looking at the person who was talking to him. He wanted to have relationships with other children, but his quirks and stifling intensity drove peers away. In his hurry to get to a destination, he would push through others, only aware of his own needs. For the same reasons, he also interrupted and struggled with turn-taking.

Utilization of scissors and crayons improved, but David's grasp and coordination were still abnormal. This hindered many fine motor tasks—especially since he resisted adult help. In relieved contrast, he performed large motor activities without issue thus far. On another positive note, David was starting to understand and use humor, and he began asking for further explanations when unsure. In summary, he was making progress, but much work remained.

Outside of school, life improved on several levels. With the discovery of David's interest in *Colorforms* and sticker books, we were able to take him to a restaurant. He stayed seated and behaved better than many typical children we witnessed. The rules were firm, and we only took him out when he was adequately rested. We maximized opportunities for success by keeping the trips short and single. We did not add them to a second errand or situation where he would likely be spent or tired of sitting during our outing. We always took additional activities and snacks to keep him occupied during delays or to compensate for occasions when his favorites were not on the menu. It was so exciting and so liberating! We could now enjoy select family events as a complete family!

Eventually, we were able to expand these to longer outings if adequate breaks were provided; we tried not to overpower David's senses and patience. An amusement park, social events at our neighborhood beach club, and even an overnight stay in a hotel were all possible that summer. Much of the success stemmed from Craig, who always mentored, engaged, and thrilled his younger sibling. Adventurous and fun loving, Craig would squeeze into kiddie rides, jump in ball houses, or perform any other feat required in order to accompany David and keep him safe. This allowed for fun and success rather than fear or anxiety.

The ultimate Craig gift was his participation in the tots' portion of the neighborhood beach club swim show. It was a huge annual production at the end of summer. Beginning after dark, it was complete with music, lights, costumes, and choreography. Each age group had performances in and around the pool, and the kids practiced most of the summer. We wanted to try David's participation as a munchkin in the Oz-themed number, but the dark, confusion, loud music, and dance steps around water all caused trepidation (mine as well as David's). Craig consented to accompany him—with resulting success and David's elation. So there he was: a thirteen-year-old basketball player, twice the tikes' height, dressed like a munchkin in front of his own peers and doing the routine with David—talk about brotherly love! From then on, David participated annually and independently with minimal prompting.

Highly anticipated, David's "sleepover vacations" to Aunt Renee and Uncle Pat's house were immensely valued. This extended family loved him and mentored him as much as we did, and they offered a separate agenda and social circle that further helped him grow. Cousin Brittany was eight years older than David and became his "Craig away from home." With these nurturing relatives and sister-like guide, David experienced fishing, kiddie parks, Christmas tree-cutting excursions, and other novel and fun activities not customary with us. They understood his idiosyncrasies and need for down time, and he was totally comfortable weaned away from us. We, on the other hand, had a wonderful opportunity for couple bonding, visiting colleges, or other activities not possible with David. These were cherished and developmentally valuable experiences (for all of us!) that occurred all throughout his childhood.

David continued his progress with communication and processing. With our new success on short outings, I took him with me to my mother's medical appointment. As Grandma sat in the doctor's exam room, David and I glanced through children's books in the waiting room. He had been learning letter sounds, so as we sat there, I explained how you could put them together to make words. I slowly and dramatically sounded out a simple three-letter word to demonstrate. Then he tried one. Not only was he successful, but he quickly figured out how to string the sounds together smoothly to form a word instead of isolated sounds. The speed at which he learned to read was astounding. Like I said before—when he "got" something, he got it. We witnessed this same phenomenon time after time during future unrelated situations. It might be difficult for David to grasp a concept initially, and it might require presentation in several different ways, but once he understood the intended message, he "had it" and would not forget it. So, in my mother goes, with David proudly knowing his letter sounds; out she comes, and he was reading words to her. When you put into perspective the speed at which he progressed from virtually no speech to fluent reading, it was incredible. Another victory for David!

Sensory differences were still an issue. David enjoyed helping me bake, but he would simultaneously hold his nose with one hand; the smells were too strong for him. His response to unfiltered noise sometimes required a limited exposure to crowds, sporting events, and social gatherings. He still disliked the feel of various textures on his skin, but with the help of bubble baths, he finally enjoyed bathing. David nicely fed himself with silverware, despite his unconventional grasp and technique: he swiftly inverted the filled spoon so that food entered his mouth while suspended from the utensil. With improvements in fine motor skills, he was learning to tie his shoes (thanks to Aunt Renee and her laced-cardboard simulation). David could not effectively hold a pencil, but with fat crayons and his own adaptations, he enjoyed both coloring and rudimentary drawing.

With his successful transition at the pre-K, we mainstreamed David into the neighborhood public school for Kindergarten; there was no special education class available for this grade level. However, David was able to receive occupational and speech/language therapy in this "typical" school via eligibility stemming from his individualized education program (commonly known as his IEP). These specialized plans and named services were available in our public school to children who met needs-based criteria. These therapies would augment Mary's private speech sessions.

Recommended by the school's occupational therapist, a rubber gadget that assisted appropriate grasp was slipped over David's pencils. As he practiced, David's muscle coordination improved; by the year's end, he could write and draw with standard tools and no device. He eventually developed beautiful penmanship utilizing a unique, backhanded style. He maintains an adaptation even today; if it works, why change it for conformity's sake?

Again, I helped in class frequently, assessing for areas that needed further intervention. The teacher and program were wonderful. David did well academically and was not disruptive. With more children in the class, I noticed that he did not get the attention or expertise with subtle issues that he would have obtained in a special school (nor did I expect him to). I also realized that the teacher was not focused on assessing for needs that would be inherent in a special-education setting. For example, an evaluation reported no problems at play time. But when I helped in class, I observed that David played with the **same** puzzle, assembling the **same** pieces in the **same** order, at the **same** location, time after time. He did not try other puzzles and did not socialize with the others. Not calling attention to himself, it was never noticed that there *was* a problem. Instead, he was assessed as being well behaved and enjoying the puzzles. I wondered what other subtle issues were being missed because of the sheer number of children and general class goals. If such issues were not noticed or addressed, I could see where he could "fall through the cracks" and not perform to the potential he might have elsewhere. My decision was reinforced: David would attend a special education elementary school. But I was thankful for the skills and adventures he experienced in this "typical" environment, and I was thrilled that he adapted as well as he did.

Mary performed a final assessment of David's speech and language status, and testing results now reflected low average to average performance. He had transcended his prior ranking of severely disabled in this regard. Though great news, we realized that he was still challenged with processing, social, and communication difficulties, along with other issues imposed by his Pervasive

Developmental Disorder. Despite his strong reading, spelling, and vocabulary skills, it was also learned that his comprehension lagged. It could definitely put David at risk if his understanding and ability were assumed to correlate with *how good he sounded*. And the risk would continue if services were not provided to improve the actual mismatch.

Mary concurred with our academic decision and highly recommended a special-needs setting that would address David's continued learning differences via small group interactions. She referred us to an exceptional school, and she also recommended replacing her individual speech sessions with social skills therapy. Language processing development would be addressed at his future school, so rather than private speech therapy, he now more appropriately required a pediatric psychologist to improve his social deficits. Therefore, with overwhelming gratitude mixed with sadness and trepidation, we graduated our care to Dr. Martin, who proved to be equally instrumental in continuing the miracle. We will never forget Mary or her precious gifts; we still correspond annually via Christmas greetings to update her on the lives that she changed and the future she enabled.

David's reading development flourished and soon surpassed expected norms. But he continued to possess a literal understanding of language and had trouble grasping abstract concepts. He had difficulty appreciating that others might have differing perspectives, and he couldn't comprehend how his actions would affect others. David said what was on his mind, and he spoke the truth—but often without social consideration or tact. For example, we once checked out in a store where the cashier had extremely long polished nails. David exclaimed within her earshot, "She looks like a vampire!" He might also comment on someone's clothing, weight, or breath. Such inappropriate remarks were potentially quite embarrassing, though never to him. He hadn't yet developed the sensitivity necessary to realize the impact or error of his words. Fortunately, social skills therapy addressed this need over time.

David's play remained very predictable and unvaried. He continued to have areas of intense interest: certain fairy tales were still central, but he was now also captivated with *Toy Story* and the pirates of *Peter Pan*. He continued to talk too loudly, stand too closely, and have other problems with voice tone and rhythm. In contrast to his early days of insufficient closeness, he now displayed an overabundance of maternal affection of almost inappropriate degree and timing, especially as he aged.

David was able to ride a bike with training wheels, but he always leaned sideways to utilize their support. He was unable to hold his balance when they were removed except on one isolated attempt during an outing with Uncle Pat. After many more trials over an extensive period, David finally aborted efforts to bike ride in lieu of a cool three-wheeled scooter my brother, Ken, bought him. We eventually purchased a tandem bike to stretch family rides for a couple more years. David then decided to hold out for his driver's license rather than risk falling off a bike, even though we later learned of a special training program that existed. He still cannot ride one and has no desire to learn.

Dr. Martin diagnosed David with high functioning autism at her initial evaluation, for she explained that his late acquisition of speech and language prevented him from meeting the usual AS diagnostic essentials. And so began our ten years of therapy with Dr. Martin, who addressed every issue I have described and much, much more. David's language skills progressed with surprising speed once speech was established, and as he aged, David exhibited new symptoms and behaviors. Based on these emerging characteristics and the evolving understanding of the relatively new AS diagnosis in the professional community, Dr. Martin eventually changed David's diagnosis to Asperger's Disorder. Regardless of this new label, the same customized treatment was still indicated, and it was continually tweaked over time to match changing needs and priorities.

Still enamored with the "Three Little Pigs," David continually drew those around him into perpetuating his fantasy. Whether it was reading the story, drawing the pictures, or playing it out, the topic was ever present. We shared with Dr. Martin our family's frustration and confusion in appropriately handling David's obsessive interests, for his antics and requests often dictated family life. Just home from a long day of work, hungry and still wearing his suit, Frank was not always in the mood to be "the big bad wolf"! Was it more beneficial to surrender to David and engage in his desired play at the family's expense, or should we defer and risk a meltdown—again at the family's expense? This was just one of the many dilemmas and problems which Dr. Martin helped us work through over the years. The importance of the issues increased commensurate with David's advancing age. The ability and luxury to seek her professional, trusted advice was a source of comfort and strength that got me through many a difficult day.

Dr. Martin worked with David individually, but she also counseled ME in how to apply strategies and continue efforts at home. Her expertise, rapport, and compassion were exceptional. She addressed the critical social and communication skills which David lacked and guided us through many challenges and crises. Sensitively and effectively, she eventually taught David about his differences, how to accept them, and how and when to communicate them. Dr. Martin was another key guardian angel instrumental to David's success, adjustment, and happiness. We will be forever grateful for her support and herculean contribution.

With our oldest son (Steve) starting his senior year and soon leaving for college, we were anxious to experience a full family vacation before time ran out. So where would you take a fairy-tale-focused child for maximum chance of engagement and success? Disney World, of course! I researched disability accommodations (thanks to Dr. Martin for informing me of their existence), planned the itinerary, and made event reservations well in advance of our departure. Tours, shows, and character breakfasts were all chosen according to David's preferences. Nothing was left to chance. This allowed me time to prepare David for experiences, stimuli, and the planned routine.

Our first hurdle was navigating the airport and flight. All went well, except for David's distress over the inner ear sensations created by takeoff—despite preventive explanations and his exaggerated attempts to swallow. His ears finally popped back to normal soon after landing, but David intermittently mentioned the return flight throughout the vacation; he anticipated and dreaded a repeat experience. Equipped with his favorite soft candies on the trip back home (he wouldn't try gum), he enthusiastically chewed more than required; desperate to prevent discomfort, he anxiously began the treatment long before necessary—and took full advantage of unlimited sweets. His ears successfully responded, but that noxious sensation was replaced by nausea related to overconsumption. David has never again eaten his once-loved treat! But back to our arrival...

Armed with proper documentation, we received a pass from Guest Relations which minimized lines for David and company. David delightedly became the VIP of our family; Steve and Craig reaped the benefits of their brother's accommodation—*their* wait times were also decreased in the attempt to prevent David from becoming frustrated or overwhelmed. In so doing, this service functioned exactly as intended: it maximized the family Disney experience. The brothers were never more bonded or jovial together.

Early risers, we began our daily park excursions when the gates opened; crowds and summer heat were reduced and bearable early in the day. Staying for only a few hours at a time, we would leave to relax and enjoy the pool long before David reached his limit. He expected this, for it was part of his Disney preparation, and he was always in favor. David loved the water activities, and he knew that naps were rewarded with a return to the parks—with fun and adventure extending beyond his usual bedtime. With planning and transitioning, the trip was an overwhelming success. Short park intervals interspersed with pool and rest times (for the whole family!) were key components to the Disney magic. David had NO meltdowns; we anticipated and prevented all triggers, never pushing him too far. He was enthralled with the characters and did not experience any sensory problems.

Amused by David's excitement, Steve and Craig actively sought out his favorite characters and assisted him with autograph acquisitions. They were good sports, for I'm sure they would have preferred other teenage entertainment. Sensitive to this, we allowed the older two to intermittently go off exploring together; they communicated with us via our shared walkie-talkies (this was prior to the cell phone era). This made the trip fun for them, as well. But the lasting memories stemmed from the thrill of experiencing David's blissful success and enjoying "normal" family bonding. It was the perfect vacation everyone always envisions—all the more special because we never thought it was possible.

Elated and recharged, I reflected on David's profound progress in the short time since his diagnosis. It struck me that he had already received three years of life-changing therapies when many other affected children his age weren't yet even recognized as *having* Asperger's. I have no doubt that David's progress and current outcome are a reflection of intense, comprehensive, and early intervention. Many experts and professionals, both personally involved and in the literature, share this belief.

So, on we proceeded with our plans to receive more interventions in a new academic life chapter. As a side note, I stopped researching "the expected prognosis" in children with Asperger's Syndrome; I was convinced that none of the studied populations had the team, plan, intervention, or determination that we did. We would define our own course...

As far as my preschool through kindergarten years, I remember a little more than the previous years. The one thing that stands out is the jack-in-the-box I was obsessed with in preschool. I played with that thing nonstop, and it was the only toy I wanted throughout my time at that school.

What my mother said about my organized food grouping is something I still do to this day. Whether it's a home-cooked meal or an "all you can eat" buffet, I will first eat the meat, then the side, and then the fruit. Basically, the only thing I do mix with my food is my beverage!

If I could describe "dentistry" in one word, I would go with "nightmare"! I can tolerate it now, but back then I would be shoving the tools out of my face, freaking out whenever they'd scale me, and much more. It's a good thing they were all professionals who had experience in dealing with hard cases.

One thing's for sure, I was obsessed with fairy tales! I remember those more than anything from my childhood. Every time the "Three Little Pigs" were brought up, I went crazy! I was hooked on that topic for many years. When I wasn't reading the story, I was talking about it; when I wasn't talking about it, I was acting it out. Or possibly, I was doing it all at once!! Another picture that I have locked up in my mind is the stage of my old preschool, which is where I had my first Christmas concert. It was while I was singing that I felt a connection to the stage, and it was something that would stick with me for many years to come.

The one thing I remember from kindergarten was that we got to draw pictures correlating with the alphabet. The teacher was a pretty good artist. She told us to be creative, but I composed exactly what the teacher drew on her board. I was attracted to her style, seeing how hers were pretty good drawings, and I was unable to create my own work. However, I eventually learned how to develop my own artistic style.

My ultimate memory is of the place where every child dreams of going for his or her first vacation: Disney World!!! The attractions such as the rides, the characters, the parades, and Cinderella's castle complimented my interests while still appealing to my family, so we ALL could have a great time. It was the first long period in my life that I could "let go" of everything, feel at ease with myself, and enjoy some time with my family without stress.

Caregiver lessons I learned:

- I repeat! If you suspect a problem or deficit, seek professional evaluation and immediate intervention. Do not adopt a "wait and see" philosophy. You cannot get that critical time back!

- Do not leave the treatments exclusively up to the therapists and educators: be a partner and work in tandem to continue efforts at home. Do YOUR "social homework" to reinforce interventions and maximize success.

- Persevere and be consistent.

- You are a KEY member of the intervention team and know your child best. If you think a novel idea might meet a need, discuss the possibility with the educators or therapists and brainstorm options.

- Enlist the help of "a Craig" who can buddy your child to offer support and maximize success with peer integration and activities. A buddy can aid with transitions or provide assistance and companionship in situations when parents are not appropriate or welcome to do so.

CHAPTER FIVE

The Primary School Years

Finally! We arrived for orientation at the school that would hone David's academic, social, and organizational skills, providing him with the building blocks for future success. With no more than ten children per class, we felt so blessed to have acquired a coveted slot in the entering first grade—but then again, I had visited the school and first communicated with the principal when David was still in preschool. It was no accident that his was one of the first applications received on the day that admission was open to newcomers! My persistence was rewarded, and I have utilized this strategy ever since. Early research of schools and programs, paired with clarifying communication, has repeatedly enabled David's maximum preparation and smooth transitions; nothing is left to chance, and the need for an alternate plan is eliminated. Our only glitch, and it was a huge one, occurred at the start of high school, but that is a whole new chapter...

Back to this most special of schools, it could be classified as sitting simultaneously on both ends of the traditional spectrum. Run by nuns, it was steeped with educational excellence, respect, discipline, and the guiding principles of the Catholic faith. Open to children of any religious affiliation, it specifically served those with learning differences. The nontraditional elements stemmed from the setting and unique methods of therapy and instruction. The school was actually a mansion set back on beautiful wooded grounds. It was donated to the sisters for a one-dollar fee to house their educational venture. The art gallery was repurposed to house a cozy, beautiful library, and bedrooms were transformed into intimate classroom settings. Children could nestle into distinctive nooks that made reading fun, supplementing the little desks of typical classroom design.

More than the beauty of this charming setting, it was the palpable love and therapeutic aura that made this school so special. It was a place of ultimate acceptance where everyone knew everyone else, staff and children alike. Free of much of the stress and anxiety present in typical schools, children thrived here through the specialized methods and pace of individualized education. Social skills and art therapy were integrated into the curriculum, and proven again and again was the premise that EVERY child CAN learn if techniques mirror how he or she understands and responds best. Lay specialized teachers joined the nuns to round out the dedicated and expert faculty, and children came from many surrounding suburbs to reap the benefits of the skillful instruction and therapeutic environment.

David's first grade teacher, Mrs. O'Neill, was the most astute, effective, and incredible teacher my children have ever encountered. She was young, beautiful, and energetic—not to mention, skilled in her craft—and the children adored her. She totally understood David and unlocked doors that changed his life forever. I helped in her classroom almost weekly, for I was eager to "give back." This volunteering also enabled me to witness David's weaknesses, progress, and social interactions so that I could better augment the school's efforts at home. In addition, I reaped the rewards of learning from a master; I tried to mirror some of Mrs. O'Neill's tactics for maintaining cooperation and changing select behaviors.

An unforeseen benefit of school participation was meeting and bonding with some of the other parents who also volunteered. It was an informal support group that helped me to cope and put things in perspective. It also provided opportunities for play situations to be arranged outside of school activities. Because of varied commutes and cities of residence, the children didn't otherwise have the chance to socialize with each other to form or deepen friendships, like commonly occurs at neighborhood schools. My volunteering extended to working on the school's annual fundraising auction. It was there that my husband surprised me with submitting the highest bid on an item I had admired. It was a beautiful handmade stained-glass piece which read, "Expect a Miracle." We hung this on David's bedroom window; every morning as I woke him, the light filtered through the colored panes and renewed my faith, hope, and determination. I do believe in self-fulfilling prophecies...

One of David's most bothersome and attention-grabbing behaviors was his tendency to audibly talk to himself, a habit we dubbed "chit-chat." He continually recited lines from television shows, movies, or stories in many different voices that were usually in a higher or different octave than his natural speaking voice. This happened when he was bored, stressed, or uninvolved in an activity, but it even occurred when he was hard at work, such as when calculating math problems. In later years, David expressed that either relaxation (stress reduction) or entertainment served as the rationale for this behavior, depending on the situation. When I asked him why he chit-chatted on a certain first grade evening, however, he responded that he liked hearing himself "do all the voices." Relaying this response to his teacher during a later conversation, Mrs. O'Neill recommended that we involve David in theater as an outlet to perhaps funnel this desire into a more appropriate expression. This novel idea of drama as therapy was brilliant and exciting—a perfect solution for finding a social niche, as well.

Discussing this quest with my mother, she directed me to a performing arts center in her neighborhood that hosted children's theater camps every fall and summer, culminating in Christmas and August productions. I met with the director (Mike), explained David's issues, and asked if he would consider my son's participation. I did not want David to ruin the performances, so I relayed my intent to sit in the parking lot during the first several practices to quickly retrieve him if necessary. In that event, we would abort further attempts and simply appreciate his willingness to give it a try. Mike insisted, however, that David's needs surpassed his own desire for a perfect performance; he took David under his wing, and since I was never summoned, I eventually left my post in the parking lot. David enjoyed the camp's summer activities of art projects, singing, dancing, and play practice. Since the limit for camp participation was eighteen years of age, there were older children and counselors to mentor the little ones. David had a chorus role in *Bye-Bye Birdie* and was paired with a teenage girl on set who gave him guidance and reassurance on stage.

Opening night finally arrived. I was shocked, but not surprised, that flowers with an attached congratulatory helium balloon arrived that afternoon—from Mrs. O'Neill. Such was her love and dedication to her students that she would remember such an occasion months after school let out. Frank and I sat nervously in the audience, anticipating any number of potential disasters that could result from David's dislike of darkness, his inability to refrain from chit-chat or vocalizations, or perhaps distress from sensory issues such as loud music, special lighting, itchy costumes, make-up, and close bodies—among countless other possibilities. But as the final curtain came down, I was overwhelmed with relief and joy. For other than his obvious initial search for us in the audience, followed by gleeful waves, he performed his part without mishap—following directions, singing and dancing in sync, and totally blending in with the other actors.

We were infinitely grateful to Mike for his patience and determination to include our son, and David had so much fun and success that we signed him up for the next (and next, and next...) production. Although the initial impetus was of therapeutic rationale, it soon became quite apparent that David had innate talent. He progressed to earn speaking roles in which he excelled, and he developed a passion for the art which has been his joy, escape, and social outlet ever since. Amazingly, though troubled with eye contact and speaking during one-on-one situations, he was in his element and in total command of the stage when elevated before hundreds. Did he still chit-chat? Big time! But the personal development and additional perks of recognition, respect, and enhanced self-esteem were benefits that transcended the original hypothesized purpose for attempting theater.

Due to the nature of David's struggles, I sincerely doubt that we would ever have explored this arena without the prompting of Mrs. O'Neill—and I can't imagine his life without it. I am certain he would have experienced much more loneliness and despair, and others would have been deprived of the astonishing talent that would have remained hidden and untapped, as well. Mrs. O'Neill's insight truly enriched and changed his life. Her incredible gift to him will keep on giving, for he has embraced theater as a permanent hobby and outlet. We were so fortunate to have reaped the benefits of her magic since she left the school shortly thereafter. Personal and professional aspirations took her elsewhere, but in a twist of fate, our paths would indirectly cross ten years down the road.

At summer's close, we packed the last of Steve's belongings into our van. Filled with ambivalence, we prepared to drive our firstborn to college. David was barely eight and would lose the support of his big brother. I hoped they would continue to grow in their relationship despite remote contact, and I was determined to get them together often to prevent estrangement. David's sadness was offset by two exciting upshots: first, he won a trip to Aunt Renee and Uncle Pat's while we settled Steve into his dorm, and second, David would inherit a room of his own! Poor Steve wasn't even gone yet, and he already lost his personal space! Moreover, we enlisted his muscle to help rearrange the furniture to convert his room into David's. Thankfully, Steve's anticipation to move on in life seemed to overshadow any hurt or annoyance.

Simultaneous with interventions employed at David's school, regular hourly sessions with Dr. Martin continued, with additive benefits. They followed a set format. She and I always began with a private discussion to 1) inform her of events that transpired since our last appointment, and 2) determine priority issues to be addressed that day. This would be followed by her private intervention with David. She would conclude by inviting me back into the conversation to 1) summarize their encounter, and 2) give us direction, advice, or an action plan for the issue(s) of the day.

Early during our therapeutic relationship, I shared with Dr. Martin that I had the great fortune to have attended a seminar which hosted Carol Gray as a guest speaker. I was thus exposed, firsthand, to the Social Stories™ method of teaching social concepts, which Gray developed. I was excited and optimistic that it could be a valuable tool to help David further progress.

Gray's Story recipe delineates a strict "ratio" of component "sentence" types and follows precise "guidelines" (Gray, "Appendix A" 8). For each given topic, without making any "assumptions" about the person's understanding, Social Stories™ explain what is happening, along with the reason; they incorporate the client's "perspective" as well as the viewpoints of others "involved" (Gray, "A Close Look" 5). These

Stories help "describe" "social cues", "responses", and expectations (Gray, Social Stories video). The technique strives for comprehension more than the mere following of dictates (Gray, "A Close Look" 7). Please refer to Carol Gray's recent works for up-to-date criteria and information.

Dr. Martin wrote therapeutic stories for David to explain and teach him behaviors and skills. These were inspired by Gray's work and were tailored to David's needs. Eye contact, chit-chat, interactions with strangers, staying on topic, and management of his special interests were but a sampling of the subjects where such stories were included in her interventions. David and I often left sessions with a customized Dr. Martin story in hand, and per her suggestion, we would read it together at least daily. This seemed to help David internalize the logic and ways to interact more appropriately.

David repeatedly demonstrated that just because he could regurgitate a statement or desired behavior, it didn't necessarily translate into appropriate performance—he first needed to "get it." Dr. Martin's stories, among other strategies, provided that link. Once enlightened, David's social functioning improved. Time and again, David exemplified that he could learn, both socially and academically, if unknown and elusive details were taught in a way that enabled him to make sense of it all. David needed to invest extensive time and effort into actively learning what everyone else seemed to innately know— and we give testimony that these critical elements can be taught, as many experts assert. Even though certain behaviors were never totally eradicated or completely achieved, David still experienced significant success and improvement in his quality of life.

The following are examples of utilized stories addressing some of David's most pressing needs. Each was composed by Dr. Martin specifically for him and always in conjunction with an individual counseling session. I will insert additional stories later in this chapter (and the next) to demonstrate their use and effectiveness in David's ongoing therapy.

My Talking Mouth

(by Dr. Beth Anne Martin)
© Cleveland Clinic 2000.
Printed by permission of the author and courtesy of Cleveland Clinic.

Our mouths are used for talking with other people. It is important to take turns when we talk to others. Sometimes, I like to talk to myself. But, when I talk to myself, it's hard to talk with others. When someone starts to talk with me, I should stop my own talking. Then I can have my listening ears on and take turns talking with them. It is also important to use a quiet, safe voice when I'm inside. Sometimes I growl when I'm mad. But, when I growl people don't always understand me. So, I will use my big boy words instead. Then when I talk to people, they'll say "Now I get it."

Chitter-Chatter

(by Dr. Beth Anne Martin)
© Cleveland Clinic 2001.
Printed by permission of the author and courtesy of
Cleveland Clinic.

Sometimes I "chitter-chatter" [chit-chat]—
that's when I talk out loud to myself and repeat
the things that people say in one of my favorite
videos or shows. If I play with my toys and
make up new stories and things for them to
say, that is NOT chitter-chatter. Sometimes
chitter-chatter can bother some people. Also,
many people would rather talk TO me rather
than hear me talk to myself. I know the rule
is that I can only chitter-chatter 2 times per
day for 10 minutes each. Also, I can only do
this when I am in the car with just parents OR
when I am at home at my play table. I will be
able to earn points every day for controlling
my chitter-chattering. Mom or Dad will help
to remind me not to chitter-chatter and rather
to talk TO people. At the end of the week, if I
earn enough points for not chitter-chattering, I
can trade them in for something fun. I will try
to keep myself from doing too much chitter-
chattering.

David progressed beautifully over the next two years,
and he experimented with new outlets and mediums
for self-expression. As might be predicted, several
inevitably became "topics of interest" to an almost
obsessive degree. First, he developed a passion and
talent for telling jokes. Challenged with the abstract

nature of humor, this was rather ironic. However, David combined his love of performance with his gifted rote memory; he became the master of knock-knock jokes and simple riddles—many of which he probably did not understand himself. He was summoned to entertain at several school gatherings and was spurred on by the appreciative laughter and attention. This lasted about a year and was then superseded by his love of drawing.

In a second irony, the child who ineffectively held a pencil in kindergarten was now a very promising young artist. When created spontaneously, David's drawings were simple, but they were still better than average for his age. However, when he drew an image while looking at another picture, his final product often looked traced. David combined his love of Disney with his new passion for drawing, and he would copy pictures freehand from countless children's sources. Many were incredible likenesses of the originals, but regardless of the quality of his work, his desire to draw to the exclusion of other essential activities became problematic. This was a classic example of when Dr. Martin's intervention with a therapeutic story and limit setting was invaluable.

Drawing Too Much

(by Dr. Beth Anne Martin)
© Cleveland Clinic 2001.
Printed by permission of the author and courtesy of Cleveland Clinic.

Sometimes I like to draw. Sometimes I draw when a babysitter babysits me. After drawing something I like to act it out. But I can't draw too much because drawing too much doesn't make you grow--I mean if I draw all the time, I'll never have time to do other fun things with kids and family. When I draw too much and my mom wants me to stop and I want to keep drawing, I just ask her if I can draw for a few minutes. Sometimes she says it's OK to finish up, but then I have to do something else like homework. I feel good about this because it helps me to get smarter. I'm gonna keep working on stopping when Mom tells me to so that I won't miss out on other great activities like going to the beach club, acting camp, soccer, and school. Drawing is fun, but you can't draw too much!

Early in our association during the summer of 2000, Dr. Martin was preparing to give a professional presentation on autism spectrum disorders. She asked my permission to use David's behaviors to exemplify certain Asperger's Syndrome characteristics. In my affirmative response, I wrote Dr. Martin a letter which explained David's obsessive drawing. I also included several sketches which illustrated his painstaking process. Piles of such pictures were stacked at home, for he valued all of them too much to allow any discard. I reproduce part of that letter here as it effectively describes an imposing aspect of "life with David" at that point in time. Accompanying artwork follows at the end of this chapter:

Dr. Martin,

[These] drawings demonstrate David's attention to detail with obsessive accuracy on topics in which he is interested. He is currently illustrating the entire Pinocchio film (from memory) and draws one frame at a time, much like the old-fashioned cartoonist, changing one subtle detail per picture. These are of Pinocchio [and an associated character] slowly turning into donkey[s]. Pictures four and five were done on separate days, and though identical [except for the added detail, they] were not copied but done from memory... [Characters] always have the same body posture and arm positioning regardless of the subject. In the past six months, we have totally exhausted [the TV show] *Arthur*, the "Three Little Pigs," and *Pinocchio*. Each theme is illustrated in every spare minute of [David's] time for approximately two months. [He] then suddenly finds a new theme and totally forgets the prior one, unless an event or person comes by which he associates with it i.e., the babysitter and the "Three Little Pigs." There is **no** creativity in re-enacting the stories. Colors, outfits, lines, inflections, etc. must be EXACTLY like the original and he directs everyone to ensure this, or he becomes very upset. This is but one small example of David's ritualism...

The copying of pictures eventually transitioned into drawing caricatures of live models, and David soon drew sketches of the entire faculty at his school, much to their delight and entertainment. So obsessive was his interest that on our annual summer visit to an expensive amusement park, David refused to go on any rides and opted instead to shadow the caricature artists for the entire day to watch the masters at work. Older parents anyway, and not in favor of riding any more coasters,

Frank and I joked that it was our easiest park trip yet: we sat nearby him and people watched, sipping coffees under welcoming shade—expensive coffees, at that, considering the cost of our three admission tickets!

As he aged, David would spend many evenings and weekends entertaining himself by honing his craft, and the subjects would change in accordance with his current fixation. We encouraged him in his efforts, for it seemed like a potential path to a career. But by limiting his work to an acceptable duration, we also helped him to eventually learn how to balance illustration time with other essential and enjoyable activities.

The ultimate victory of David's primary school experience was his successful participation as the ring bearer in my brother's wedding. With much advanced preparation via counseling on expectations and behavior—and with the assistance of another therapeutic story from Dr. Martin—David was well versed on his duties and social cues. The only child participant in the bridal party, he had no one to model or accompany on the long walk down the aisle. There was so much potential for disaster and embarrassment—reminiscent of his first theatrical performance. But once again, David rose to the occasion. The shoes and tux shirt were perfectly sized and were paired with ideal undergarments to minimize irritation. Church duties were repeatedly rehearsed, and responses to relatives' likely comments were practiced. I brought bags of snacks and quiet activities, and I arranged for him to have break times and an early exit. David was perfect: good manners, no chit-chat (except during breaks), and no growling! Second only to the newlyweds, David theatrically "stole the show" during bridal party introductions, proving once again that acceptable behavior *can* be learned if thoughtful effort and time are taken—along with preparations to troubleshoot unforeseen deviations.

The Wedding

(by Dr. Beth Anne Martin)
© Cleveland Clinic 2002.
Printed by permission of the author and courtesy of Cleveland Clinic.

I am going to have an important job in my Uncle Kenny and Aunt Patrice's wedding--I am the ring bearer. That means I will carry the ring down the aisle during the wedding. I won't have to worry about it falling because it will be tied onto a pillow. I will try to remember to look straight ahead at Craig, who will be [by] the altar. I can think of it like a play where I am doing my acting job.

I will have another important job after the wedding--being in the wedding pictures. I will have my listening ears and looking eyes on for what the photographer tells me.

I will also get "breaks" from my jobs--there will be plenty of time to take a break and have some play or drawing or reading time. Mom will make a schedule for me so I know when my break is coming. If I need more breaks I will let my parents know.

I also know that I will probably meet a lot of grown-ups that I don't know or haven't seen in a long time. I will remember my manners.

These are a few things I can say: "Hi," "It is nice to meet you," and "thank you." I definitely will not growl at anyone, even if I have a growly feeling inside. Instead, if I am feeling growly or tired or frustrated, I will tell my parents and they can help me take a break.

Being a ring bearer will be fun. I am proud that my uncle picked me and I know I can do a great job!

Just like his brothers before him, David joined a city soccer league. It was an ideal sport for him, as team sports go, because even if he didn't make game altering plays or have frequent ball contact, David still felt involved in the action just by running alongside his teammates. A lower skill level wasn't as obvious, and *everyone* played in every game. He reaped the benefits of sunshine, exercise, and team camaraderie and gained exposure to working in a group towards a common goal, pun intended! His first coach was a family acquaintance who knew David's issues; more importantly, this respected man valued the benefits of childhood exercise and team participation more than the mere winning of a game. He was patient and encouraging, and he transmitted his enthusiasm for the sport. It was a wonderful experience, despite the irritation of the shin guards and feel of wet or muddy clothes. However, as the teams became more competitive and coaches became less accommodating, soccer was abandoned in search of other attractive options that matched David's expertise.

Appreciating that swimming might be an independent activity void of the stressors of a team culture, we enrolled David in lessons at a young age. He could thus reap the benefits of the exercise while hopefully finding a means of stress release, relaxation, and prowess. David participated in weekly instruction for years, and he climbed to the top skill level offered. Despite his success, however, he felt no joy or passion for the sport. So other than for its practical value, swimming was also abandoned as a potential extracurricular interest.

Finally, despite the potential challenges associated with dribbling and shooting, we turned to basketball, for it was a favorite family sport and Craig's ultimate passion. Wanting to emulate his brother and bond further with the neighborhood kids, David joined our church-affiliated team. He transitioned well, for Frank volunteered to be a coach, and Craig helped him learn basic rules and drills. Gross motor deficits did not seem to impact David until later in his childhood, but even despite this, he really enjoyed basketball and possessed a decent skill level. He therefore continued participation in this same league up until entering high school.

David advanced to occasional speaking roles in his theatrical endeavors, and he began to socialize more in school and neighborhood activities. By third grade, he progressed academically to the extent that he required increased intellectual challenge. David's perceptive and innovative teacher supplemented his class work with extra assignments (such as writing short reports). This appeased his hungry quest, addressed his weaknesses, and kept him engaged and learning. But at his midyear evaluation, his teacher introduced a most interesting notion: perhaps David should skip fourth grade to obtain the most appropriate academic placement for optimal success. We all agreed that he was not yet ready to mainstream; he still needed specialized instruction, and his social issues required continued intervention. As I considered this proposition, however, I believed that he might be ready to mainstream by junior high. Skipping a grade would result in David being the youngest in his class when he was already disadvantaged and somewhat immature. To prevent this, my plan was to advance him a grade, keep him at this specialized school through the completion of grade six, but then mainstream him *repeating* the sixth grade. This would ease his transition to larger classes and a faster-paced environment, and it would restore a more appropriate age differential. After discussion with the principal, multidisciplinary testing was scheduled to see if the results would find this plan to be in David's best interest.

The results of said testing placed David's intellectual abilities in the average to above average range, with no problems illuminated in any specific subject area. There was consensus that, although unusual, skipping fourth grade would not be harmful—as long as the missed work was independently mastered. I firmly believed that the academic benefits outweighed the negatives, so I embraced that challenge and plans were made accordingly.

The testing also revealed that David still struggled with deduction, adapting to change, and appropriately advocating for personal needs or assistance. Social interactions remained suboptimal, and he still had difficulty initiating conversations, utilizing eye contact, and performing school work without the guiding suggestions of adults. Of note, he thankfully no longer "growled" to communicate frustration or disagreement. He had also transformed from an aggressive, argumentative, and headstrong little boy into a polite child who was willing to be helped.

Often, David required repetition of directions in a variety of ways before he understood the intended message. First noted in preschool, a lingering and important finding was his tendency to "give up" if a task or question was too difficult. Instead of trying, he would opt out with his standard response: he "didn't learn that yet." It was as if he was afraid of failure and would rather not make an attempt if he was not guaranteed success. I wondered if this same rationale prevented him from trying to ride his bike. Clearly, special education was still imperative; these subtle needs and skills would be addressed in that setting but quite possibly missed with the time constraints and goals of a mainstream classroom.

Further, David continued to perform frequent repetitive behaviors while at his desk: smacking his lips, pulling his ears, and tapping either his foot on the floor or a pencil on his head. He audibly verbalized to himself while completing lesson work. These practices all required expert intervention to become socially acceptable and yet still allow him to function in whatever capacity these behaviors assisted. Understanding this concept helped my tolerance and empathy of his idiosyncrasies, but they still set him apart and required continued social skills therapy for acceptable adaptation. He definitely needed more time in this therapeutic school for many obvious reasons.

That summer, David and I spent a few hours every day learning the history he would have studied in the fourth grade. In asking him to explain the information back to me to verify his understanding, I soon saw his problem with grasping abstract concepts. I also then realized the great difficulty he had in going from "point A" to "point C." In other words, he could not make an inference or extrapolate—he could only learn the facts as presented. David readily answered any questions requiring rote regurgitation, but he struggled with those necessitating the application of information (and often responded with his pat answer, "I didn't learn that yet"). I worked on these skills as best I could, but they needed years of cultivation before he could perform critical analysis and arrive at a personal conclusion.

David was very cooperative with the summer tutelage, for he was extremely excited with the prospect of moving ahead in school. Summer studies were nothing new. I had always required all my boys to read daily during this hiatus to maintain skills and, hopefully, come to enjoy reading. David was additionally accustomed to short periods of math and grammar drills. But this summer, we added private math tutoring to ease his transition to fifth grade and to strengthen his skills and confidence; he was particularly challenged by word problems. The tutor was a family friend who had assisted my other sons before David; her expertise and kind counsel continued to unlock mysteries, dispel panic, and enable grade-saving epiphanies for David for the next eight years. Our family could not have survived without her!

Besides the drudgery, there was plenty of time left for summer fun. David continued with theater camps and socialized at the beach club and pool. There were a few boys in the neighborhood that David loved to play with, and he was delighted with occasional invitations to come to their houses. David's safety skills had improved, so we allowed him to walk to neighborhood destinations alone or ahead of us; he was thrilled with gaining this independence. In addition, since Craig was often charged with watching him on my workdays, David experienced great fun (and an education of sorts, I'm sure!) tagging along with the high school group. He went with the guys to the beach, mall, or whatever activity was planned (if Frank or I approved). Finally, it was time to get ready for another year of school, and David embraced this with great anticipation, for he would be in the fifth grade!

Starting at this school is a little bit fuzzy, but the general scenario is that it was a warm and safe environment. It was run by teachers and nuns who cared about each and every one of us kids and wanted to see us succeed. (It still remains a big part of my life to this day.) I do remember the time in first grade when I mostly kept to myself and spent much time "chit-chatting." I remember doing it when I was bored, happy, excited, and even when I was frustrated. I remember Mom telling me she had a talk with Mrs. O'Neill. My teacher suggested an activity that could be an outlet and a way to express myself: theater! I headed off to a performing arts center close to where my grandma lives, and it was there that I met Mike. Throughout my time at the center, Mike took me under his wing and treated me and all the other kids in the camp like talented and important individuals (the whole responsible adult/friend role). From the first production I was in, "Bye Bye Birdie," I fell in love with it. I continue to act to this day and hopefully will do so for the rest of my life.

Something I recall well is Dr. Martin working with me by using stories. Reading these with Mom took up a great amount of our time, but it's something that all paid off in the end. Subjects such as my chit-chatting, interacting with people or friends of the family, and not talking to strangers were some of the topics that the stories helped me with in my real-life experiences. But there were times when they did not resolve certain situations: bugging and teasing were still problems.

Throughout my primary years, I gained a reputation as the kid who would bring in bags of the "popsicle" sticks with jokes inscribed on them. I would tell these jokes to the people of the school during early announcements and even at special events. Some of the jokes I didn't understand, but I did my job for the day if they got a good laugh. I also had a tendency to go around the school composing portraits of the faculty and staff. I thought they were pretty good back then, but looking at them now, I can do ten times better. Drawing was another great outlet for me and something I also saw myself doing in the future. I liked to watch people sketch portraits. When my family and I would go to amusement parks, there was a time when I wouldn't do anything except watch the cartoonists compose caricature portraits of their customers. I was fascinated by it to the point that I didn't want to do anything else.

In addition to theater, I also played some sports here and there. I started off with soccer, which helped me see the purpose of hard work and teamwork. My coach motivated me to just try my best, work hard, and most of all, have fun. I don't remember much about how I interacted with my teammates, but I do remember the uncomfortable feelings of playing in rain and mud. I also recollect the scratchy sensation of the goalie jersey. Eventually, I lost my interest in the sport and haven't played it since. After soccer, I started to swim. I would go to the YMCA for swim classes once a week, and it was a great way for me to get exercise. Plus, I felt really good in the water. But it was just too boring for me, so I dropped that as well. Finally, I found a sport that was to my advantage: basketball. I found it to be a great tool to bond with Craig and the kids in my neighborhood. I thought I was pretty good at the time, and I enjoyed being on a team—especially the year my dad helped coach; it was some great father and son bonding time, but he did not cut me any slack.

By the time I hit third grade, I remember spending most of my time writing reports, particularly about sharks and the great Walt Disney. It was like I had a private tutor teaching me extra work in addition to the curriculum. I also took these special activity tests that helped me with deduction and comprehension. I didn't know what all the extra work was for until the last day of school. I was eating lunch with my friends in the grade above me, and they said that I was going to be a part of their class next year. I was surprised to the point where I thought it was a joke. I came home and I told my mom, expecting her to be shocked. Surprisingly, she told me she knew because she had arranged it herself. She then told me all the key facts she explained in this chapter. We were both excited, but we also knew there was a lot of work to do before this change could go into full effect.

During that summer, I experienced a healthy balance of work and play. I spent a great deal of time with my mom working on material like math and social studies that I would have learned in the fourth grade. It was hard at times, but I knew it would all be worth it in the end. BUT I also got to experience some fun with my summer. Craig let me hang out with him and his friends whenever they were doing something. It was at that time that I considered myself very fortunate to have a brother who thought of me highly enough to invite me to places with his high school friends. And with all of that, plus knowing I was on track to move on to the fifth grade, the summer came to a positive close.

Drawn by David
at age 7

Drawn by David
at age 9

Pinocchio Turning into a Donkey*
*note: Dave drew one image per page; grouped here for space and comparative considerations

#1

#2

#3

Boy amid Change to Donkey*
*note: Dave drew one image per page; grouped here for space and comparative considerations
(drawing prior to #4 is missing)

#4

#5

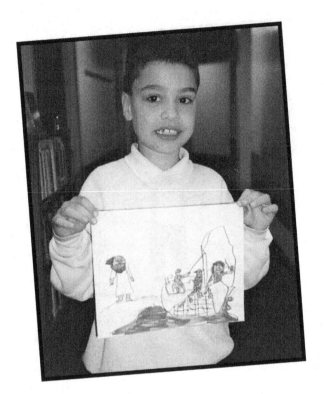

Caregiver lessons I learned:

- Anticipate, research, and prepare for the child's NEXT phase of life.

- Volunteer at places where your child is involved. Observing him or her firsthand in school and social situations gives incredible insight that is not gleaned from others' accounts and reports (including your child's).

- Interact with faculty to customize your child's education to best fit his or her needs. Do the adult homework necessary to maximize your child's success.

- Find and enroll your child in a group, club, or activity that matches his or her passion.

- Provide summer activities for your child that aim to prevent regression—intellectually as well as socially.

MORE SAMPLES THAT IMPACTED DAVID'S SOCIAL LEARNING:

Friendship

(by Dr. Beth Anne Martin)
© Cleveland Clinic 2001
Printed by permission of the author and courtesy of Cleveland Clinic.

It is fun to play with lots of different kids. I have some friends that are boys; some that are girls; some that are my age; some that are older. Some kids have lots of different friends, so they can't always play only with me. When two people want to be friends [they] have to both agree to spend time together. Some kids want privacy to play with other friends. I'll know this when my friend is in another spot playing with his or her friends. Sometimes it's OK to ask if I can join them. I have to listen carefully to their answer and if it is not a good time to play, I know I can try again another day. If I don't give them space and privacy, they might get frustrated with me and not want to play later. I have to keep remembering that both of us have to agree about our time together.

Showing My Close Feelings

(by Dr. Beth Anne Martin)
© Cleveland Clinic 2001
Printed by permission of the author and courtesy of Cleveland Clinic

We all have big feelings sometimes, especially when people are leaving or when there are changes in our lives. Sometimes people accidentally show their big feelings with big behaviors. At times these behaviors might hurt someone. For example, if I hit a friend of mine hard on the back as a way of showing I'm having a big feeling about seeing them or leaving them, that might hurt them. Then, they might think I was trying to be mean when I was really trying to be nice! I will try to show my big feelings in safe ways. Sometimes I do big behaviors because I see that happen in the plays I'm in. I have to remember that when I'm in "real life", I can use my safe words and safe behaviors to show my feelings.

CHAPTER SIX

The Middle School Years

David was very well accepted by his fellow fifth graders. Because children were always grouped according to ability, the students were accustomed to a mix of ages in each class; it was also common for participants to change from class to class. David had associated with many of these peers in preceding years, so there really was no transition to be had. He did experience, however, the novelty and temporary popularity that often accompanies being "the new kid," and he enjoyed the attention (especially from the girls) that it brought.

Academically, David was now perfectly placed, and he thrived in this custom environment with its expert and dedicated staff. Modifications existed in the general classroom setting for the benefit of all, and individual attention was additionally given to him for issues that were solely his. I will provide an example of one such issue. David demonstrated above-average abilities in both reading and spelling, as was evident from his recent testing as well as his actual performance. But there was a hidden problem too unexpected for average detection. David could smoothly read aloud a passage or script he had never seen before; amazingly, though it was totally foreign to him, he would include just the right inflection, emphasis, or dramatic pause. One would thus assume that he perfectly understood the selection, but to the contrary, his comprehension of the meaning or implications often did not correlate. This subtle but very significant discrepancy was noted by the faculty and was addressed for years to come (Mary had found this earlier on a simpler level, as well). I sincerely doubt that recognition or intervention for this problem would have transpired in a typical school.

David demonstrated similar inconsistencies in the world of math. Certain aspects of mathematics were extremely challenging for him; they just didn't make sense. For example, he studied excessively, both alone and with tutors, to try to grasp word problems and abstract material. In contrast, other numerical skills were second nature to David: he could quickly perform mental math computations and could also instantaneously recall or calculate dates of occurrences, such as how old Grandpa would be if he were still alive. Such were the dichotomies of David's presentation of AS.

Beyond academic needs, David continued to exhibit other characteristics necessitating specialized intervention. He frequently daydreamed in class, and he required prompts or redirection to get his focus back on the task at hand; repetition of instructions was commonly needed. David also continued to talk aloud to himself in order to get through assignments. For the next couple years, faculty worked with David consistently to help him overcome two shortcomings: 1) improve his ability to stay "tuned in" and 2) complete his assignments with a decreasing need for reminders as well as decreasing distraction to others.

During these years, David's clumsiness in sports and large motor skills became more apparent. He also developed a characteristic gait to his walk, and we fondly saw similarities in him reminiscent of the fictional TV characters "Barney Fife" of *The Andy Griffith Show* and "Steve Urkel" of *Family Matters.* David's desire to please—along with his naivety, increasing politeness, and commitment to rule following—also won him the private parent pet name of "the Beave," a reference to Theodore Cleaver on the late 1950s sitcom *Leave It to Beaver.*

Speaking of television shows, David watched his share in lieu of actual peer entertainment. It often seemed to Frank and me that he was inadvertently socialized by Disney or tween-targeted programs. Having few real-life peer situations to learn from, he seemed to internalize lingo, unrealistic expectations, or responses based on fictional plots. This became even more apparent when we role played how to extend invitations, handle situations, or talk to friends. We thus needed to reteach appropriate and realistic modifications.

David gave new meaning to "reality TV"—it often became his reality. He would research the participants and talk about them as if they were acquaintances. *American Idol,* for example, became a fixation during this time frame, especially with his love of entertaining.

To this day, he can state full names and life details of participants, including the year of their TV competition, contestants they vied against, and the specifics about candidate eliminations per episode. He often, still, relates continuing details about their recent lives with the assumption that we will know who he is talking about. The fixation and discussion of competitors' personal developments spilled over into other reality shows in his future, as well. In his teen years, he often spoke of the life events of guests on The *Biggest Loser* or *The Bachelor* as if they were people I should know. For example, he might ask, "Mom, guess who's breaking up?" But, back to age ten...

In terms of David's topics of interest, his rambling speech could finally be curbed with visual cues. A look at Frank or me giving a preset signal was enough to remind him to stop. Besides learning to control his desire to expound, he was improving in asking others questions to include them in a reciprocal conversation. Nonverbal cues were also more successfully utilized in class to keep him on task and appropriate. He still exhibited a lack of social common sense, however, and often felt like an outsider with the neighborhood kids, stating that he didn't "get" what they talked about.

Much of our family's winter social life revolved around Craig's high school basketball participation. Attending every weekend game, Frank and I bonded with other parents, and David enjoyed playing with the younger siblings of Craig's teammates. We treasured this added opportunity for David to associate with kids his age. Sitting through both junior varsity and varsity games was often too challenging for David, however, especially on Fridays after an already long day at school; the noise, cheering, bright lights, and constant activity were frequently bothersome to him. But he did enjoy watching Craig and their mutual friends compete, and David was also gaining a better understanding of the game in which he himself was a team participant. Socializing with the other kids (and visiting the concession stand, of course!) provided a welcome distraction after David hit his limit courtside. Rather than push our luck, we occasionally attended only one game or opted to keep him at home with sitters. We utilized the services of a few great teenage guys who played video games with David and engaged him in male-oriented activities when they watched him. This option was more acceptable to him than having female BABY sitters; he actually enjoyed staying home and being thus entertained, for it was more like hanging out with friends.

In Craig's senior year, he arranged for David to assist the team as a water boy. This was a wonderful role for him, and he was able to be right on the court, bonding with the team and participating in the action. It was a distraction from bothersome stimuli, and Craig was nearby to offer necessary guidance. It gave David a sense of pride and belonging, and it filled his long winter weekends with anticipation and memories. On the downside, witnessing Craig's high school world also provided David with unrealistic, preconceived high school expectations; few adolescents experience the friendships, successes, and popularity that Craig enjoyed. It was a very uncommon and skewed perspective for *any* child to emulate, and it "set the bar" ridiculously high for David.

It was around this time period that David became increasingly distressed with teasing or sarcasm. Attwood describes the common "literal interpretation" of those with AS and demonstrates how intended communication and funniness can be missed. He recounts a case in point: a child had misperceived a lighthearted jest, for the boy had responded only to the words actually spoken and was seemingly oblivious to nonverbal clues and the occurrence of kidding. "[T]easing" can be quite perplexing and the same with "sarcasm, pretence or lies" (76-77). Though all of this had implications for David, the following declaration had the utmost significance for him. Attwood states that the child's "naivete" may delightedly be taken advantage of by peers (78).

Beyond his perception of comments or actions, I believe that problematic teasing was aggravated in David's life largely due to his exaggerated responses. David grew increasingly defensive, for while it was true that he sometimes blew innocent exchanges out of proportion, he also more and more encountered peers that possessed less than good-natured intentions. David was emotionally and physically oversensitive— whether to verbal remarks viewed as offensive or to sensory stimuli invading his space. Both were perceived as noxious and intolerable. Regardless of his acting skills, David could not mask his feelings when experiencing either. His extreme reactions became fuel for his amused teasers' fire. So, considering all of the above factors, the stage was set for huge challenges.

Regardless of the setting, David was always plagued by someone "bugging" him. Even in this school's unique atmosphere of love, acceptance, and intolerance for this sort of behavior, the variations in student challenges sometimes combined to create a conflict. The difference with this school, however, was that it appropriately addressed the issue in a manner that taught the students valuable problem-solving skills. In addition to the adult intercession and rendering of apologies that usually occur, students here were encouraged to consider and explore underlying issues to achieve resolution. Peer mediation, depending on the student, circumstance, and age, was one such method utilized during David's attendance. Though formats might change with time, this conflict management training became a helpful tool that David independently tried at other facilities in order to solve peer confrontations.

Even at David's beloved acting camp, his fun was ruined by the antics of two boys who continually sought *their* fun at David's expense. Successfully dealing with such issues became the focus of several Dr. Martin sessions over the years. The names and settings changed, but the problem remained the same (or worsened). It was an issue as pervasive and problematic to David's life as was his chit-chat. David simply could not ignore his teasers. And if a situation WAS eventually resolved, he seemed unable to generalize the strategy (that is, apply what he did or learned to other occurrences). I frequently found myself questioning what he might be doing to invite this type of behavior, but in retrospect, that may have made him the victim twice. We turned to our experts to help us work on solutions for resolution, and this effort and process continued for years. Again, Dr. Martin's therapeutic stories were components of the interventions used to help David understand and respond appropriately. Here is one such sample:

Problem Solving

(by Dr. Beth Anne Martin)

I go to acting camp every Saturday. I really like acting camp, except there is a problem. There are two boys there named [X____] and [Y_____] who tease me all the time. They call me names and try to get me to believe I am those bad things. Am I those bad things? NO!! They also try to boss me around. Are they my bosses? NO!! If they can get me to get upset then they think they've won the teasing game. Am I going to let them win? NO!! Even when it really bothers me, I try to not let them get me upset. They'll never make me believe I'm the dumbest kid in the camp. Am I the dumbest kid? NO!! I'm not going to waste my time at camp talking back to them. I have more important things to do. I won't let them spoil my fun. Next time they bother me I can do any of these things: Ignore them so they don't think they got me; use my conflict management 4 steps with them; or if I really can't concentrate because of their teasing, I'll tell the teacher. I might even just try to see if they'll be friends with me because I'm a good kid. The one thing I have to remember is not to let them bug me!!

The summer vacation was crammed with all the aforementioned activities. But this year, there was one crowning jewel: David would spend an entire week at camp! There was a wonderful facility within an hour's distance that was the epitome of any kid's ultimate camp concept: swimming, hiking, crafts, horses, campfires, cabins, and much more. The big imperceptible difference was that, for this one week, the campers had the additional criteria of an AS or high functioning autism diagnosis (our thanks, again, to Dr. Martin for making us aware of this incredible offering). The counselors and professionals were trained in the special needs of this population, and therapeutic interventions were incorporated into the program.

David was thrilled, but I was apprehensive as we drove past the totem pole and up to the check-in station. What if he didn't like the food? Could he remember his hygiene needs independently? What if he couldn't handle a hectic day of events? Would he get along with the cabinmates and minimize his chit-chat? Anticipating parental concerns, the counselors were wonderful. I handed in the many required forms specifying David's needs and idiosyncrasies and gave them a bag of his dietary mainstays—something all campers were invited to bring for comfort and routine, despite the new "experiments" David was prepared for. I hoped that the camp could help wean his dependence, increase his flexibility, and improve his willingness to try new things. It achieved all these goals and more.

Following the opening activities, each family was invited to their camper's assigned cabin to help make up the bed, provide a reasonable transition, and then say good-bye. It was a long week with no communication between us, but David fared beautifully. He met wonderful people, bonded well with other campers, and experienced many "firsts" successfully. He looked happy and none the worse for perhaps having less than the usual number of home-required showers or fruit servings. We attended the awards ceremony and witnessed his pride, sense of achievement, and obvious comradeship. It was fantastic and helped us all to grow up a bit.

Questions began the minute we hit the car: "Do I have something wrong with me?"... "How did I get it?"... and so on. Apparently, the campers shared openly and therapeutically with each other, and David quickly realized the common thread bonding them. We talked about it much of the way home. He was not angry, just incredibly curious. It was the topic of conversation for the next few days, and I answered his questions to the best of my ability. There had never been any secrecy, and I guess I didn't realize that he didn't already know. We had been going to therapies for years, and he had been present for countless professional conversations, but again I must have assumed that he could make an inference. The only frank discussion I recall was when he started first grade. He questioned why he could not go to the neighborhood school like his brothers, and I responded that he had more difficulty with certain subjects that the chosen school could better teach. He accepted my explanation without rebuttal or further comment, so I offered nothing more. He seemed too young to comprehend the details, so I figured I would just answer his questions as they came. No more had come. I never gave it another thought.

The camp increased David's confidence and, I assume, gave him novel insight into challenges that had historically plagued him. His sudden willingness to try new foods was an added bonus. David had a very selective palate and severely limited his dining choices based on texture, seasoning, or time of day. He also insisted on moderate temperatures: entrees and drinks could not be hot, but merely warm. David would not try ice cream other than soft serve vanilla; even cake, chocolate candy, and other desserts were adamantly refused, so you can imagine his response to healthy meal choices. Vegetables were an obvious challenge, especially with their pungent odors that plagued his sense of smell.

With a bit of peer pressure, limited options, and the extreme hunger that followed a day of outdoor activities, David ate what was available—and he was amazed that he actually liked several experimental tastes at camp. It made him realize that he could be hurting himself in his refusals, so that was the start of his willingness to expand his options. Since he loved *McDonald's* sweet 'n sour sauce, we had purchased it for years to help with palatability, for he would eat certain foods *only* if dipped in *this* sauce. We continued to use it from then on to encourage more variety, for the camp changed his attitude. This continued for years, and with the added use of ketchup and barbecue sauce, sometimes even on grapes and other unorthodox choices, David finally began rounding out a healthy diet—especially since he never did come to eat most desserts.

Interesting to note, it was at that time that I began making inquiries into high schools—and even to one college—regarding programs, requirements, and offerings. Though I was still amid deciding David's elementary school path, I always felt it was crucial to consider future steps. As introduced in the last chapter, this has repeatedly enabled better decisions and preparations to be made at each successive institution, putting us in a more optimal position to attain our (his!) ultimate goals. I did not believe, at that time, that David could handle the coursework required of a baccalaureate program, but I still made the inquiry at one local college because the wonderful Mrs. O'Neill was involved with the initiation of a novel program there. It aimed at assisting students with learning disabilities, including AS. The director was incredibly helpful and followed our conversation with a detailed mailing, despite David's young age. Filed away for future reference, and believing at that time that he would instead find more promise in an artistic venue, it was fate that it resurfaced seven years later while I was cleaning out files...

Sixth grade proceeded with continued progress in academic and social skills. David continued his theatrical involvement and began to participate in the annual productions at our church's affiliated school. He loved his involvement there and started to ask why he couldn't attend and walk to that school, like his brothers had before him. Recalling our prior plan to mainstream David after skipping fourth grade, we gave the matter fleeting consideration, but we again postponed this option since he was so appropriately placed where he was.

Social skills and specialized interventions were inherently and maximally woven into the curriculum at David's current school. With a solid base established in reading, writing, and math, all other secondary subjects could then be more easily learned. But of equal (if not greater) value, the belief in the uniqueness and importance of each student permeated all interactions. This translated into David's development of amazing self-esteem and confidence. As a family, we always believed in David and showered him with positive reinforcement and praise. But having this also occur outside of the home from different adults in response to different challenges, a child was created who would keep on trying in the face of any adversity—and one who believed in himself.

This school recognized David's strengths and utilized them everywhere possible. He was placed in leadership roles, was invited to welcome guests at fundraising events, and was asked to participate or entertain at ceremonies—whether by acting, singing, or reading. He learned and internalized key lessons that would help him for life: 1) organization and preparation are worth the effort, 2) everyone is special and deserves respect, and finally, 3) it is okay and desirable to ask for help— do not be embarrassed if you need assistance! Rather, take advantage of the potential for aid in order to do the best that you can, and advocate for this assistance in the appropriate manner taught. These lessons reshaped David's future.

So, we made the decision to remain at this special school for at least one more year. Junior high brought new challenges, increased independence, and greater expectations. David required the expertise of this highly skilled team to maximize his preparation for his eventual move into the mainstream, and he looked forward to the leadership status and social opportunities that junior high conferred.

The period when I transferred into the fifth grade was probably the easiest transition I've ever had in my life. In the beginning, I was able to bask in some instant popularity with the kids, especially the girls. Eventually the excitement died down, and I became just a regular kid in the class. I didn't fall behind as the schoolwork began to pile up. In fact, I even saw myself get ahead of the pack a little bit. I feel that the tutoring during the summer led to me being on top of my game in school. I got good grades, and I even saw myself being a resource to some of my classmates. Overall, the transition and the grade skipping were not stressful because I was prepared. Going a little off topic here, but up until the age of eighteen, I was completely unaware of my secret nickname, "The Beave." I actually embraced it when I found that out from my parents, and it's something we still joke about to this day—but back to middle school. It was during this period that I had a fixation with the Disney Channel and reality television. It was through all those programs that I developed my own "natural way" to go about social situations, or at least what I thought was the right way. I would watch reality shows that involved contestants. After the show was over and a few years had passed, due to my quick memory, I would see something about the contestants on the internet and remember them. Once I read it, I would shout down to my parents and give them the news, but their reaction would be more like, "Who is that?" I never really viewed it like they were true friends; I just saw it as me doing research on my area of interest.

In terms of social situations, whenever we went to a party, a friend's house, or a school function, my parents kept me in line with some social cues. Examples of these were my mother's facial expressions and my father's stare, which I like to call "The Frank Petrovic Stare." If I was talking with someone, whether it was a friend or someone my parents knew, I would glance over at my parents; if I saw either of them giving me a certain look, I knew that was my cue to back off a little on the conversation. (It's something that still stays true to this day.)

These signals particularly came in handy when we went to Craig's basketball games, which were some of the best social outlets during that time of my life. My brother's teammates had younger siblings close to my age who I developed a strong connection with over time. It was cool knowing I had kids to hang out and bond with while our brothers were on the court. Also great was that Craig was able to pull some strings and make me one of the water boys for the team. It was a very enjoyable experience for me to be a part of the team and experience the action on the court.

As the school year progressed, I started to experience some slight teasing and bugging—nothing serious, just some typical kid stuff. Yet it still annoyed me. What was more frustrating was that I didn't know why it was going on. I just saw no use for things like that. It was also true that I just could not differentiate between the aspects of fun teasing compared to bullying. I looked for ways to resolve it, which led to Dr. Martin developing more stories that focused on the content of teasing and bugging. I tried the concept of ignoring, but it backfired with the person escalating his inappropriate behavior. No matter what I did to try to resolve the situation, nothing seemed to work.

At the end of a successful transition to fifth grade, I had the opportunity to go to summer camp for a whole week. I thought to myself, "Cool. It should be good." During that week I got to experience all the traditional summer camp activities: bonfires, hikes, recreation, camp food, etc. But I noticed something different about the camp. After talking with some of my friends I made there, I realized that it was a camp for kids with special needs. It was from that moment that I started to question who I really was: throughout my whole life, I never assumed anything was wrong with me. I never suspected my school as one for kids with special needs, and I never viewed the way I interacted with people as strange. I always saw myself as just a regular kid who did regular things. So when I got back from camp, I became very intrigued about who David Frank Petrovic really was.

Once sixth grade rolled around, I came into school with the knowledge I had gained that previous summer. Knowing that my school was one for kids with special needs, my feelings and attitude towards the school did not change. I didn't think more or less about anyone or anything, and I still looked at my classmates as my friends. I feel it was the way the school was set up that contributed to my accepting and nonjudgmental personality. And it was the morals the school taught me from first grade onward that were also key contributors. To be honest, I had never even noticed anyone's differences, and I was still very happy there.

Caregiver lessons I learned:

- Networking with other parents and professionals often leads to great ideas and information about unknown programs or events—and may also give you greater insight into your child's progress and public behavior.

- Encourage the child's organization and preparation.

- Help the child experience success. Seek opportunities that utilize and reveal his or her strengths.

- Recognize even small victories with praise and positive reinforcement. Increase the child's self-esteem and confidence at every opportunity.

- Help the child realize that effort pays off.

- Encourage the child to request and accept assistance without embarrassment. Work with him or her on the timing and manner of such requests. Start to plant the seeds of self-advocacy.

CHAPTER SEVEN

The Junior High Years

It was a highly eventful August. David had just concluded a summer theater camp that was affiliated with a different, professional fine arts group. We hoped that this would open the door to diverse future opportunities that could potentially continue into adulthood. Meanwhile, he busied himself with reading and math reviews in preparation for seventh grade, and he enjoyed rehearsals for the annual beach club swim show. David also watched as bedding, office supplies, and boxes of clothes piled up in the dining room: we were preparing for Craig's imminent departure to his chosen college four hours away. Steve had just graduated from this same university and had settled in the surrounding area, never again to come back home. We were thus all acutely aware that we would perhaps lose Craig for good, too - but we knew we still had a few summers to enjoy his return. This thought was not much consolation for David, who would dreadfully miss his companionship, mentorship, and fun-loving nature during the upcoming, stressful adolescent years. We watched as they said good-bye with awkward words and custom handshakes. And then there were three of us.

Seventh grade was definitely different. There were no-nonsense teachers, more class changes, more homework, and much more to remember independently. David soon realized that "growing up" brought added responsibilities in addition to the privileges he sought, and the stress of the former began to play on David's mind.

The "cough" began in July. Occurring with very rhythmic spacing and repetition, bouts were frequent and uncontrollable. Coughing became increasingly disruptive to David's daily functioning and had no medical basis according to his examining pediatrician. Within three weeks of starting seventh grade, a neurologist diagnosed David with a specific type of tic. He explained that stress could be a factor and prepared us for the possibility that it might last for years. The specialist described a potentially helpful physical intervention, which we tried twice daily for an extended period to no avail; he also prescribed medication to control the cough's intrusion on life. Clearly, Craig's departure and the rigors of junior high took a greater toll on David than we had anticipated.

It took a few weeks to regulate the medicine in order to balance its side effects with adequate tic suppression. We quickly realized that neither would be optimal. It was nearly impossible to know if David's subsequent meltdown in school was related to stress or to the effects of the titrated medication. But attention to all possible variables finally began to restore normalcy. This included a discussion between David and a teacher he found intimidating as well as continued sessions with Dr. Martin. David began to adjust to the advancement in expectations and workload, and he improved his organization and ability to work independently. As he began to relax and enjoy, his tic receded to almost unrecognizable existence. I realized, more than ever, the extreme importance of transition for David at every new stage of development.

We welcomed October after the intensity of the preceding quarter year. David enjoyed another season of basketball in our church-affiliated league, and he also earned his first major speaking role in the school theater group associated with this same parish. This was the performance that illuminated the extent of his talent. It brought him neighborhood recognition for his acting ability—over and above the stigma of his differences. Even we, his family, hadn't realized how natural and good an actor he truly was. David, of course, enjoyed the compliments and attention, and his requests to transfer to this local school resurfaced.

I began to seriously entertain that idea myself. I was not dissatisfied with David's current situation. I simply anticipated high school demands and wondered if a period of mainstreaming would ease his transition— especially given our still-fresh experience with adjusting to junior high. I researched high schools and had several possibilities in mind.

With only three of us left in our nuclear family, we sought to downsize into a home more fitting for our future needs. We decided to move anywhere that would maximally benefit David. Seeking the camaraderie that often occurs among neighborhood kids who attend the same school, we decided to let David's high school location dictate our new area of residence. We hoped that might optimize his opportunities for new friendships. David had come so far; as an added impetus to move, we wished to escape the stigma of his early behavior and reputation. We sought the opportunity for a fresh start, void of preconceived notions.

After an extensive search on all sides of town, we finally set our sights on a private coeducational high school with a spectacular fine arts department, including both theater and art. It was close to an excellent community college as well as the fine arts center that David attended the previous summer. It was the perfect choice—now he just needed entrance. The more pressing question was this: would mainstreaming David *prior* to high school be better for him, assuming he was ready to move on?

It was again time for a multidisciplinary team evaluation of David's status and needs, and I welcomed it for the objective assistance it would provide for our decision. The results were predictable and mirrored past findings. David's scores for reading, spelling, and rule-based calculations or tasks exceeded his nonverbal measurements. He was still challenged in areas requiring analysis, extrapolation, application, or advanced understanding—the same areas that were always impacted by his presentation of AS. David remained literal and thus continued to struggle with related reasoning, language forms, or abstract concepts. Beyond these issues, social interactions, independence, and creative writing all required further development.

I supposed that many of these areas would challenge David, to some degree, indefinitely—despite the marked progress he had absolutely made. Would they radically improve with one more year of special education? Perhaps mainstreaming would require more use of these skills and hence facilitate further advancement and comfort with them. Since kindergarten, David had never experienced a class size greater than fifteen students—and usually even less in the core classes. This undoubtedly was a huge factor for successful learning up until that point. But we realized that David aspired to attend a typical high school with a higher student-teacher ratio. I reasoned that eighth-grade experience in a similar environment would make high school less foreign and intimidating to David. He would also be exposed to a faster paced and perhaps more advanced curriculum, all while shouldering an increased need for independence. At the very least, the experience would let us know if a "typical" high school was beyond his range of options. Finally, we reasoned that mainstreaming prior to high school might enable David to acquire more "street smarts," for his naiveté would be more challenged. The reasons to transfer seemed to outweigh the gains of remaining at his current school.

It appeared that we had made our decision—again, not because of discontent, but rather, as a testament to the success of the special school. They had accomplished their mission: David appeared ready. A new question emerged: should he repeat seventh grade in order to be more age appropriate, or should he move on to eighth? I reviewed the curricula and spoke with the principal at the typical school; it seemed that David was academically prepared for the more advanced placement. Maybe his memorization skills would help compensate for his areas of difficulty. Bearing in mind his good organization practices and outstanding work ethic, success seemed probable. There was one other nonacademic factor to consider: the stigma associated with "flunking" was huge at David's age—especially since the neighborhood kids already knew his current grade level. Perhaps repetition of seventh grade would have a more harmful social outcome than promotion to eighth.

Ultimately, we presented the options to David; as a family, we made the decision to send him on without repeating the year, taking into account his self-esteem and pride as important components requiring consideration. A successful and exciting shadowing experience in the upper grade solidified David's choice, and it confirmed his assumption that he could handle the academic demands. As an added safety net, many teachers and students knew David and our entire family quite well at this neighborhood school. Thus, there would be a familiarity for David. And maybe more importantly, there would be "guardian angels"; they could assess problems at their inception and swiftly intervene to optimize the chances for success. It was the ideal scenario in which to attempt mainstreaming, and we decided to take advantage of it; we would never know his capabilities, or limitations, unless we tried.

In retrospect, I am confident that these decisions were ultimately the best choices for David, though I admit to subsequent occasional doubts. I believe that the ensuing challenges he battled were inevitable; they had to be fought, and won, regardless of how or when he mainstreamed. It was a necessary part of the journey. Experiences were presented that I believe would have been encountered, eventually, on *any* chosen route to "the real world." For us, better sooner than later; we chose to get on with it. Leaving the comforts of his beloved school, David felt ambivalence and anticipation akin to a young adult "leaving the nest"—both taking love and lifelong lessons with them.

David had an eventful summer, several weeks of which were spent in a day camp sponsored by his brothers' high school. It was a program for young men entering the eighth grade and was geared toward academics and athletics. It exposed participants to various classroom subjects and group sports (some of each were new to David), and it also incorporated team activities and exciting field trips. We felt this would be a great transition to David's mainstreaming: he would meet a diverse group of guys, would practice his social skills, would remain intellectually stimulated, and would exercise in novel, practical ways. Though it seemed a bit intimidating for David, my other two boys loved it at his age. Besides, we had the benefit of an added safety net and support person: as one of Craig's summer jobs, he just happened to be a lead counselor for the program, though David was not his direct charge. It worked out beautifully, and David was able to participate fully and independently—with one glitch. Distressful "bugging" by one of the other campers (someone known to David from his past) marred the experience. It proved to be an omen: David was troubled with teasing, or worse, at every school or program he attended throughout his adolescence.

In preparation for mainstreaming David at our neighborhood school, I met with the new principal and each of David's four prospective teachers; the upper grade students rotated classrooms and received instruction from the entire junior high faculty. I provided testing and narrative reports from David's special school and explained his differences, challenges, and needs. Together, we developed a plan to maximize his potential to succeed and to provide some of the accommodations he was accustomed to. For example, he was to sit near the front of the class, and he would be encouraged to seek clarification or ask questions beyond that usually required for most students. I emphasized that David might need to hear explanations presented in different ways before he would comprehend the task required of him. Preparation was necessary for the school personnel, as well as for David, in order to minimize miscommunication and frustration. All parties were prepared to the utmost extent that anticipated needs allowed. The school community could not have been more accepting, willing, accommodating, or supportive.

The school year finally began, and David was able to joyfully walk instead of riding a bus, just as his brothers had before him. He was thrilled and well received, and he again enjoyed another "new kid" honeymoon. The faster pace and intensity were indeed stressful; David responded by increasing his studying and tutoring to keep up. He continued to utilize the regular assistance of our family friend for mathematics, and I worked with him on the remaining subjects or concepts which required further explanation. Frequently, we read difficult material out loud in turn. I would then reword it in a different way, often using analogies or tangible examples to help him "see" the idea. Visuals such as diagrams or models often assisted his comprehension. I would then request that he repeat the information back to me to validate his understanding. We would follow this with the summary and review questions that often existed at the end of a section. This would reinforce the material and help David apply his new knowledge.

David's difficulties with inference, deduction, reasoning, and analysis really began to surface as work became more demanding. He could memorize facts without flaw and regurgitate them back with understanding, but if he was required to answer a question worded differently than the exact text he studied—he was lost. For example, if definitions were learned for vocabulary words, he could state them exactly and choose the matching word being defined. But if the word was used in a sentence he had never before seen or heard, David could not figure out its meaning even though he could recite and explain its definition. The teacher voluntarily worked with David using sentence examples as part of her personalized instruction; he eventually improved on quizzes, for we also practiced similar types of questions during our studies at home. David struggled if a test did not ask *what* he studied or *how* he studied it (hence his problems with standardized tests). In addition, he often needed to clarify *what* the question was asking, or *which* thought process he should follow—even when he understood the material and actually knew the answer.

Similarly, David had difficulty answering the exact question that was asked in an essay. He provided true facts and details in his response, but they were often irrelevant and never actually addressed the required issue or made a point. This skill did improve and develop with time and practice. Patient mentors (including myself) explained the problems with his replies, and they pulled the known information out of him via leading questions which took him down the right path. But the process was unnerving, and it jolted his self-confidence in the academic arena. David was called upon to utilize more advanced mentation at this school; though extremely difficult, it was necessary for him to progress.

Thankfully, the fall play provided a fun respite from all the hard work. David enjoyed a leading role and entertained us all with his still-emerging talent. Rehearsals provided opportunities to socialize, but as time went on and the novelty of being new wore off, they also highlighted his social deficits when he was offstage. David became increasingly aware that he was often out of the loop and didn't understand what the others were talking about. The content and lingo were sometimes perplexing. During interactive times between classes, such as lunch or recess, he was frequently picked on and began to experience teasing, misery, and ultimately, bullying.

Many conversations eventually ensued between David and the principal, whom David sought out to gain assistance and counsel with such encounters. I sometimes became involved in these discussions as well. It soon became evident that David had difficulty discriminating between teasing and bullying. When is that line crossed? Similarly, what is the difference between tattling and the unequivocal need to inform an adult of an inappropriate act? Poorly defined and confusing for most people, discerning their difference was a total mystery to David. In addition, when he needed adult input most (realized retrospectively), Frank and I worked on weaning him away from our involvement in conflict management; instead, we promoted his independent resolution. Right or wrong, in the situations he described, we felt it was not in his best interest for us to speak with offending peers or their parents on his behalf (though I must admit it was often difficult to refrain).

Separately from the adults at school, Frank and I continued to give David suggestions for potential strategies that might help him handle troublesome interactions. The incidents were usually harmless childhood antics, but there *were* instances when adult intervention was necessary, and the school personnel did take appropriate action when informed. Peer situations were also a continuing topic of counsel with Dr. Martin. At home, Frank and I regularly assessed the status with David, but he was so unnerved by even the simplest peer comment or invasion of space that I believe we may have inadvertently disregarded certain accounts as overdramatizations. In these circumstances, we may have failed to offer the help David so desperately sought. We encouraged him to confide in trusted adults, yet in response, I fear we minimized his concerns and offered empty verbalizations—probably intensifying the despair and frustration that were brewing. Though names, settings, and incidents changed, this was a large and exhausting part of life for the next couple of years. Seeking to intervene appropriately and ease my son's struggle, I read articles and attended presentations. David and I both felt helpless at times, but I hoped and prayed that he didn't feel alone, abandoned, or hopeless.

Among the highlights of junior high were the occasional Friday evening tween dances held at a neighboring school. David looked forward to these with great anticipation and enjoyed the first couple with fulfilled expectations. But as academic demands intensified, commensurate with the bothersome antics of certain classmates, dances punctuating a long school day of a long school week proved to be a bad combination. David began to experience a degree of rejection and uncomfortable solitude at the dances, simultaneous with watching others enjoy the social experiences he desired. But even worse, the attention he did receive was often harassing in character, imperceptible to chaperones, and entertaining to his bullies at David's expense. We were phoned by David or adults on several occasions, requesting that we pick him up early because he felt "woozy." He complained of being lightheaded and felt like his heart was racing. He described a pressure in his chest and hyperventilation. In an extreme occurrence, the security person called us to hastily retrieve him, and the official demanded a doctor's note before future admission would be permitted. What was going on?

We were all upset and frustrated, but in hindsight, Frank and I did not appreciate the intensity of the situation from David's perspective. We were only familiar with the "typical" experience of a dance—I recall the loud volume of the music as being the lone irritant. Unfortunately, it wasn't until many months later that I read the following supposition (which may shed light on just one facet of the complex dilemma). Attwood describes "three types of noise" that "people with autism and Asperger's Syndrome" can experience with exceptional forcefulness: 1) abrupt, unanticipated, and piercing (exemplified by "a dog barking"), 2) shrill and constant (illustrated by certain household appliances, like a blender), and 3) intermingled and multifaceted (like a crowd or mall) (129-30). Attwood likens them to nails on a chalkboard to gain typicals' appreciation for the distress of these seemingly innocuous sounds (130). In pondering this, David has indeed demonstrated past difficulties with all of these at times (and additional examples will be revealed in future chapters). Certainly this trio exists at a dance, separate from the music's high volume; could it have been a factor in David's reaction? Recall, as well, his differences and challenges in other areas. And especially consider his inability to escape distressing individuals within the confines of the dance hall—a plight we also minimized.

Unfortunately, Frank and I did not realize, at that time, the gamut of coexisting stressors which David endured. It wasn't until years later that David shared with me the gravity of his reaction to experiences at these dances—and the potential for adverse consequences that we fortunately avoided. Despite the mystery for what transpired at these socials, we instinctively limited Friday evening outings for David and encouraged restful breaks in his activity. Luckily, there were no similar events for the remainder of junior high.

Finally came the time to officially apply to our chosen high school. Despite the more difficult, fast-paced curriculum of eighth grade and the class size of thirty-four students, David was very successful academically. This was largely due to his diligent studies, conscientious nature, incredible work ethic, and intense motivation. He didn't perform well on standardized tests, however, and I was concerned that he did not score high enough on the school's entrance exam—especially since he took it without accommodations. To compensate for potential poor scores that were not reflective of his actual abilities, I sent an explanatory letter to the school and enclosed materials which spoke to David's AS and past needs and behaviors. This was done intending to illustrate his progress, qualifications, and strengths. I also communicated that a personal interview with David would be welcomed if questions existed regarding his admission.

It possibly backfired, for while at work, we received frantic calls from a devastated son. David had raced to the mailbox after school on a Friday to excitedly open his anticipated acceptance letter. Instead, he was alone and unsupported as he read the worst news possible for a child who had already suffered so much rejection: he was denied entrance. Compounding the situation, schools were closed by then and unreachable until Tuesday because of an extended holiday weekend.

David was inconsolable—and I was panicked. I feared that my well-meaning intercession had instead convinced the admission committee that David's needs were beyond the school's scope. Why had they not contacted us or his current school officials if there were any questions or doubts? Why had they not asked to meet with him in person as I had proposed? We knew that this was the perfect school for David to fulfill his potential in every facet of development. And we also knew that he could contribute to the school, in turn. Incidentally, we were so confident of his admission that we had already started construction on a home in that area. He had to get in! It was the longest weekend of our lives, only made bearable by the decision to continue with plans to visit Steve and Craig. Steve now worked in the same city where Craig attended college, and the laughter and distraction provided by the brothers and their friends served to ease our anxiety and pass the time.

With the support of my coworkers, I left work early on Tuesday morning and sat in the high school office until an official could speak with me. I realized and respected that other scheduled obligations pre-empted my meeting, and I was willing to wait the entire day if necessary. Talk about advocacy: David was qualified and deserved decision reversal. If I had inadvertently complicated the process, I most certainly was going to right the situation. And I wasn't leaving until given that opportunity. David's eighth-grade principal was also surprised by his rejection and was independently intervening from her end. Finally, my turn arrived; as I sadly suspected, it was misinterpretation of my submitted material that put David's admission in jeopardy. I clarified specific concerns and was promised that the committee members would re-evaluate their decision. David's acceptance was communicated to me on the following day.

We were relieved and thrilled, of course, but the news was not in time to spare David the long and hard Tuesday at school. He endured the excited announcements of fellow classmates celebrating their admissions while he still nervously awaited his fate. He could not participate in their joy and solidarity, and he fumbled to respond to their inquiries regarding his destiny. By the time he was able to happily join the party, it was yesterday's news and not really the topic of class interest. Such was his luck and life, often striving to catch up with the others. But this time, it was largely my fault, and I've always wondered if his test scores were enough to merit his admission in the first place. Despite my lucky history of generally making good decisions on David's behalf, I was also taking a blind journey and was learning from my mistakes (and this, unfortunately, would not be the last of them). Wanting to shield David from the rejection, I told him only that an error had been made. I did not confide the complete story to him until he was a successful high school graduate and able to understand the circumstances—which he graciously accepted without assigning blame.

It was always two steps forward and one step back, and we had to constantly remind ourselves that the net movement was forward. So, after regaining our composure, we proceeded.

I have elaborated on the above incidents to illustrate David's challenges and Asperger journey, but I don't mean to portray that all was negative. David's experience during that mainstreamed year was predominantly successful, positive, and full of fond memories for all of us. Academically, he progressed in weak areas; notably, he learned to read quietly to himself rather than aloud. He became less sheltered and very much enjoyed his growth and exposure to the larger world. Aside from the handful of bothersome male peers, he was very well accepted at this school and experienced friendship among many wonderful classmates. The faculty could not have been more helpful or accommodating, and David transcended his entry status to rise to a whole new intellectual, social, and emotional level. We were convinced that the transition had provided key experiences for his high school readiness.

In the spring, David ventured outside of youth productions and entered the world of community theater. He landed a supporting role in a wonderful musical and shared the stage with actors of all ages; he greatly enjoyed his experience and growth in this venue. At some point, "rap" became a talent and "special interest." David attracted spectators as he spontaneously rapped familiar or customized songs to any open ears: at the mall, sporting events, or social gatherings. It was during that time that David Petrovic became more commonly known as "D.Pets." He was actually quite good, but as with most AS topics of interest, we worked with him constantly to limit his craft appropriately. We always feared that he would outwear his welcome or set himself up for ridicule.

The school year was swiftly approaching the anticipated graduation festivities. I tried to contain the mixed emotions that fought to surface as David processed into the church, flanked by a fellow graduate. He had battled so much and yet rose above so many others. Selected to perform the Scripture reading, his theater background served him well; he strongly and eloquently seized the attention of the congregation. I am always amazed at others' startled reactions when they realize the extraordinary abilities of people with disabilities— people who they assume to be generally *unable* just because they are, in some way, *disabled*. David was given additional recognition several more times that evening, most notably for achieving second honors. He earned a high school tuition award based on a competition and would later receive a second scholarship from a private outside source. No one was more deserving.

David attended the graduation parties which followed that evening while I hurried home after an abbreviated celebration. I needed to complete packing for the following big day. For while most of the graduates would enjoy a final group outing to the amusement park which once held David captive at the caricature station, our family would leave the neighborhood that was central to cherished child-rearing memories. We jointly chose this day to move, for David was still distressed by the continual provocation of a few of the guys; we felt that a huge park, void of constant adult oversight, would pose too much opportunity for misery. Rather, we chose to end this life chapter on the high note of graduation and the pride and fond memories it imparted.

Hope and anticipation dominated any ambivalence as the three of us said our final good-byes and sped off to a new life. We welcomed a new home and a new school, and we felt uplifted by the rare opportunity for a fresh start for David. We couldn't wait to begin!

Starting junior high was probably the toughest transition for me up until that time. The teachers, the curriculum, and the homework were way harder than middle school. In addition to Craig leaving for college, the stress was at its greatest. A symptom of the stress was something that I remember specifically starting in my art class in seventh grade: as I was sitting there listening to the teacher, I started to develop this cough. At first I didn't think that much about it, but over time it grew into a very disturbing habit. There was a periodic intense pressure in and on my chest to the point where I needed to cough to release it. After going to a specialist and learning it was a "tic," I sought remedies to resolve it the way the doctor instructed. This didn't work for me, but the cough did decrease over time with the help of some medicine. I still struggle with tics to this day.

As the days of junior high got harder, I found myself falling victim to anxiety and stress. I distinctly remember breaking down during school just because of a bad grade I received on one of my homework assignments. Even though it didn't count for much, that poor mark hit me hard; with all the emotions bottled up inside of me, I had to let it all out. Eventually, with the help of organization and time management, I learned to balance my schoolwork and deal with my emotions. Adjusting to the teachers, responsibility, and independence solved the problem.

During dinner at our favorite restaurant, my parents and I finally discussed my possible transfer to the local school. I never really thought that much about the switch until one night at basketball practice. I was talking with some of my teammates when they brought up the idea of a possible shadow day for me. I strongly considered it, ran it by my parents, and we decided to check it out. I thought I was well received by the teachers and the students when I went to shadow. I enjoyed myself, and I could see myself going to school there. My parents and I made the decision to transfer. By the time seventh grade finished, I walked out of my special school with tremendous accomplishments, proper tools for moving ahead, and a place I could always call home.

That was the summer I decided to go in-depth socializing with new peers. I was able to get involved in a cool program that Craig was a counselor at. I thought it would be a fun way to enjoy the summer, learn, and get the chance to socialize with boys my age. It was an overall good experience, but there were times during the program when I experienced upsetting teasing. And it was the teasing that prevented me from enjoying the program to the fullest.

Once the summer was over, the day came when I could finally walk to school and begin a new experience. Like the switch to fifth grade, I basked in another short-lived popularity from being new; I just became an ordinary part of the class once that died down. After getting my feet wet in my studies, I saw that the work was a lot harder and even frustrating at times. But with the help of my parents, teachers, and different approaches, I kept up with my studies. I've always *had problems with tests: if they do not correlate with how I studied or memorized the material, I struggle to answer the questions. But thanks to teacher interventions that year, I was able to improve and broaden my horizon on test-taking abilities.*

As time went on in junior high, teasing began to develop into bullying. In addition, it was hard for me to develop an understanding of slang and lingo; with my literal views, it was usually difficult to interpret phrases such as "lol" and "brb." I also met with the principal at times to go over ways on how to deal with this teasing/bullying situation. There were days when it was very subtle, but there were other occasions when it was at its worst.

Throughout the year, I was able to go to some dances at another local parish that served junior high kids from schools throughout our area. They were enjoyable at the beginning, and I had the time of my life at the last one, but the ones in between took a toll on me. Among problems that came with dances, I was a target for some of my bullies. Verbal, physical, and emotional abuse occurred as well as alienation— sometimes all at once by different people. It was basically their amusement to see me suffer at my own expense. In addition to that, there were times when I found myself getting light-headed and my heart would race uncontrollably. This happened to the point that chaperones and an officer would have to help me out of the dance.

The way I felt was bad, but I felt even worse when the officials had to call my parents to pick me up early from a dance. I felt like I was putting my burdens on my mom and dad; at that point in time, I don't think they really understood what I was going through. After I came home one night, I was distraught to the point that I questioned my self-worth. The fact that it was going on daily and for so long, no matter what I did, made me feel like this was going to be my life. As my parents slept, I stayed awake thinking about how I could not survive one more day of this. I kept all the bad thoughts to myself and only told my mom years later. Eventually, I was able to sleep. The next day, I pushed it all down and I just continued with life.

On top of everything going on, it was during that time when I received a rejection letter from the high school of my choice. When I got that letter, I dissolved into tears—not because I was angry, but because I didn't understand. I had good grades, I had plenty of extracurricular activities under my belt, and I just did not get it. Eventually, I did get my acceptance, and I was greatly relieved.

I don't remember how the bullying stopped at that school, but it eventually did, even though teasing continued. I didn't go to the next few dances in agreement with my parents, but I really wanted to go to the last one of the year. Before the dance, I met a girl who I really liked and who actually liked me, too. We agreed to meet up at the dance, and I got to hang out with her and her friends. Throughout the night, we danced and chilled, and I hung out with a good group. Luckily, I was able to avoid my bullies. I got to live it up with friends, and no one gave me any grief. With no one around to tease me, I could finally let loose and enjoy myself without feeling uptight or stressed. Not even the music amps or vibration bothered me this time. Overall, it was the best way to end the school year.

I didn't have the time of my life at this school, but I'm glad I transferred. It taught me how to grow up a bit, become a more independent person, and adapt to an academic setting similar to my future high school. I had a feeling it would all pay off, which came to culmination senior year. So, while my peers were off to the park on their Last Hurrah, I would go and visit with my aunt and uncle for a few days until my parents got our new house all together. Though I was reluctant to leave my friends, I was eager to see what my future held. And so began the next chapter: my high school career.

Caregiver lessons I learned:

- Optimal transitioning and advocacy remain paramount for success.

- Work with the professional teams to customize the academic path.

- It may sometimes be necessary to educate the educators.

- Accommodations can still occur, within limitations, in "typical" schools – and can be essential for successful mainstreaming.

- Your journey is unique, and no one is perfect – do not chastise yourself for mistakes. Learn from them and move on.

- There will be setbacks, but continue to forge ahead. What is the alternative?

CHAPTER EIGHT

High School:

FRESHMAN YEAR
(The Longest Year of Our Lives)

David and I spent our down time that summer exploring our new community and settling in. It was all very exciting, but I was at a loss for how to get him immediately involved with peer events. An exhaustive search did not reveal any plausible theater options, and David didn't yet know anyone in the area. Falling back on the venue which my older boys enjoyed, we opted to enroll him in a summer basketball camp at his soon-to-be high school. He still enjoyed the sport and looked forward to making some connections with classmates. It proved to be one of our biggest mistakes and set him up for years of grief. It was a most inappropriate choice, and we brought it on ourselves. Live and learn.

I should have realized that many of the participants at that age level were serious contenders for the various competitive high school teams. While not terrible at the game, David was totally out of their league athletically, not to mention socially. He walked in, naïve and alone, and the seemingly harmless teasing began almost immediately. David was distressed and frustrated and could not wait for the week to be over. The problem was, however, that it was merely the beginning; while some guys soon lost interest in the entertainment, a couple escalated their behavior and expanded their scope.

So instead of a quiet and slow acclimation to this new and exciting venture, David walked in on the first day of class already in receipt of negative attention; he projected an aura far from that intended. I couldn't help but wonder, time and again, how life might have been different had we avoided this sports camp and found instead the activities enjoyed by the theater crowd. But that is a pointless question that will never be answered—and so began David's tedious uphill battle to "break out" and "catch up."

Academically, the decision was made to defer foreign language during this first year, acknowledging David's continued challenges with English basics. This proved to be a very wise choice, in stark contrast to this second seemingly logical decision: in order to hopefully ease the workload and transition, a study hall was advised instead of an elective course. Due to the loose nature of study halls, this decision was another that backfired. Had we opted for choir class in lieu of said choice, life may have taken another turn. But again, we learned this only retrospectively, and we deferred to the judgment of those more experienced in curriculum design and student needs.

David had performed well in coursework during his mainstreamed eighth-grade year, so I decided that no accommodations would be utilized at the start of high school. Due to his turbulent admission process, I did not want to begin our association with extra requests that made David stand out as needing more help than the "typical" student; I didn't want to raise any red flags or confirm any suspicions that his entrance might have been a mistake. And if I am being totally honest with myself, I may have assumed that he had been "fixed" academically because of the preceding year's successful experience. I may have been fleetingly in denial of his actual lifelong needs. I just wanted to start off "normal," not calling attention to ourselves or setting David up for any prejudgment. Ironically, it would take about two months for the opposite to occur and everything to unravel, resulting in anxiety, distress, and negative attention beyond our wildest dreams. I quickly relearned that David would always have special needs but that anticipation, preparation, and intervention—rather than closed eyes and wishful thinking—would put him in a position for success and "normal" goal attainment.

Despite turning down the school's initial offer for academic accommodations, I personally addressed David's needs for transition and alternate teaching strategies. On receiving his schedule, we walked the halls together prior to the actual first day, finding each classroom and learning the buildings. This was followed by his independent and successful quest for the same, aiming to increase his comfort. When school officially began, four short minutes were allotted for class changes. Requirements during this brief timeframe included opening his combination lock under duress, exchanging books in his locker, and independently remembering to gather all detention-avoiding necessities. The ensuing trek through crowded corridors was punctuated by a shrill bell that potentially signaled tardiness—and all this repeated nine times daily! The stage was thus set for stress even before course demands and social problems were added to the equation. We spent extra time practicing the lock manipulations, preplanning locker runs, and mastering the routes, for these are issues that worry even "typical" students, much less someone with issues like David's.

I called the city office to investigate the exact transportation plan. David would need to transfer busses at a local school during the morning commute but would take a single bus home. We learned the vehicle numbers, pickup locations, and time schedules. He would have only a few minutes after his last class to gather all needed homework supplies or would risk missing the sole ride home. This posed additional stress, for David would have to wait, some days, up to three hours for a parent ride home in the event of a missed bus. He was thus under pressure to recall and pack all the evening's required essentials. We planned that David would utilize assignment books (completed at the close of each class) and check lists to expedite this process and prevent omission. We rode the routes by car before his first actual trips, and I wrote the bus numbers and details down for his referral. We explored all the pickup locations, and he seemed comfortable with where and when to be at each. I thought he was adequately prepared...

During this first semester, David initially proceeded with class work and home studies independently. We both wanted to see if and how he could handle this feat. I helped him get organized with the tabbed binders and assignment notebook that were vital in the past, and we reviewed study tactics and nightly plans. David denied problems and stated all was well, but after a couple of weeks and the first few quizzes, it became apparent that he didn't know what he didn't know.

Different from elementary school, reading and study needs existed beyond assigned work, and students were responsible for class discussions and material that often did not appear in any written form. But David seemed to learn better from seeing, rather than merely from hearing. Compounding the challenge, taking notes on verbal presentations was difficult and daunting for him. Bolick details the skill's complex process: one needs to hear the content, deliberate on noteworthy information, record the chosen essentials on paper, and resume focus on the presentation (30). She asserts that for a learner with Asperger's, supplying "notes" can help ease this burden—pending the teen's use of a fitting learnt method that enables self-sufficiency. The person's mind is thereby freed up to concentrate on the lesson (30, 68, 76).

Alas, this service was not occurring for David at that point in time (though I advocated for it later). In attempting to accomplish this feat, David often missed important communications and became lost in the discussion. Thus, he instead opted to mostly listen rather than write, hoping to hear and remember what he needed. Unfortunately, he didn't always comprehend or retain— and then had no way to study class concepts that were not present elsewhere in text.

On discovering the first quiz results in two separate courses, I requested a look at his sketchy and inadequate notes. Questioning him on their content, I further found poor understanding of the meager information he *did* possess. A discussion revealed that he had not received a book in one class, related to a temporary shortage of available copies, and was not permitted to take the book home in another. He finally admitted his stress over demands and performance; game over – our experiment with independent learning came to an abrupt halt.

Private math tutoring sessions were reinstituted at least weekly via our family friend and savior. My correspondence with a teacher and the school psychologist resolved the lacking text information in the two subjects previously mentioned. I began to read sections of his course books and correlating notes daily in three of his subjects. I would reteach the information in a format he could understand, building on the techniques we used in his previous mainstreamed year. With the increased difficulty and volume of material to be learned, the time and means we employed also intensified.

I will reiterate and expound on our methodology since it was so vital for David's comprehension. He and I would alternate reading difficult passages out loud together, with me often interrupting to reinforce, refer to a diagram, or restate critical concepts. I utilized examples, analogies, acronyms, and word associations. I relied heavily on repetition and the use of models or illustrations (some that I would create). Following instruction, I would ask David to answer questions and/or restate the material in order to verify his understanding. I would never merely ask, "Got it?" For that would inevitably generate an affirmative response with no proof that the material was correctly mastered; he sometimes *thought* he knew it when misperception still existed. Rather, I requested him to explain or show me the newly acquired knowledge or skills—a technique that I learned and regularly utilized in my professional nursing practice. This would validate either an understanding of the provided education or illuminate further need for clarification. Obviously, we both invested significant time in all these processes. And this occurred in addition to David's ordinary studies and assignment completion. But it was well worth the effort for him to understand, relax, and keep up; he was a willing and appreciative participant.

Nightly, David and I studied the class work presented earlier that day. This made the following day's class more understandable, meaningful, and valuable (easing *that* night's review). More confident in his knowledge, David's class contributions and enjoyment also increased, positively reinforcing his desire to continue our methods. We prepared for tests incrementally beginning a few days prior to the scheduled exam. Even when he mastered the material, test scores were dependent on his proper understanding or interpretation of the questions. So solid test preparation alone did not ensure David's success—his scores did not always reflect his actual knowledge of the subject matter.

I contacted each teacher to discuss David's general and test-taking challenges, and several responded with wonderful alternatives. Continuing this approach throughout his high school years, many teachers provided him with their own accommodations. Some offered one-on-one reviews to assess and maximize his understanding. Others suggested variations in testing locations or strategies. And surprisingly, others allowed nontraditional and unique venues to accomplish the assignment goals within David's skill set. The most amazing example of the latter was an English teacher's response to David's difficulty with critical analysis and creative writing. While the other students were given a traditional assignment, she agreed to David's request to instead create and perform a "rap"; he was still required to read the literary selection and incorporate the mandatory components the same as everyone else. Though writing an essay was stressful and difficult for David at that point in time, the computer keys clicked away with amazing speed and seemingly little forethought with this revised and exciting challenge.

When David quickly announced that he was finished, I thought it impossible to be comprehensive enough in such a short span. My skepticism melted into stunned admiration as he performed his interpretive rap – not only did it fulfill all the criteria, but the message, creative rhymes, and cadence were outstanding. Even I, who knew him better than anyone else, was humbled and surprised by how intelligent and capable he truly was. These realizations were solidified later that year when I came upon a collection of songs he had written but left untidily strewn in his bedroom. Skimming them to determine if trash or not, I was shocked at their depth and emotion – and this from a person initially insensitive to others' needs and perspectives! Truly, he had come so far – and demonstrated that he possessed the same hopes and desires as any "typical" adolescent. He had learned things that were inaccessible in the past and had gifts and talents unknown to the assuming outsider. He just expressed himself differently and needed the opportunities that worked for him. How cool of that English teacher to recognize this and allow him to use his strengths to succeed! She had opened a door for him, and his fellow classmates gained a new appreciation and insight into the person he was.

From that point on, after a week or two of classes elapsed during each new semester, I communicated with David's teachers via phone, email, or personal appointment. I reasoned that meeting David prior to my revelations might prevent them from forming preconceived notions possibly generated from our discussions. I would explain the issues that challenged David relevant to their particular classes, and we would discuss measures that helped him compensate and overcome his difficulties in the past. I found that the teachers had a greater understanding and appreciation for his needs after they first observed and interacted with him in the actual classroom setting. But I also felt that the conversations yielded the highest mutual benefits when they occurred very early in the courses. This allowed communication and adjustments *before* the teachers experienced misperceptions or missed signals and *before* David experienced stress or substandard performance. Seat changes, opportunities for clarification, and revision of note or test-taking strategies were examples of outcomes from such discussions. The faculty was incredibly open and generous with their time and consideration. They, too, wished for his optimal success and often surpassed the boundaries of dedication and responsibility to achieve it.

Beyond academics, David was challenged with every aspect of high school adjustment. Because he needed to exclusively focus on general orientation and scholastic demands until they were manageable, David did not immediately join any extracurricular activities. It was difficult for him to socialize or make any friends. He navigated those early weeks alone and then began to draw from tactics that helped him fraternize in the eighth grade. Gaining prior attention and fame for his impersonations and rapping skills, he once again called upon these one-sided talents to break into a conversation. Surrounded by others—and enjoying their attention—David often performed customized raps on the spot. His listeners seemed entertained, at least for a while; occasionally, certain individuals had ulterior motives and unusual requests that could have caused repercussions for David. (Exemplifying this, he was once asked to stand on a cafeteria table to perform his rap.) The trusting rule follower that he was, we feared that David would innocently comply with occasional inappropriate wishes. We tried to teach and protect him by explaining reality without hurting his feelings. We also clarified that he was not obligated to comply with all requests; he *could* refuse and not follow "orders" if they were not in his best interest. And this he ultimately learned.

It appeared, however, that most students and staff enjoyed the raps that launched his recognition. His skills eventually propelled him to participate in sports rallies and school announcements; later, they even resulted in his complimentary hire for delivery of a unique prom invitation. But despite this positive attention, we were all too aware of his tendency to take his topic of interest overboard. Frank repeatedly counseled him to stay "down low," or "DL," as he still periodically cautions. (By this, Frank meant that David should tone things down to be less noticed; David's interpretation of the definition was to "stay cool": not too much, but not too little.) But the fact is, "DL" is not who David is—nor ever will be. And it is David's sincere, outgoing, and forthright self that makes him the endearing, unique person that others often find so refreshing. Thus, we continue to work on timing, extent, and refinement in lieu of "DL."

Finally, the time came for the fall play tryouts. Despite not being a musical, it was an opportunity to become associated with the group he so longed to be a part of. Unbelievably, the format for the audition was improvisation – the very skill that he struggled with in writing. He was given a scenario that he broke a lamp and was asked to explain it to his parents. Rather than test his acting skill, it tested his creativity. He was stumped for *what* to say – not *how* to say it. He was rejected after one attempt and never had an opportunity to show his ability. Had he received a script with that specific scenario, I am confident he could have revealed his talent. We swallowed the disappointment and unfortunate methodology, knowing that the spring musical would require far more actors. I was confident that David would meet the criteria when a bigger, better look was taken. Meanwhile, he would focus on the academic challenge – but that still left no avenue for socializing or enjoyment.

School had only been in session for one month, but it seemed so much longer with the extent of stress packed into "a David day." Keep in mind that many issues taxing for him were not even conscious considerations for "typical" students; they were just routine, background occurrences in their lives. When not working, I would frequently pick David up at his day's end to give him a break from the bus ride home. He would burst out of the school, wide-eyed and in a panicked half run. He was unaware of his fellow students, who, in striking contrast, laughed casually in relaxed banter with each other. David was in a totally different place, and only retrospectively did I realize that he was in survival mode, merely trying to get through each day. As he approached me, he would blurt out homework assignments and test results much like a younger child imparts to his mother, oblivious to his peers' reactions. I tried to redirect his verbalizations and defer these details until we were alone and out of earshot; I tried to protect him *socially*, not realizing, at the time, his actual priority of physical and emotional needs. And the situation would get worse before it got better as the following month unfolded.

David was basically alone while in a group. He didn't have lunch partners and often ate hurriedly to retreat to the library for the remaining period. As for the few acquaintances he had from the past, they were making new friendships and associations; in some cases, they added to his problem rather than providing support. An embarrassing past incident was resurrected and circulated. Other historical material was also divulged, setting the stage for ridicule—so much for trying to start out fresh in a new place. David's phone number was released by someone, and organized harassment ensued which could only be squelched by changing his cell number to one unlisted.

There is one profound experience that I would like to share with parents and professionals alike. It's very easy to tell others to ignore negative behavior directed towards them (and I've advised this myself), but I was astounded at how very difficult that truly is when I was confronted by such a situation firsthand. Driving David home from school one day, we were stopped behind a bus at a red light, the back of which contained a few of the teasing perpetrators. I witnessed their taunting antics toward David and could sense his stiffening and reaction. One person was most active, but others' supportive laughter was still offensive. I could not believe their impudence to carry on in my full view and wondered at what must be possible when unobserved. Glancing at David's face, and reading his pain, humiliation and despair, it took all my strength to refrain from reacting inappropriately myself. And David just sat there passively as previously instructed, taking it all in with a multitude of emotions erupting within—the finale to another tough day at school. In that moment, I finally realized what he was up against and why he had always had trouble "ignoring" his teasers.

What an epiphany to experience life from David's perspective (which is the ultimate intention of this entire book). It was clear that he endured upsetting scenarios from more than one circle of students, and frequency was escalating. Frank and I struggled with the best action to take; we tried to help David as best we could. We did not, however, get personally involved at that point in time. I impatiently waited for our next visit with Dr. Martin to receive her input.

Shortly thereafter, we began to receive calls from the school's nursing personnel. David frequently visited that office with symptoms of chest pain, difficulty breathing, and stomach upset. Occasionally, I could speak with him by phone and convince him to go back to class. But depending on his specific complaint, it was the school's protocol to ask parents to provide a ride home.

So began such calls to us at work, with Frank being called out of important business when I was unreachable in my duties. My husband was frustrated with the minimal ninety-minute disruption of his packed day for a seemingly noncritical issue necessitating the transport. From a different viewpoint, I was distressed that David was missing valuable class information because of the nurse visits and potential dismissal home. I was also concerned with the assumptions probably forming among students and faculty regarding psychosomatic complaints, and I thus missed the hidden urgency and causes underlying these nurse visits.

We explained our concerns to David and reassured him that he was physically fine—which he always *was* when he arrived home. He, in turn, sincerely assured us that he was not trying to get attention or get out of class. Frank's good-night expression to David frequently ended with the admonishment, "... and no visits to the nurse tomorrow!" In retrospect, we added another layer of fear and stress, for David could no longer gain relief from his symptoms in the manner he had relied upon; instead, he tried to keep things inside to prevent our disappointment at home. More appropriately, we should have *encouraged* short breaks to the nurse, or other safe preplanned escape, to allow him to de-stress and recharge. Surely the few minutes of instruction lost could have been recovered easier than the consequent alternative.

A bus driver called me during one of David's transports home. He feared that David was having an asthma attack, for the latter complained of shortness of breath and was hyperventilating. David again complained of chest pain. I met the bus and examined David on our arrival home. Listening with my stethoscope, I assured him that there was no wheezing present; as usual, the symptoms disappeared after an interval of rest.

If only David had an outlet for fun to counterbalance all the demands and drudgery! His invitations to other students did not result in successful ventures, and none had come in the opposite direction. Gone were the days when a mom could arrange a playdate. I was powerless to intervene. I longed for the spring musical tryouts— the avenue for *all* our hopes—and realized that they were only eight weeks away. Meanwhile, we encouraged David's attendance at football games and school events to facilitate engagement and companionship. We were amazed at his willingness and courage to always go alone; often he did enjoy himself, mingling with other students and holding private rap circles. Frank and I also regularly attended the football games. We provided his ride, sat elsewhere, and frequently "spied" on him—the latter was to assess his appropriateness of interaction (for future guidance) as well as to witness any purported improper behavior imposed on him by peers.

Such was the setting on a beautiful October Friday evening as we watched the homecoming festivities. We saw an ambulance pull up with its lights flashing in obvious answer to a summons. While wondering what had transpired, since all was safe on the field, Frank's cell phone rang. It was the emergency medical team – and it was David who was the patient in the ambulance!

We hurried to the scene and found David quite unlike himself; oxygen flowed and an IV infused fluid. The events leading to the call were unclear at the time, but David later recounted distress, dizziness, problems breathing, numbness and tingling - with these symptoms occurring soon after a confrontation with a harassing peer. Evidently, the football game was fraught with emotional challenge: being conspicuously alone—and yet scoping out persons to avoid; trying to say and do the right "thing" to fit in—but not surely knowing what that was; and attempting self-assertion—while apprehensive about the consequences. I watched David intermittently stare off without breathing or responding for several seconds and then finally resume movement, speech, and respiration. Transported to the emergency room, he was treated and discharged; there were plans for a detailed neurological evaluation to follow. A past EKG had verified that there were no existing cardiac issues, despite complaints of chest pain. The subsequent tests thankfully did not reveal seizure activity or other maladies. With no physical cause determined, the event was attributed to stress and anxiety.

Further communication with his pediatrician followed; plans for continued sessions with Dr. Martin were arranged to focus on stress management and coping strategies. It was obvious that the increased demands and problems in high school had taken a toll on David. It was equally obvious that despite success with only minimal adjustments the previous year, accommodations would be required long-term for David's optimal outcome. Challenge was essential to his progress, but it had to be of reasonable and achievable degree. More work was necessary to hone underdeveloped skills, compensate for differences, and regain the confidence and comfort to be happy and fulfilled in a world of typicals. Central to this was assistance in dealing with new and complex social issues. No job can be done well without the necessary tools of the trade, so how could I have assumed that I could throw David into this environment and expect him to thrive (or even survive) without his tools for success? What had worked in the past was clearly no longer adequate, and he was ill equipped in various ways. The bar had been raised and his life stage and world were more complex – with distress and demands further magnified by the meanness and escapades of insensitive peers. Wishful thinking could not deny his reality of ongoing, evolving needs. I was still sure he could flourish, but a revised formula was essential. In addition, David's life required more balance; it was all work and very little play.

We regrouped toward that end, and I suspected that renewed personal education was an essential and obvious starting point. After all, I hadn't read any new Asperger information for years because of the gloomy prognosis often conveyed. But now David was mainstreamed without the benefit of intervention specialists to guide the way. I was the head of his team and needed to teach him to transition into that role himself. I began to reread Attwood and my stack of other resources, and I found a wealth of new information that had always been available to me under my own roof! Concepts and topics that were formerly irrelevant, forgotten, or overlooked were suddenly very enlightening. I read from a different perspective since David had advanced in life stages and experiences. I have since vowed to regularly review favorite materials for new pearls not applicable previously, and I always learn something to assist us. In addition, I continue to seek new sources, both live and in print, that speak to specific challenges and age-appropriate issues. And of significance, David is now willing to read recommended works himself.

Shortly thereafter I came across Teresa Bolick's *Asperger Syndrome and Adolescence: Helping Preteens and Teens Get Ready for the Real World.* I have found it to be an outstanding, valuable, and practical guide full of insights, revelations, and useful strategies. One section was particularly enlightening. Bolick discusses the physical, involuntary "reaction" (the fight-or-flight response) that comes into play in times of perceived hazard. She explains some of the consequent "adrenaline" effects, including acceleration in pulse and respiration, which assist with either action or escape. Separate from perilous scenarios, she explains that in pupils with Aspergers, this can result from "invasions" of stimuli that are common in ordinary life. Providing examples of potential multisensory contributors in the school setting, Bolick expounds on the human and locker noises that occur between course periods, the scent of kitchen lunch offerings, and the unintentional touch of passersby. She further brings to mind separate issues that the teen may be experiencing, such as interpersonal challenges or even the continual discomfort of a bothersome article of clothing (27–28). Considering such real sources of distress for David, also remember his ever-present concern for beating the shrill bell to his next classroom.

Bolick describes how a repeated barrage of stressful input, both "sensory" and "social," could cause an almost continual "fight-or-flight" condition. In such a situation, very little additional stimulus might be needed to tip the scales, with a pupil's response perhaps appearing too extreme for the actual circumstance (28). She explains that the "load" can accrue with time (29). An added dimension, Bolick discusses that the teen with AS may also be challenged with handling the "emotions" that coincide with "fight-or-flight"; she exemplifies how hard it can be for the person to move on from such "feelings" and situations (24-25, 39).

Reading this section of her book, I was shocked to realize the enormity of what David continually experienced. I recalled (*and newly understood*) his adrenaline-ravaged expression and demeanor as he burst out of the high school at dismissal: "David days" were filled with various, repeated stressors which attacked him from all sides. I reconsidered, with new insight and appreciation, multiple past scenarios that dated as far back as the botched-homework meltdown in seventh grade. (And what about those tween dances??) Most importantly, I returned to the present and vowed to reshape the future. I reflected on the last two months' repeated bombardment, and I pondered Bolick's reminder that the stressful burden can snowball as time goes on (29). Clearly, drastic change was imperative...

I reassessed the situation with newfound knowledge and perspective. Changes were incorporated immediately and evolved over time. They were inspired by multiple sources, both live and in print; they included our instincts and trial and error as well as the recommendations and counsel of professionals. Importantly, breaks were scheduled into David's day. On his arrival home from school, David relaxed with special-interest activities before discussions, my questions, or homework began. Studies were preplanned into timed intervals to ensure intermittent mental refreshment. A written plan was developed with the school nurse delineating when David's visit warranted a phone call to me versus a brief respite from the outside world. In time, he also vented to other supportive faculty members; eventually, trips to the nurse subsided - per *David's* substitution and resolved need rather than per parental directive. Friday evening activities were limited unless preceded by quiet downtime. When they did occur, David often chose to keep them brief (one to two hours at a party, for example, was all he desired). He frequently elected to stay home at least one evening per weekend to relax and recharge. Of course, the latter had more appeal as he progressed to a more active social life; he was then home by choice and not because he felt isolated and rejected.

Essentially, intervention occurred on three fronts over time. **1) We worked on lessening or eliminating the stressors or triggers that we could control.** Bolick has suggested looking at probable sources in the surroundings as well as at factors that weigh on the teen's "cognitive" or interpersonal capacities—bearing in mind the timing of these and possible alterations that might decrease their impact (29-30). Besides those listed in the previous paragraph, examples we employed will be shared throughout future chapters. Included, of course, were our continued efforts to manage and eradicate distressing behavior from peers. **2) We strove to help David's coping mechanisms and stress management—especially with factors beyond his control.** Besides learning to cope with the situations, personalities, and actions of others over which he was powerless, David also needed to improve how he handled the emotional components of life. Dealing with his sentiments—and getting past them—was often hard for David; just as discussed and exemplified by Bolick, he often got stuck on certain occurrences and the "emotions" that went with them (39). Dr. Martin (and later, other professionals) was instrumental in addressing these varied needs. Stress-reducing/

relaxation techniques were valuable tools that David increasingly learned and utilized as he aged. **3) Lastly, David was encouraged to participate in nonacademic activities.** Desirable goals were a decrease in stress, an increase in friendships, and - FUN. Noteworthy, David still employs the bones of these strategies today, for they continue to be relevant and effective for him with the evolving life situations of young adulthood. Also significant, these interventions help(ed) David both prevent and relieve stressful episodes.

Per Bolick's suggestion, I have studied David and have learned to recognize markers and behaviors that indicate when his tension is mounting to "overload" (29). Specific changes in his facial expressions, quality of speech, breathing, and demeanor provide clues to increasing severity - as do his more obvious verbalizations or occasional symptoms. Through our varied personal incidents, I have discovered (the hard way) that further discussion with David is useless when he is saturated, and it can even worsen the situation. A separate consideration, Bolick has cautioned that grown-ups' reactions perceived by the teen to be "critical or impatient" could instigate the latter's "fight-or-flight" anew (30). I agree, for I have witnessed David's deterioration in such instances. An epiphany to me when first read, I have thankfully taken heed and have since worked on my calculated responses. Regardless of my frustration, my struggles with patience and tone of voice have paid off greatly in helping to prevent David's stress escalation (and have additionally promoted his growth, confidence, and comfort via my increased receptiveness in daily interactions).

Based on Bolick's detailed "LOW and SLOW" strategy (32-33), I have found that my use of simple, composed, and unhurried statements during David's spiraling stress are very effective in aiding him, among other suggestions she proposes (see Bolick 32-33). Most difficult for me, I have independently concluded that, in occasional scenarios, my best intervention is no intervention: I need to just keep quiet rather than further add to his burden; I need to give him the silence he needs to get himself together.

Following sufficient time for David's recovery, I initiate appropriate discussions with him. David and I try to troubleshoot the causative factors that pushed him to his limits. We implement action plans to address these problems, and we seek out resources, if necessary. We strive to learn from each occurrence to 1) improve our recognition and handling of contributing factors, 2) perfect our management of similar situations, 3) learn and change from any mistakes made, and 4) hopefully prevent future incidents. Notice the "we," for many scenarios indirectly involve me, even as David ages. We function as a team; our experiences, behaviors, and interactions mutually affect each other. David will live his own life - but we will always support and advocate for each other.

Preferring, of course, to avoid problematic episodes altogether, I am *always* watchful for behaviors that indicate *any* elevation in David's stress or nervousness. For example, increased tics and chit-chat (in certain contexts) have clued me into his emotional state since their origins, and other hints have since emerged. With his "potential need" already on my radar, I can assist David early on if *his* self-management begins to deteriorate. He can thus grow but not drown. David has also learned to earlier confide feelings of rising stress or anxiousness. I have found that timely, preventive intervention can reverse the trajectory. Encouraging David to take a break with a relaxing activity (such as a walk or computer/TV escape) often enables a deferred, constructive effort or conversation with a better outcome or collaborated plan.

Over the years, David's independently developed self-awareness has allowed him to increasingly adjust for himself. He has learned from experience when he needs to breathe deeply, take a break, or seek advice. He better regulates his schedule to adapt to his needs. He prearranges what he calls "chill time" and works it into his daily plan, with an extended period to recharge on the weekend. He is organized and can pace himself—procrastination never occurs and would not be well tolerated.

I have just expounded on the evolved strategies that have worked for David in the past and continue to help him still. Let's return to the period when they were first initiated in less sophisticated form: ninth grade.

With time, David adapted to the academic challenges of freshman year, and his improved study skills and better outcomes further alleviated stress in the scholastic department. As daily demands became routine, he calmed in other areas, as well. Continued extracurricular involvement and counseling from Dr. Martin also improved his social situation, which will soon be revealed.

Interestingly, as David became busier over his high school career, his stress decreased instead of the expected reverse. It seemed that a healthy balance, our interventions, and renewed hope enabled David to juggle more demands than ever before. He became engaged in meaningful activities that brought him joy and fulfillment. Feelings of accomplishment and belonging seemed to neutralize noxious input. I suspect that armed with happiness, burdensome intake could either be better tolerated or less noticed—it took much more to push him beyond his limits. In addition to the positive developments discussed in the preceding paragraph, David finally attained coveted peer relationships and a respite from bullying. His stress level was therefore drastically reduced. The resultant breathing room seemed to amply cushion David from reaching his ceiling, even with new and continued bombarding input. My supposition revisits and refers to my earlier discussion of Bolick's "overload" concepts (27-30). Keeping with this same frame of reference (Bolick 28), I envisioned David as situated on a better part of the slope; less chronically stirred, he lightened up and came down from the brink. Living with more leeway, David finally had the freedom and confidence to blossom.

Over time, David appeared to become somewhat desensitized to stimuli that bothered him before; however, certain sensory issues remain even today. As the challenges of life increase with age, David will need to be mindful that the potential to be overwhelmed still exists. His lifestyle must incorporate preventive management strategies—as must all of ours—and he will undoubtedly need to continue and expand fitting interventions.

But, sorry to say, David would experience further disappointment and rejection prior to his life taking this upward turn.

While David impatiently waited for the drama auditions, he tried to get involved with other on-campus activities to improve his social balance. He "rapped" at occasional football rallies, submitted sporadic sketches for the school newspaper, and served as a tour guide for prospective students at open houses. David continued to endure isolation or humiliating, hurtful behavior, but he never once balked at getting up for school. Frank and I often marveled at his stamina and courage. He just kept on going, reminding us of the drumming pink bunny in the popular battery commercial. He started each day with fresh determination, and though possibly filled with private trepidation, he never complained or gave up. I believe that he developed an incredible coping system out of necessity, which enabled both survival and accomplishment.

Our private efforts to handle harassment suddenly changed one November day. A school representative called to inform me that a peer had inflicted a small skin-penetrating mark upon David's arm during study hall. It necessitated a visit to the nurse's office, but more significantly, it led to involvement of the administration for disciplinary consideration. I appreciated the school's concern and prompt attention, but in light of the emotional injuries of the past three months, this minor incident paled in comparison. I relayed these thoughts to the school official that I was asked to meet with, and I was questioned as to why I never communicated these prior incidents. With no knowledge of problems, the school couldn't possibly intervene. I understood this but explained both our fear of making things worse as well as our desire to help our son learn to manage such issues. We henceforth urged David to confide in the appropriate school officials; we could then work as a team in our attempts to resolve problems, eradicate unacceptable behaviors, and improve David's social skills and experience.

A resulting suspension for the guilty student prohibited the teen's participation in that evening's sporting competition; by that day's school dismissal, word was out that David was the snitch who caused the suspension. Fault was assigned to David—not to the person whose own misjudgment caused the root problem—and many students communicated this blame to David as he hurriedly caught the bus on this downhill Friday afternoon. Entering our home haven, David was frantic and feared retaliation. A victim for being a victim, he worried all weekend. It was precisely why he had feared speaking up in the first place.

When Monday finally came, however, there were *no* repercussions. It seemed that Friday's events were now forgotten, and no further mention or reference was ever made. Relieved, David also felt that negative attention receded for a while. Could guilty parties have feared that he would name them as well? Was the message received that inappropriate actions would have consequences? David enjoyed the temporary reprieve and became comfortable confiding in this take-action administrator. Gaining hope and a powerful ally, David's burden was reduced, and the school reaped benefits, as well. Informing school personnel of improper student behavior was clearly the correct action for us to take, and I regret that we did not do it sooner. Along with this support, David continued to receive counseling to improve his management of these types of issues (indeed hoping that such skills would never again be needed).

Like study hall, lunch was another problematic environment for David. Whereas most students loved these periods to socialize and relax, David dreaded them. The stress of ambiguity left him anxious regarding where to go and what to do. And without a "group," he was reminded daily that *he didn't belong*. He also worried about the potential: the ill-defined, ever-changing nature of these periods enabled would-be harassers to perform unnoticed. David solved the study hall dilemma by signing out to use the library, but lunch was a tougher issue. He was hungry and needed to eat – but where? Social dining is valued in our society, and it was so humiliating and unnerving to continually seek somewhere to sit so far into the school year.

Our prayers were answered when a compassionate senior noticed David's plight and invited him to sit at his table. Finally welcomed, David gratefully accepted and returned daily for the remaining year. How brave was Tony for this simple gesture? I wondered at the internal reactions of his tablemates, for wasn't this the rapping freshman who now interrupted the flow of their senior group? If Tony ever received flack, he never wavered, and David finally found a lunch home—a respite in the middle of the day to provide a reprieve from stress rather than compound it. Luckily, the others embraced David and appreciated his talents. A window into senior life, David looked forward to the conversations, in which he was actively included. He gained a new perspective of the student experience and was no longer available to his teasers. More importantly, he found a mentor and friend in Tony, quite possibly providing the link that kept him from transferring out of the school. Tony's intervention had a huge impact and quietly screamed volumes to anyone sensitive enough to notice. A kind, courageous, and incredible person, he has remained in warm contact with David beyond high school. I am forever grateful to Tony. He turned the tide.

Auditions for the spring musical were finally announced. The talented Tony would eventually land the male lead, and he selflessly helped David learn the requisite dance moves during the last several minutes of lunch. Entering my waiting car following the first song and dance round, David felt confident in his performance. However, he did not receive a callback the following day. Realizing that he was a freshman, I did not expect him to read for a part, so I was not surprised by this occurrence. Surely he would still "make" the ensemble in a production with such a large cast. Possessing this mindset, I was shocked when he came to the car on the following afternoon and reported that his name was not on the posted cast list. I imagined his fervent searching amidst the celebratory clamor of those whose names were displayed, and my heart sank.

It was impossible and unfathomable! He possessed so much talent! And more importantly, all our adolescent and developmental hopes were dependent on this absolute prerequisite. More than simply not making a play, David now had no social alternative. Others who were turned away had their sports, friends, and other extracurricular interests – David had nothing. I was devastated and desperate; I could no longer hold it back, and I could barely see through my tears to drive. True to form, David calmly tried to console *me* rather than the reverse. He was more concerned with my reaction and feelings than his own and had already called his highly practiced coping skills into play. He would weather this storm like many before it.

I was less experienced than David with this type of loss, and I was clearly taking it harder, hurting for my son. I was less prepared and less accepting. It just seemed desperately unfair that again he was "cut" before he could reveal his true acting talent. If script reading had preceded dance, maybe he'd have had a shot. At the very least, a full assessment of his ability would have better enabled my acceptance of the decision. But what if his unpolished exterior prevented him from *ever* getting that chance? What if no one was interested in seeking the potential below the surface—or even of the mindset that potential could possibly exist? Would the joy that lent him freedom be unattainable because of circumstances beyond his control? My imagination compounded my distress.

I was sure that the director would understand our extenuating circumstances and reconsider. This was not Broadway, after all; wasn't high school meant to provide opportunities for students to foster their development? The stakes were too high; I had to advocate swiftly. Despite my familiarity and respect for parental deference to the decisions of a sport's coach, I gambled with this protocol and met with the director on the following day (unbeknownst to David). I fully explained our position, but the director would not deviate from the posted cast list; he felt that David's dance abilities were inadequate for the advanced choreography anticipated. But he listened and "got it." He saw that I was not a disgruntled, subjective stage mom. He was empathetic and realized that David had suffered more than his share of rejection and disappointment – exposure to these life lessons was not necessary. The director further understood that David had no social alternative to fall back on; as a compromise, he invited him to work on the production's stage crew. David cautiously accepted the director's offer when it was personally extended to him the next day; activities were scheduled to start after the winter break. It was not our dream outcome, but it was a step in the right direction. Most importantly, it presented the opportunity to find a friend or social niche. We were thankful and optimistic; with the proverbial door closed, we would work at prying the window further open. We needed to regroup, keep trying, and move on.

Was it FINALLY time for the holiday recess?

Had it really *only* been four months since high school began?

Exhausted and in need of time off, we gladly headed home. David looked forward to his brothers' visits and cherished the family celebrations of the season. He attended high school basketball games (one ruined by bothersome peers), but otherwise, he received no calls or communications from fellow students. David utilized the break mainly to study: final examinations were scheduled two weeks after classes resumed. This would be his first experience with cumulative exams that spanned semester material. Together we strategized varied preparations for each test; we developed plans and a daily schedule. Some review was independent; some was with my assistance. He arranged math tutoring sessions and devoted many hours to the extensive review of challenging subjects. By the vacation's conclusion,

David felt less intimidated; he was confident in his knowledge *and* in his ability to prepare for comprehensive exams. He was ready for finals week and rightly felt accomplished and relieved. In addition to academic and familial activities, this respite provided time to receive extra counseling from Dr. Martin for needs previously described. David was nourished on all fronts: socially (with the focus on skills), emotionally, intellectually, and spiritually. Good food and the luxury to sleep late completed his physical recovery. David returned from his very therapeutic recess ready to again tackle the challenges before him. I also felt refreshed, and we sought activities to substitute for the rehearsals that would never materialize, for the play's crew participation demanded far less time than initially anticipated.

Final exams went smoothly because of David's advanced preparations, and his successful first semester results reflected his hard work and dedication. Second semester included a "dramatic interpretation" elective; it would be fun as well as an avenue to meet students who shared his passion. We further hoped it would bring to light some of David's talent and assist him in the audition process.

Looking for activities, I contemplated another venue for widening David's social circle, and this one provided simultaneous therapeutic benefits. During our holiday visits, Dr. Martin mentioned a teen social skills group that a colleague hoped to initiate. It seemed like a wonderful idea, but David's response was surprisingly cool and resistant; he had always been in favor of any recommendation suggested in the past.

I scheduled an assessment visit with this referred psychologist soon thereafter. The doctor described her vision: 1) the nature of the potential group, 2) planned activities and topics of discussion, and 3) the possibility that interactions might be videotaped to enable participants' guided study of self-behavior and responses. While I found this to be an ingenious method to lend a fresh learning perspective, David was uncharacteristically belligerent and adamant that he would not participate. He seemed quite intimidated by the taping and was not at all interested in socializing with this group. I respected his wishes because forced involvement would not yield results worthy of the time and effort. In the end, this group never did materialize. But David's response and refusal were not lost on me— they were my first indication that he was either in denial of his differences, or he could not understand and accept them. He did not want to associate with anyone who would remind him of his reality. And most especially, he did not want to see himself interacting in any way categorized as abnormal or "different" - he just wanted to be like everybody else.

A few weeks before the high school musical, David was finally summoned to assist with the set assembly and associated crew duties. I was a bit concerned as I envisioned the potential combination of power tools, heights, and David's poor coordination. I forced myself to focus on his opportunity to learn practical new skills and increase peer relationships. David initially had some difficulty opening himself up to the new role; quite frankly, I believe it was painful for him to constantly hear and see the action on stage—where he longed to be instead. It was the only production where he could have shared the stage with Tony, for the latter would soon graduate. And he couldn't help thinking that he COULD have performed those dance moves. A week before the performance, David shared with us that he would never again be on crew. We understood and empathized with his decision, but we insisted that he fulfill his current commitment, to which he totally agreed.

Frank and I attended the opening night performance in David's support, and we were stunned when he jumped into the car following the play: he was ecstatic and dedicated. Whatever ceremonial events and camaraderie occurred prior to the curtain rising, David finally belonged. He was part of a special group that possessed mutual appreciation for *every* contributor; it was powerful enough to result in his proclamation that mere participation transcended an acting role – he would definitely work behind the scenes if he was not cast in the plays next year. We were thrilled for him; it was the intended and hopeful outcome of him joining the crew. As an added benefit, David was included in every cast party; he thus finally experienced an "invitation only" high school social event. The fact that David was truly invited was more important than the party itself. He often chose to stay only a short time rather than risk becoming overwhelmed by stressful small talk after a long day. He had the opportunity to dance and socialize like any other typical teen, so he better understood and participated in Monday's lunch recaps.

An emptiness followed the play as socialization and excitement reverted to the old norm. David returned to his lone existence, and I sought avenues to fill the void. The nearby community theater was holding auditions for *High School Musical*, one of David's favorite productions. The choreography would require the added coordination of combining dance moves with basketball-handling skills. Despite his careful preparation, David again received the phone denial which sank my heart. Normally resilient, he instead seemed resigned that his acting career was ended; I worried at the sadness, quiet, and solitude that transpired. Hopelessness is a dead end. How could hope be restored for this actor that I knew had talent and passion to share? Despite the challenges with coordination that AS imposed, I did believe that there was a niche for him. I was certain that I was not merely colored by maternal subjectivity, and I needed corroboration.

I called the director the following day to find out the rationale behind David's denial. I also requested some constructive suggestions to help David improve the causing deficits. I did not question the actual decision; I merely sought to find out if, in fact, David *had* future potential. If not, we would acquiesce and seek other interests, sparing ourselves the pain of further rejection.

The director could not have been more compassionate or helpful. He absolutely saw potential in voice and acting skills, but as suspected, the nature of the choreography required a grace that David lacked. The director strongly recommended dance instruction; he shared personal experiences and an assessment of David that inspired hope. Giving us specific direction regarding an avenue fitting for a male teen, he encouraged us to persevere. It was all David needed; his tenacious spirit took over, and he was enrolled in hip-hop classes by the end of the week. It was the perfect choice to improve confidence and coordination—wearing preferred sweatpants instead of leotards—and it complemented his rap skills beautifully. At least we felt like we were taking control instead of caving in, and the lessons filled his time with an enjoyable outlet.

Simultaneously, I had just completed reading Luke Jackson's *Freaks, Geeks and Asperger Syndrome: A User Guide to Adolescence*. Jackson dedicated an entire chapter to *tae kwon do* (154–62), which enlightened me to the sport's value for so many issues that David was facing. Prior to reading this work, I knew nothing about *tae kwon do* and thus never considered it. I was thrilled with this exciting prospect; I researched programs and found the perfect establishment. David loved it (especially since Craig thought it was cool), though he eventually switched to karate for a better style match. It was the ideal intervention at a critical time! Between the dance and martial arts, David felt empowered and uplifted. Guided by the wisdom and experience of others, I found therapeutic, enjoyable activities which improved David's physical and emotional performance; they put him in a better position to attain his ultimate theatrical goal.

David's refusal to read the above-named book confirmed my suspicions of his struggle and denial. Regular and frequent summer appointments were scheduled with Dr. Martin to focus on these barriers, for understanding and acceptance were paramount to move on. How could he advocate for himself or help others become properly informed if HE did not come to terms with his Asperger's? We would use the time off to our advantage and return to school properly equipped in the fall.

Meanwhile, David busied himself with intramural basketball and school ambassador activities, in addition to the dance and karate previously explained. As mentioned earlier in this chapter, I discovered some songs and poems he wrote during his idle hours. I was amazed at his sensitivity and understanding. I never anticipated or appreciated how smart he truly was. It was clear that he possessed the same romantic hopes and future aspirations that any "typical" teen contemplates, for exceptionalities do not preclude the desire for relationships. David wasn't verbally smooth at that time, but he was very effective putting his thoughts on paper in rhyming fashion, and he spent significant amounts of "chill time" doing just that.

Ironically, while David still struggled with writing essays, he was able to create and communicate skillfully in other formats, drawing on his rap experience and special interests. I would like to share three of David's works written during that time period. These will help you enter his mind, but they are far less effective in print than with his actual performance. (The syllables fit and the rhymes work when expressed as intended!) The first is a birthday "rap-wish" for Craig - about as mushy as they got with one another! The second is a song David wrote about a beautiful classmate he admired. And the third is a creative writing piece that was assigned for a class that freshman year. Though grammatically imperfect, it is the imagination and cleverness that speak to David's progress. Note that he still used his beloved fairy tales as known springboards from which to jump to originality. Though he was no longer obsessively fixated on such tales, they remained a fond attraction that provided his frame of reference in two of the samples below. He additionally drew from rap methods, Shakespeare, and other commonly known poetic lines.

SAMPLE #1 (rap)

Happy Birthday Craig, this one's for you
And this will be the day you turn twenty-two
You're the big brother that I love and know
But do you annoy me sometimes? Yeah for sho
But that's what makes up our brotherly love
And I'll still feel that way with
every push and shove
That's all for now—that's all I have to say
But before I forget: Happy Birthday!

SAMPLE #2 (song)

Fairy Tale Flavor and Shakespeare Spice

Lyrics
I'm Prince Charmin lookin for his Cinderella
And I'm not gonna lose you to some other fella
When I looked into your eyes I suddenly knew
Like a poem "Roses are red, and violets are blue"
I knew for a fact that we were meant to be
But if you think different, I'l l still be happy
So listen girl, and listen true
I won't belong to anyone except you

Refrain

Love, girl, it's a beautiful thing
And I'd express it by buying you a diamond ring
I swear to thee by Cupid's strongest bow
That everything I do will be my love to show
So love me girl and I'll love ya too
I mean that girl and that's the truth

I guarantee every word that I say
And I'll keep thinking of you every day

<u>Lyrics</u>
"Shall I compare thee to a summer's day?" *
I swear to God our love will never fade away
I know that our love will last forevuh
And it won't happen if people keep sayin "nevuh"
As long as there's beatin inside my heart
I know our love will nevuh grow apart
So I hope you remembuh all these words
And respond with the voice of those pretty birds

<u>Refrain</u>

<u>Lyrics</u>
Now, girl, is the closing of my rap
I guarantee, girl, this is not a trap
My passion burns for you like a blazing fire
But I hope our relationship grows higher
So, girl, consider what you just heard today
And remember our love will never fade away
So holla girl; I'll see ya soon
Hopefully we'll meet under the bright full moon

<u>Refrain</u>

* (Line 1 of Sonnet 18 by William Shakespeare)

SAMPLE #3 (story/play)

Character List**

** [Note: David's inspiration for the following cast names came from creating rap-style "take offs" on the original tale character and/or rap/hip-hop artist named in the correlating parentheses]

G-Locks... (Goldilocks)

Pin-YO-Cchio... (Pinocchio)

Lil' Red... (Little Red Riding Hood)

Master Double P... (Peter Pan)

Da Shoe... (The Old Lady Who Lives in the Shoe; Soulja Boy)

Rumple-Fly-Skin... (Rumpelstiltskin)

Tri Pi G's... (Three Little Pigs)

Cinderalizzi... (Cinderella)

P. Charm... (Prince Charming)

Lil' Wolf... (Wolf from "Three Little Pigs"; Lil' Wayne)

The play's stars are Agents: G-Locks, the hot spy with the golden curly locks; Pin-YO-Cchio, the nervous spy that when he lies, he destroys anything wooden; Lil' Red, the gloomy spy that with her red hood, she can transform into anything and anyone at will; and Master Double P, the sweet, innocent one to some people, but to his team, he's the mastermind and leader of the whole group. Together, they are the Fairy Tale Quad. One day, they're chillin' in their secret lair, Da Shoe, when they're contacted by their Commander-N-Chief, Rumple-Fly-Skin. He's reported that the Tri Pi G's, the most deadly gang in the fairy tale hood, has kidnapped the most beautiful, and richest dame in the whole hood, Cinderalizzi. It seems she was abducted from her castle when she went to bed. When her husband, P. Charm, went to go wake her up, the window was shattered from the outside and her bed was sloppy (Note: She's a neat freak). So the Fairy Tail Quad is on the mission. In order to find Cinderalizzi, they have to find the Tri Pi G's hideout. So, they use Pin-YO-Cchio's wooden tracking device and insert Cinderalizzi's hair they found at the scene of the crime. It's revealed that the Tri Pi G's are keeping her hostage under the Buh-Ridge. But when they try to do so, the group is captured by the Tri Pi G's. When they're taken to their hideout, it is revealed who is the Tri Pi G's leader. It's actually Cinderalizzi's husband, P. Charm. He actually had his gang kidnap Cinderalizzi because he wanted the castle to belong to himself (that means no wife). So he has the Tri Pi G's dump the Fairy Tale Quad into a poisonous acid that will destroy them for good. But, Lil' Red still has her hood, so she transforms into a giant axe in order to easily cut the ropes that bind the four of them. So, they escape easily, and then, the four split up. Master Double P and Pin YO-Cchio try to find Cinderalizzi and G-Locks and Lil' Red fight off the Tri Pi G's. Lil' Red and G-Locks are in a tussle. It's two against three. But, with Lil' Red's hood, she transforms into the Tri Pi G's biggest fear: Lil' Wolf. He's the original founder of the Fairy Tale Quad and he's actually Lil' Red's adopted cousin. So as the fight begins, which doesn't last very long, Lil' Red, whose form is Lil' Wolf, was able to gobble up two of the Tri Pi G's. Now, the third of the gangsters was the toughest of them all. So, what happens is, G-Locks flips her hair so the third gang member is distracted, so Lil' Red is able to sneak behind him and gobble him up in one bite. That's what happened with G-Locks and Lil' Red. Now, what happened with Master Double P and Pin-YO-Cchio was that they were using Master Double P's tracking device in order to see where they're holding Cinderalizzi. It's revealed that she's trapped behind a mahogany door, the strongest wood in the whole hood. So what happens is Master Double P makes Pin-YO-Cchio tell a lie, so when he says the lie, he goes berserk and destroys the mahogany door. And behind the door is Cinderalizzi, bound and gagged in the middle of the room. So Master Double P and Pin-YO-Cchio untie and remove the gag from Cinderalizzi and they finally reunite with G-Locks and Lil' Red. But as they're getting out of the lair, they hear a ticking, and it's revealed that P. Charm installed a bomb in the lair before he left, to make sure the Fairy Tale Quad would be finished off once and for all. So, they make a break for the door, and they get out just in time for the lair to explode behind them. And finally, they return Cinderalizzi to the safeness of her castle, P. Charm was arrested, and Rumple-Fly-Skin announced the Fairy Tale Quad, a job well done.

As faculty and staff became more familiar with David, extraordinary efforts were individually undertaken by several to draw him into activities and harvest his talents. He was sought out by two such guardian angels and was invited to join Music Ministry, a group that sang for liturgical services. Because it was uncustomary to join extracurricular activities so late in the school year, David carefully considered entry into this established group. Tony was a current member, and with his encouragement as well as ours, David became a dedicated participant and enjoyed this association through his remaining high school days. It was an opportunity for service and self-expression, and singing became a medium for joy as well as socialization.

Toward the close of David's first year, I met with a school official to discuss curriculum considerations for sophomore year. Leery of the challenge that geometry's abstractions presented for his literal thinking, I requested that David be placed in a remedial geometry class—despite his high algebra grades. Because this course was a unique animal, his geometry level would not dictate an ongoing math track of lesser challenge; he would resume standard placement junior year.

My second request was more unconventional than the first: I asked to defer foreign language for yet another year to accommodate choir into David's schedule. I realized it sounded ludicrous to prioritize song over college preparation, but I felt it was the more vital choice. Choir was essential to fulfilling three of David's desires: learning music basics, becoming involved with key persons, and creating a stepping stone to drama. David loved to sing, and he sought to improve his skills. He also longed to create tighter associations with the group from the play. What sense did it make to live in the future? We wanted David to be happy NOW. High school needed to be a forum for joy and accomplishment, not solely a place to prepare for life beyond. First things first.

Much to my relief, the official fully agreed, and both requests were approved. We further discussed that class timing and instructor styles were as critical to

David's success (and stress reduction) as was course selection. It was decided that he would have access to individualized consideration and priority prescheduling every summer. This ensured David's ability to take challenging courses during periods when he was optimally fresh and alert. It also enabled scheduling with teachers whose style and personality best matched his learning needs. This latter arrangement was probably the most important component of his accommodation plan. It was implemented via my intercession and without David's knowledge.

Two additional components were discussed: tutoring would continue as needed, and I would meet annually with David's guidance counselor and the school psychologist to update accommodations. Examples of these were as follows: 1) optimal choice of seats in the classroom, 2) extension of time for testing (for finals only) in a monitored location separate from the class (if deemed needed by David—he selectively chose this option), and 3) the acquisition of notes for verbal presentations if material was not available from the board or written/ electronic formats. This school and its dedicated staff did everything possible to enable David's success. They were accessible, flexible, and open to every idea I had— and they enhanced my suggestions with proposals of their own design. They were phenomenal!

I was thankful and relieved that I was once again supported by an experienced team, an option I greatly preferred over my solo expedition through uncharted territory. I was confident that David would thrive academically with this mainstream support, especially given his motivation and work ethic. He had performed respectively even without this assistance, albeit with a high stress level and huge expenditure of grueling effort; imagine what he could do with help! With hopes renewed for increased extracurricular involvement during the next three years, new approaches were welcomed to free up time for rehearsals and fun. For in David's life, I felt that the latter was our highest priority, in vast contrast to the hierarchy of many other parents! Graduation was imminent and the Baccalaureate Mass signaled the beginning of the end. I watched from the back of the church. I had chauffeured David for Music Ministry participation, and I stayed to see the exceptional men and women who had been so kind and protective toward him. Having lost their senior members, each remaining singer's voice was that much more vital. I enjoyed watching David's pleasure as he ended the year both needed and involved.

Tears welled in my eyes amid the thunderous applause— Tony was announced as a recipient of an admirable Christian award; I had nominated him, undoubtedly among countless others. Without his kindness and light of hope, I am confident that David would not have lasted the year. What a loss to all involved if David had not fulfilled the subsequent journey.

Tears continued following the service as I watched David seek out his senior friends. He gave them congratulatory hugs that were both appreciated and reciprocated. He *had* made some bonds and he *did* experience some good moments. We talked excitedly all the way home, and I vowed to him that next year would be different. I was energized with optimism. We had learned the hard way but the impactful way; we already revised plans and strategies based on lessons learned. The year of the unknown was thankfully complete. The "green" freshman would soon be a seasoned sophomore. For added measure and confidence, we would utilize the summer to help him accept and explain his diagnosis— both elements were essential to his happiness and progress. David, himself, summarized his first year of high school best with the following proclamation: "I wouldn't say that I'm popular, but I'm definitely well-known." I couldn't agree more!

At the end of my eighth-grade year, my parents and I packed up all our belongings and moved on to my new hometown. We immediately started looking for any programs that I could get involved in, particularly in the theater aspect. Unfortunately, our endeavors did not prevail, so we checked out a basketball camp at my future high school. Now even though I loved the sport, I didn't see myself as being athletic compared to some of the other guys who were committed to sports. I also didn't make connections with these guys, and I even saw myself developing some enemies. I got nothing out of the week, and it was more like a failed social experiment. Despite what happened at basketball camp, I had a good feeling about freshman orientation. Among the countless activities meant for developing connections with your peers, there was one in which we had to introduce ourselves to the first person we ran into. I remember the first guy I talked to, and he would later become one of my greatest friends. After going through orientation, I thought it would be a good year. **Boy was I wrong!!**

Let me just say that in high school, nothing makes a fresh student more uptight than having to transition between classes with only a four-minute break; that is the main factor that shot my nerves up. Because of my prior year in eighth grade, since I already used a locker with a lock on it, I was more prepared for the lock combination than the time crunch.

Once I figured the timing out, I eventually got everything organized and found my way around. I was very rushed in the first weeks; after that, I felt like I made a good transition and made it to class on time. As the schoolwork began to progress, I found myself always struggling with note taking (something I still struggle with to this day). There were a couple classes where the books weren't being supplied. I solely had to rely on what was being said in class, and I struggled with trying to determine what I needed to know.

I discovered my unknown talent for rapping in the seventh grade. It's always helped me express my emotions and was a way to have fun and impress people. It was a contributor to me being positively well-known in my freshman class and in the entire high school. Soon enough, I was dubbed "Petrofly" by the upperclassmen. It was through my rapping skills that I was able to show who I truly was. I remember rapping at the pep rally as the overall greatest experience of my whole freshman year. I owed that opportunity to the teacher who headed the rally committee. She saw greatness and potential in me even when I couldn't see it in myself, and she became my greatest motivator throughout my high school career. It was after that particular event that the kids in my class started calling me by the names Petro or Petrofly; I was climbing the ladder slowly but surely. One time in my English class, while discussing the literary elements of a novel we were currently reading, I asked my teacher if I could write a rap instead of a report (which I like to call a "rap-port"). She allowed this. After presenting my rap to the class, I received the highest grade of any schoolwork to date, and I even started to develop a positive reputation.

As the months went by, the fall play tryouts were approaching, and I was eager to get my first taste of high school theater. BUT when I got to the audition, it was to my surprise that the tryout was strictly improv (which, to this day, is not my strongest suit as an actor). I was given a certain scenario, and I was just pulling random responses out of the drama hall air; I didn't even recall what was coming out of my mouth. The results matched my performance—bad. I did not make it. I didn't expect to, but I wasn't crushed because this play didn't really appeal to me. I WAS uneasy about future shows though. If improv was the layout of every audition, I could kiss my high school theater career good-bye.

Not only did I have to deal with the autism, but I was bullied mercilessly by kids who might have felt like they could target me and pick on me because I was different. Whether it was the things I said or did, there were always those kids who I think tried to make themselves look good by making me look bad. It had progressed from the start of early high school. It didn't happen every day; it depended on the people I ran into or how I responded to certain situations. Even with the love of my family, everything I endured just made me feel small, weak, and worthless. I mean, I didn't even do anything to these guys, and I didn't understand why they were coming after me. Maybe they felt like they could be the tough guys and the cool kids through their actions. By making someone else look small, they could make themselves the bigger person, at least for a few minutes. Incidents such as prank phone calls, fake love notes, and other things they did to me made me feel helpless—and so alone.

Because of the bullying, I didn't have the opportunity to form the connections that a lot of freshmen were making with other people. Even on the good days, I was very defensive and unable to trust. Everywhere I went, I was uncertain and nervous about who I would run into or what might happen. I was trying to fend for myself and survive all my problems. Even being surrounded by eight hundred kids in that school,

I had never felt more alone in my whole life. I felt like I didn't have anyone that I could lean on—like no one had my back. I was secretly livid because the philosophy of the school was that we were all united as a community, yet no one would step up to the plate and help me. I felt like I was cheated and they were breaking their promise.

Nurse visits were pretty frequent my freshman year; I was always experiencing an unsettling feeling in my stomach or a sensation in my chest that made it difficult to breathe. My dad constantly reminded me not to visit the nurse. Honestly, I felt like he didn't get it. I felt like no one understood what I was going through or how I just wanted everything to stop.

The most significant "problem" overall was at the homecoming football game. It started off good. I was having fun watching the game and rooting for the team with a group. Then this annoying kid a few seats up started saying things to me that pushed my buttons. When I tried to approach him to tell him to stop, he took off. I followed him, and for the first time, I stood up for myself. I went back to watching the game, but I kept replaying this situation in my head. Soon afterwards I started hyperventilating, losing feelings in my hands and feet, and getting lightheaded. When I got to the lower level I collapsed, and the EMTs got there. You know what happened next from my mom's segment.

*Lunch was very difficult for me in terms of finding my own group. One day, a senior named Tony saw that I was wandering around the cafeteria looking for a place to sit. He came over to me and invited me to his lunch table to eat with HIS friends. I ate with them for the rest of the year, finally able to relax and even socialize at lunch. Although I was a little uneasy at first, I was wholeheartedly accepted, and the upperclassmen saw me as part of their pack. **I was accepted**—something I* *hadn't felt in a long time. Because of this, I started to gain a newfound confidence that was the kick-start to my drive to get involved at school. To this day, Tony remains a part of my life, and I am honored to call him a friend.*

The spring musical auditions finally came. I was able to try out and go through the traditional audition process. Unfortunately, I did not make it—and the worst part came when I told my mom. She started crying, and that was something I did NOT expect. I tried to reassure her that everything would be okay; I didn't know it at that moment, but eventually it would be. The director talked to me, and he offered me a position on crew. I took the job, seeing it as a good way to still be involved with classmates, hang out, and make connections. For most of the experience I grew jealous seeing everyone on stage, but I came to know many of my classmates and gained a deep appreciation for crew. Being on the stage most of my life, I never knew what it was like to work backstage, and I saw it in a new light. I also feel like I solidified my place in the theater department; despite what happened that year, I was hopeful for the next year. But that's in a whole different chapter.

*Dr. Martin had suggested that I join a group of kids just like me for a social outlet. I wasn't comfortable with the idea because, at the time, I was very "closeted" about my Asperger's. I had very little knowledge about it. I was mostly in denial—I couldn't see anything wrong with me. So I did not go through with it, and I simply continued on with my life. The academic part was getting easier towards the end of the year because I then knew the routine and the process. I was up for **that** challenge. The greater challenge, for me, was to combat my social struggles.*

After the musical, I looked for other ways to be involved. The local community theater was doing "High School Musical," a personal favorite of mine. I tried out, but once again, I did not make it. At that point, it was like "three strikes and you're out" for me. I didn't know what to do and I gave up hope. But, of course, my mom called the director. I was offered some ideas on valuable resources to help improve my coordination, such as hip-hop dance classes. I was enrolled within a few days and embraced the experience. I met new people, including a great instructor who would later help me in future theatrical endeavors. With other activities such as "tae kwon do," intramural basketball, and being an ambassador for my school, I can confidently say that I grew a pretty good deal from the first day up until then. I joined the Music Ministry with the help of Tony and many others, and it was an activity that I exceeded in and enjoyed all throughout high school. Involved in that group, I did what I loved and met new people.

By the time my senior friends' graduation Mass rolled around, I had attained the greatest goal any freshman hopes to accomplish: I was known! I had made my mark. And as I walked away from that experience, I was confident that next year would be completely different.

Lessons we learned:

- The need for transition, preparation, advocacy, and accommodations is ONGOING, though it may change in nature and scope.

- Confer with teachers sooner and more frequently than is typically scheduled. This highlights needs in a timely fashion and may result in interventions to help achieve maximal outcomes.

- Try not to minimize concerns expressed by the teen. Some may require further exploration and additional input.

- Ask your teen the tough questions; listen and truly hear the answers. Seek assistance as needed.

- Reread favorite resources as life stages and challenges change. Interpreted from a different perspective, overlooked or forgotten messages may now be very pertinent. Supplementing these with new, reputable information may provide additional support, insight, and helpful ideas.

- Involvement in enjoyable activities is a priority. If preferred avenues don't work out, stay open minded and keep looking! Something foreign and never before considered may be a perfect choice!

- Even in high school, do not hesitate to request alterations in scheduled classes. One change could make all the difference...

CHAPTER NINE

High School:

SOPHOMORE YEAR (Finding His Way)

David met with Dr. Martin throughout the summer to facilitate his understanding and acceptance of his Asperger differences. She secondarily helped him decide who should be privy to this information, and she explained "how" and "how much" to share. Obviously, he shouldn't blurt it out as an introductory statement to every person he encountered, but disclosure was appropriate in many situations. This ambitious agenda was quite a delicate matter; it required the expertise of our cherished professional to appropriately and gently impart the knowledge and develop the judgment— while simultaneously promoting David's confidence and positive self-image.

Dr. Martin customized a plan to address critical concepts. She utilized verbal approaches in conjunction with two texts (which David and I chose from suggested options). These latter works provided practical exercises to stimulate thought and discussion, and they enabled instruction via various modes. This seemed to augment his grasp and application of the material. David and I found Catherine Faherty's *Asperger's...What Does it Mean to Me?* to be enlightening and beneficial. Relevant exercises were chosen to fit his specific needs, in combination with other therapies Dr. Martin utilized.

The summer proved to be very instrumental in helping David understand himself; his individuality and relationships with others were both addressed. More introspective and willing to analyze himself, he often divulged difficulties and behaviors and asked me, "Is that because of my Asperger's?" Though still a little apprehensive about how and when to share, David was well on his way to accepting his AS. Consequently, he seemed both relieved and more at peace with himself. As David digested and practiced newly learned concepts, he eventually gained a matter-of-fact attitude toward the diagnosis as well as a comfort with its revelation to others. It took him to a whole new level. He even found humor in poorly communicated statements or confusing circumstances, and he was able to laugh or joke about it—relieving tension and catching surprised listeners off guard (an example appears in the chapter after next). This in itself was a victory, for somewhere along the way, he learned to pick up on sarcasm, "get" a joke, and even contribute original witticisms himself. Even today, however, he must still occasionally clarify, "Is that a joke?" or "Are you being sarcastic?"—but at least he clarifies to receive the intended message.

Besides attending the above sessions with Dr. Martin, David busied himself with required sophomore reading, geometry tutoring, and the dance and karate activities described earlier. Craig came home for this last summer before his college graduation, and he often took David to the movies, mall, or pool. They went together as a twosome or joined Craig's friends. David cherished these outings; he couldn't very well hang out with Mom any longer, and he idolized his brother and associated pals. David still had not found that "best friend" he sought for himself, but we frequently discussed how many people don't have that special relationship until later in life. He maturely understood and patiently and optimistically awaited that experience.

David enjoyed going to the area church carnivals that were staggered throughout the summer. We constantly marveled at his courage to venture out alone. He always ran into people he knew, and David was gratified simply with the passing conversations he had with acquaintances. He was free to stay as long or short as he desired, and he called us for a ride home whenever he hit his limit. David was aware enough to blend in with styles and trends but comfortable enough with his own individuality and tastes to be his own person. He was actually more mature in this regard than many teens who strove relentlessly to "fit in."

School was once again upon us. In true form, David optimistically looked forward to the coming year, shaking off negative freshman memories that would have likely daunted others in his shoes. His study skills were sharpened, and he took comfort in knowing that safety nets and support people were now available. He loved his perfect schedule (he never knew that I had primary input until reading this book) and continued in the art/college prep track. He was thrilled to be in choral class, albeit a year behind his peers. Regardless, they would perform together, and he hoped this experience would lead to further friendships. It was a start. He knew the lay of the land and was comfortable after practicing class routes and locker runs on the scheduled preparation day. The prior autumn's fear of the unknown was replaced with a surprising nostalgia, and he was armed and ready.

The first week was remarkably smooth, except for an isolated incident of being "picked on" during day one. My biggest worry was the lunch arrangement, for Tony and company were gone. Luckily, David shared a common lunch period with a few of the guys he knew, so their claimed table became the year's routine. Our first hurdle was resolved. Equally fortunate, a few of the key harassers—each from different social circles—did not return that year. David was breathing easier already. I hoped that other students would take the chance to associate with someone "different" as they matured and became more secure within, opening David's world to friendships. At the very least, I prayed that bullying behavior would not resurface, for most classmates were now socially situated and thus hopefully free from the need to prove superiority.

David continued his involvement with the Music Ministry and school ambassador activities from the onset. He participated in occasional pep rallies, performing his now renowned raps, and he gained more comfort and ease in navigating the school. Growing familiarity with others even brought enjoyment in doing so, for the increase in uplifting smiles and hallway greetings drowned out more noxious sensory input. Stress still existed, but it was no longer his whole world, and he was now more equipped to handle it.

My own change in jobs seemed to better fit David's needs, as well. No longer working the occasional evenings that inevitably coincided with the eve of a tough exam, I was always available to improve his study preparation and increase his confidence. These both served to reduce or eliminate test anxiety.

Parent "Back to School Night" occurred annually soon after the year commenced. It was an opportunity to hear key speakers, network with other parents, and follow your teen's schedule to experience his or her day. This was invaluable, for teacher expectations and a syllabus were explained per class, and David's challenges were then much easier to anticipate and troubleshoot. He and I would discuss our concerns and share ideas to deal with them. Shortly thereafter, as introduced in the last chapter, I would routinely communicate with each teacher to discuss David's needs and issues, brainstorming plans for maximal outcomes. He was blessed to have an elite group of talented and caring instructors. The ensuing teacher/mom associations, with their generated strategies and wonderful results, were mutually rewarding.

In a school which supposedly did not provide "special education," David's education could not have been more specialized within the mainstream. We will be forever grateful for the willingness and creativity of the countless professionals who welcomed me to their team. They listened and labored on our behalf and always carved out time for us. This team truly made a difference in our lives and futures, for David's experience and happiness impacted our entire nuclear family. But, humbly speaking, I also believe that tireless effort and cooperation from David and me enhanced the faculty investment and made the ultimate difference. The responsibility for educating cannot be shouldered solely by the school—home behaviors must augment formal endeavors. Students and their supporters must take on their share of the burden, and great harmonies and symphonies can be created from unique orchestration.

On that note, pun intended, let's segue to talk of choir and drama progress. A new faculty member was added to the department for that single year. In nine short months, he hugely impacted David's happiness and high school career by opening the door of opportunity. Following a traditional style of audition, David earned a role in the fall nonmusical production and was finally able to demonstrate a facet of his acting and comedic ability.

David's drama debut led to a stronger association among coveted peers, but it also exposed him to some degree of social discomfort during offstage rehearsal downtime. He claimed that he didn't always understand the conversations which the tight group shared. He wanted to join in the talk, but he merely hung on the periphery; he was politely allowed to stay, but he was not drawn in. David felt alone even in the company of others. We tried to explain that many of these members had been friends for years and had a history and bond that he could not expect to infiltrate. But beyond this truth, David inherently knew that he was not "getting" the dialogue on a different level—despite all his social skills therapy. He often felt awkward and confused in these situations. Not involved, he was on the outside looking in. David desperately yearned to "belong" and wanted to bond with someone. He therefore made sporadic, inappropriate comments in his effort to merely participate.

Earlier in the school year, a female classmate rudely compared David to a "creeper." He had gained valuable understanding during summer therapy, yet he quietly endured her hurtful words without rebuttal. I encouraged him to educate people in such circumstances. As sessions progressed with Dr. Martin, David became more secure in his knowledge and effective responses; he finally felt equipped to take the plunge. Slowly and selectively, he began to reveal and explain his diagnosis in response to caring inquiries. This was huge—and was a far more therapeutic conclusion for both parties than what previously occurred in the "creeper" situation. And so began David's "coming out" process regarding his autism.

The perfect venue, David was taking a speech class and needed to prepare an oral presentation on "Five Facts about You." Stumped for what to say for fact five, I suggested that David could reveal his Asperger's and very simply explain its major characteristics. We discussed the pros and cons of this exposure, and he ultimately decided to proceed, receiving the approval of the teacher to do so. A sounding board to his speech, I felt it was appropriate and well delivered, and it was received in class without negative ramifications. In fact, as he became better understood, he seemed to enjoy improved comfort and acceptance at school (his presentation's content likely spread beyond the speech class). Further and more profound disclosure would continue throughout his remaining high school years and will be revisited in the chapters to come.

Though Tony's presence was hugely missed, another guardian angel "miraculously" appeared to fill the void. A beautiful senior, both inside and out, Katie met David during her acting role in the previous spring musical when he served on crew. Her kindness grew into a friend/confidante role, and David eventually befriended her entire gracious family. Trustworthy, caring, and wise, Katie sustained David through some of the hardest days of his adolescence; I will be forever grateful for her friendship, advice, and support (and that of her family).

Homecoming rolled around quickly, and David would be accompanied by a freshman young woman he knew from past association. Since he did not yet drive—and because his multiple requests for group inclusion were declined—David and his date were the lone riders in the chauffeured town car we hired. House pictures and restaurant dining were reportedly fun and not awkward, but after entering the dance and posing for the requisite professional photograph, David's date promptly left him in search of her friends.

David regrouped to survey the room and plan his evening, but he truly did not mind, for he was not romantically interested in this girl. More important to him was active participation at his first high school dance. He found many acquaintances that either came alone or paired with a friend, so potential dancers were available for the asking. Bottom line, David danced all night with a variety of schoolmates, including Katie and her friends. He had the time of his life! Thankfully, he wasn't at all bothered by the factors which haunted many tween dance experiences! He found his date at the night's conclusion, and after Frank and I drove her home, David expounded excitedly for the remaining commute. His expectations had been altered, but they were more than fulfilled. In fact, I'm sure David had more fun solo than if he remained coupled with his date. One fact remains undisputed—it sure beat the previous year's homecoming experience!!!

A first real glitch in the year's academic plan surfaced in geometry class. The problem did not involve poor understanding, for David's private tutor kept him on track. Rather, it centered on select disruptive students who interfered with the learning process of the majority. Besides David's frustration with the distractions and disrespect (rules, honor, and "rights" were very important to him), he was agitated by a student who continued to call him names, throw things at him, and push his buttons. Upset, David left class on more than one occasion. I met separately with his counselor and the course teacher, and David was transferred into another comparable class with a much-improved dynamic. Optimal learning was restored, and no further harassment occurred for the remaining academic year.

The above counselor appointment was an addendum to a prearranged meeting. As a first order of business, David's sophomore year accommodations were to be determined on that snowy November morning. The conference itself was very productive, but unexpectedly, it was career altering for me and impacted my entire family. For I slipped on ice as I returned to my car; I suffered severe ankle injuries that required surgeries, rehabilitation, and weeks off my job. Recalling our family mantra that "everything happens for a reason," I must admit that this turned out to be most fortunate for David. I was not cleared to return to work for four months, and even then, I had restrictions and shortened days. It so happened that I was therefore home for an extensive portion of David's biology course: the most challenging and time-intensive class of his high school career. Its difficulty was closely trailed by junior year's chemistry class; this course ironically paralleled the timing of my second surgery and time off work—ah, fate (or heavenly intervention).

It is only in retrospect that I can view my plight optimistically, for I do feel that my extended home convalescence was critical to David's academic success. I was always available to reteach the sciences in ways that he could grasp, and I could coach and tutor him in other areas, as well. In addition to honing his study skills, my limited mobility and extended use of crutches necessitated David's independence. He needed to assist with laundering, cooking, and other chores. And he was now forced to walk to the bus on cold, dark mornings rather than wait in the comfort and warmth of my car. I realized that he was capable of much more than I had delegated prior to that time; I further learned that he enjoyed his freedom, contribution, and accomplishment. I was proud of how our family rallied and used this wrinkle for the best.

David worked extremely hard to learn biology, and he was rewarded with good success. Following the formula which worked in the past, he conquered each day's lesson nightly. He comprehended more fully after my translation illuminated missing pieces or misperceptions (often via analogies and visuals). We read chapters together and prepared for exams starting days in advance. David additionally transferred useful study habits to other courses; his organization and work ethic would serve him well even beyond high school.

David had continued his hip-hop and karate classes to prepare for his musical theater debut. Efforts paid off, for he was cast in the ensemble of the finest musical production of his high school tenure. Finally! He was chosen! He found himself among all those he had longed to associate with—including Katie. It was the best Christmas gift ever!

With the addition of extracurricular rehearsals, David's time management and juggling of course demands became even more important. Teachers were wonderfully flexible in preventing any last-minute crunch or undue burdens for David. Informed of the long rehearsals that preceded opening night, the biology teacher supplied David with her class notes days in advance, per my request. David learned this material with my assistance earlier than his classmates. The lessons were then reinforced during actual classroom instruction. Adequate pre-test review time was therefore possible regardless of evenings monopolized by the play. An alternate accommodation occurred in David's history class. His teacher (counselor, mentor, and confidant) provided him with individual reviews prior to each test to assure David's correct understanding of the material. And most optimistically, there were a few courses that David successfully navigated with total independence, despite his extracurricular involvement.

We adjourned for the holiday break very appreciative and cognizant of the striking contrast from the prior year.

Yes, we still spent considerable time reviewing for finals together. And yes, David still reviewed independently and attended sessions with his math tutor. But past experience with cumulative exams had calmed our nerves, and stress was replaced with family and holiday festivities. David knew he was in control of the academic piece, and everything else seemed to be falling into place. It was the most optimistic we had felt in ages.

The new year quickly recaptured the preholiday momentum. Finals were exhausting, but David was prepared, so they moved along smoothly. He took advantage of his extended time accommodation for his most challenging exams, and he performed admirably well. Conveniently coinciding with the start of play rehearsals, I was finally cleared to drive. Life got simpler for all of us as I slowly resumed tasks traditionally mine. Not yet back to work, I was David's private chauffeur, and I arranged his transportation to best fit his needs. Though he would soon be of age to obtain a temporary driving permit, we never discussed the possibility. The mere prospect terrified me; I was uncertain if he possessed the skills, perspective, and judgment necessary to make timely and safe decisions. If *he* wasn't posing the idea, I surely wasn't bringing it up! This goal was so far removed from his mind that he actually asked one day, "What are temps? Everyone is talking about it." David had multiple other priorities that were never even conscious considerations for his peers; driving was the last thing on our minds.

Early sophomore year, David informed us that classmates were ordering school rings. Never really asking his preference, Frank and I discouraged the idea. We told him that Steve and Craig never bought one, and it would likely just sit in a drawer. "You're right," he said—and never mentioned it again. Then came this winter evening when he needed a ride to school to sing with the Music Ministry for an event. As I dropped him off, I recognized his classmates and parents filtering in, very nicely dressed. Responding to my inquiry, David informed me that tonight was the ring ceremony. I was horrified! He should have been among them; instead, he was with students of the other classes singing accompaniment. I turned and asked him if he had wanted a ring; he emphatically said yes, but he didn't want to go against our wishes. He never contested our earlier presumption in order to share his real desire. It wasn't the hardware as much as the special class rite of passage. Steve and Craig had attended an all-male school. Rings were merely distributed when they arrived—it was no big deal or cause for celebration—it was a purchase. I had no idea that there was a ceremony at this coeducational school, and I didn't realize that almost everyone participated.

I felt awful. David was alienated and out of sync again, but this time it was our fault. We never asked; we never listened. David was so eager to please us that he never told us about the specialness surrounding the ring; he simply trusted our judgment. I instantly thought of the homecoming dance. We had encouraged him to wear his white shirt and navy blazer as was customary at his brothers' school. He told us that most guys were wearing suits or black shirts, but we were against buying a suit he would quickly outgrow. Again he acquiesced without protest, but sure enough, he stood out from the others when we came to pick him up. David was more respectful of our wishes than of his desires. He accepted the evening and handled it gallantly, but he admired everyone's rings and took notice often. Luckily, we bid on a school ring at the annual fundraiser later that year, and David was thrilled to customize it exactly to his liking. Contrary to our expectations, he wore that ring constantly for his remaining high school days—long after the others' rings disappeared from their fingers—and he treasured the symbol with pride. Lesson thus learned, you better believe he sported a black shirt under his choir robe at the next choral concert!

A probable offshoot from *The Bachelor* television show (one of his topics of special interest at that time), David had an idea. He would present a dozen young women with roses on Valentine's Day in appreciation for their kindness and acts of friendship. He worked out the details, and I visited the florist. I drove him to school on the special day, and he hurriedly carried in his two aromatic shopping bags. With the blessing of certain staff members, David hid his stash behind their desks; he presented the roses individually to preselected candidates when he saw them throughout the day. He loved their reactions and associated hugs (sometimes even a kiss on the cheek), and he quickly gained a well-deserved reputation for being thoughtful and sweet. He truly appreciated and respected these young women and appropriately used this day to show them. Even the guys gave him a "thumbs up" for being smooth. And so began his Valentine tradition. The gift changed annually, but the message, sentiment, and surprise element became standard. He always came home gratified and elated on this day—when his expression of "care" was accepted and appreciated. He also proved the adage that "giving is better than receiving" as evidenced by his joy.

As opening night neared, rehearsals and excitement both escalated. It was an awesome experience for David, and he felt increasingly more connected and in sync with the others. With organization and preparation (such as the study modifications previously discussed), David was able to handle the schoolwork without a problem. There was a special bond among the actors and crew during this joint venture; the quality of the production transcended high school theater—and David was part of it! He felt more comfortable socializing at the cast parties, and for the first time ever, he received occasional rides from peers rather than relying on us. This enabled "the entire high school experience" and helped him ease into a whole new set of teenage expectations and responsibilities. It was the culmination of his prior year's dream. I anticipated that the days following the play would bring the letdown typical of every postproduction period. But I also knew that the void would be filled. David had grown in his skills and experience. I tried to focus on my gratitude, soak up the memories, and simply enjoy the moment.

Turning to an update of David's personal characteristics, his smile was becoming more natural and his eye contact had consistently improved. Small talk still had its challenges, and nonverbal gestures remained relatively predictable. Time after time, David displayed identical facial expressions and body positions in photographs. It may have been possible that a go-to pose eliminated any indecisiveness over what to do or how to act— kind of like scripted responses. Or perhaps David liked his "look" and found it conducive to peer blending. Regardless of the rationale for standard and inflexible poses, years of pictures document David showing the peace sign. This was largely replaced, for another long stretch, by an unsmiling, pensive-faced teen whose arms were either crossed at chest level or straight down in front of him, fist in fist. Posed photos only recently demonstrate his increased variability; they now depict a more spontaneous and smiling David instead of his routine and plastic predecessors.

David continued to exhibit hypersensitivity, but he coped and expanded in many avenues. His evolution to more sophisticated dining choices was most noticeable. He developed a passion for Italian spices and cuisine and would experiment with foods in that vein; he would eat calamari, shrimp, or new dishes in tomato sauce—even when still refusing chocolate candy, hard ice cream, or baked goods. Salads with basil or seasoned grilled vegetables were now enjoyed over the common junk foods of teens. So discerning was (and still is) his palate that he could detect if I substituted a brand or changed any ingredients. New food samples were willingly tried if they were topped with ketchup, *McDonald's* sweet 'n sour sauce, or tomato sauce. But certain routines were still rigidly followed: he ate one food group in its entirety before moving on to the next, and he ate a restricted breakfast menu. After years of dining on the same waking meal, David finally tried one new option: my banana and cinnamon oatmeal formulation. He then alternated between this dish and his customary fiber bar with extra peanut butter—the standard which is surprisingly still current. I continue to pack the bars for any overnight stays, for he refuses to try toast, cold cereal, or other commonly enjoyed options, even extending to fast food or restaurant offerings.

Many of David's skin sensations differed from the norm. He didn't like tickling or light touch, and his hugs were overly zealous, threatening to topple my shorter self. I often noted that he desired to wear a waterproof hooded jacket even in a light drizzle, which is uncharacteristic for a male teen. As if in fear or dread, David ran through rain as fast as he could. I once joked that while wetness would not hurt him, a slip or fall could. It was only then that he explained the situation: wetness did not cause the distress—the irritant was the prickly sensation of pelting drops as they hit his skin. (Remember his aversion to cut hair landing on his body?) In a way, rain DID hurt him, as he was hypersensitive to its touch. That realization prompted me to stash a hooded parka in his backpack for accessible protection; he still willingly uses this barrier when caught unprepared for rain.

Luckily, given his passion for choir and theater, it seemed that bands and louder music no longer universally distressed David. Intolerance was now more dependent on the situation, and it worsened when he could "feel" vibrations that "made things jump" (per his description). Still, David visibly cringed at isolated, unanticipated sounds or if yelled at. And it was the explosiveness of the shouter's voice rather than the message that seemed more painful to him. Of interest, I noticed that David often activated the closed-caption option on the television to augment "hearing" the dialogue. In addition, he always wore headphones when listening to selections on his computer. I am not sure if this was to enhance the audio or to screen out background noise. David slept with the ceiling fan on, regardless of the temperature, and loved when it heavily rained at bedtime—he claimed that the "white noise" of the fan and rain blocked out other stimuli and greatly assisted his sleep. Note how all of this compares with the discussion of bothersome noise found in the junior high chapter.

David's incredible sense of smell is most remarkable to me. He can accurately detect a change in my skin or hair care products from a considerable distance away. Likewise, he can identify cooking ingredients, entrées, or other odors that are not discernible by the average person. I was concerned about his biology lab experience for obvious reasons; I feared that this sensitivity, combined with his squeamishness and touch aversions, might hinder his dissection tolerance. His teacher wonderfully understood and suggested that perhaps a virtual means might be an alternate option. Thankfully, the requirement was minimal, and he handled the typical format with the assistance utilized.

As the biology class shifted its focus to genetics, David and I spent a considerable amount of time using examples and diagrams to learn. Among other topics, we studied inheritance and the concepts of dominant, recessive, and sex-linked characteristics. Discussing family traits and real issues made it much more interesting and understandable—practical application always solidified concepts for him. David possessed an appreciation for the beauty of vivid color. He also loved his coveted best feature: thick and easily styled hair. The latter was a genetic gift from Frank's father. My mother's side, in contrast, passed down premature male balding. Additionally, David was stunned to learn that Steve and Craig were both color-blind, just like my father. Tracing the genetic pathways, and aware of David's above-mentioned passions, my jaw dropped at David's most astonishing quote ever: "Thank God I'm not color-blind! Thank God I'm not bald! Thank God I only got autism!!" Talk about an optimist—no wonder he coped so well! Clearly, everything is relative!

In the summer heading into my second year, I was honestly very confident that my sophomore experience would be a complete change from the year before. I felt like I made it past the "fresh" stage of freshman adjustment, and I had made myself well-known in the halls. The first week of classes was a great kickoff because I recognized new freshmen who had gone to my old school. But I still wanted to make stronger connections with the kids in MY grade. With Tony and the upperclassmen from last year gone, the ultimate test for me would be to find a core group to sit with at lunch. Surprisingly, I found that group, and it wasn't just random kids who I bumped into in the hallway. These were peers who I had classes with, who I was able to have great talks with, and who were also kind of in the same circle. It was that particular lunch arrangement that made me feel like I accomplished something big. Now, for most sophomore kids, it doesn't necessarily sound like a big deal, but with everything I went through the year before, any stepping stones accomplished to build that core group were huge. I would be willing to climb the Mayan Temples to get where I wanted to be, and I was determined to make it happen.

As the weeks passed and the schoolwork progressed, there was a completely different aura in the school: I wasn't a newbie, I had some connections, and I was sort of well-known due to my rapping status. I was even starting to open up more to my fellow peers and teachers. Because of the events that happened the previous years, I struggled a lot with trusting people in general. But over the early course of the year, I saw myself becoming more social, especially with teachers. I found myself walking into their offices to say hi, to ask questions about assignments, and even to simply converse. I especially grew close to five of them during that year, all of whom would make a drastic impact on my life throughout the rest of my high school career.

Even with being well-known and more open, things were still awkward for me socially (especially with girls). Now, for any high school boy, talking to pretty girls always makes one flustered. But for me, being a young autistic man inexperienced in the complex game of love, I needed tremendous work on my game! I'll describe the general scenario: I would see a pretty girl at her locker, I'd take a moment to catch my breath, I'd walk up to her, and I'd say, "Hey." Then she would respond with, "Hey," or even a, "Hey David," if I knew her well. I would stand awkwardly for about twenty seconds, tell her I'd see her later, and walk away. Yep, that was about as awkward as you could get. And it was because of such encounters that social scenarios, like homecoming, made me quiver. But I'll get to that later; a more important event was coming up first: the fall play tryouts!

After last year's fiasco, I was determined to be cast in this one. Thankfully, the new director was also my choir teacher, and I developed a pretty cool connection with him over the first couple weeks of school. The time finally came for the auditions. While on the outside it seemed like I was composed, on the inside I was freaking out! After what happened last year, I couldn't help but feel self-conscious about the audition and my abilities in general. What was going to happen? Would the director like me? My mind was basically going a million miles a minute. I felt like I did very well in my audition, and I eagerly awaited the results. A day went by, and the cast list was posted: I made it!! Now, even with my parents trying to instill in me the concept of "DL" (down low), that did not stop me from skipping down the halls and doing my "D.Pets Happy Dance"! Obviously, my physical reaction showed complete happiness, but I also felt accomplished on the inside, and I regained a new sense of hope. In simple terms, I was basking in an all-time positive high. I looked forward to the months of play practice when I would hang out with my own group.

Aside from the play, homecoming was coming up. Since freshmen weren't allowed to attend homecoming without an invitation, I decided that I would step up to the plate and ask a ninth grader. There was an acquaintance from one of my past schools who was now at my high school; I decided that I would ask her. But, since my game wasn't at its best, I decided to seek advice from the family—specifically my mother. The way we planned this out (as well as all other future dances) was that we would role play. We would come up with the exact words to ask the girl. That way, I would get my point across, and it wouldn't be awkward. After finding the right words through many attempts, it was the next day at school that I finally asked my friend the question—and surprisingly, she said yes! So within a few short weeks, I not only "made" the fall play, but I also had a date to homecoming. Already, you can see the difference from my freshman year, and I knew it could only get better!

The days went by, play practice was going extremely well, and homecoming weekend arrived. Because of the school my brothers went to, it was a tradition in my family that I would wear a navy blazer to this homecoming dance. With my parents' help, I went through the whole process of buying a corsage, getting a chauffeured car, and finding a color-coordinated tie. I picked my date up, and we did the traditional photos outside the house with her family. We then went back to my place, took photos there, ate at a restaurant, and headed to the dance. We got there, took our formal picture, but then afterwards, three minutes in, she said she wanted to hang out with her friends. So, kind of confused as to what just happened, I let her do her "thing," and I proceeded to the dance floor, hoping to find mine. At first, I felt a little uneasy about what happened, but as soon as I got to the dance floor, my senior friends included me in their fun. Some of my senior female friends even wanted to dance with me! I had a fantastic time!

*At the end of the dance, I found my date, and we went home. As you can see, homecoming wasn't exactly what I pictured, but the main lesson that I took away from that night, which I still hold to this day, is to **not** have any expectations. Just go with the flow and roll with the punches.*

Opening weekend of the play arrived, and I felt really good; I would finally have a chance to step out onto the stage. Following my first performance, I met with my family and felt very accomplished; I had fulfilled my hopes and wishes for the start of the year, and I had the drive to do more. After the play had concluded, I decided to focus on school before worrying about the next round of auditions. Overall, I was doing well, but there was one class that I particularly struggled with: not grade-wise, but concentration-wise. I was in a remedial geometry class because math wasn't and isn't my strongest suit. Every day I went into that class hoping that there wouldn't be any disruptions or inappropriate behavior. Unfortunately, this did not prevail, and it got so bad that it was unbearable for me to even be in the classroom. Thankfully, with the help of my mother, I was able to transfer out of the class; I still had the same teacher, but the students were better behaved.

Aside from the schoolwork, there were scenarios in classes that brought up issues way beyond the academic subjects. I found myself facing my biggest insecurity: my Asperger's. There was one situation that sticks out in my mind. I was finishing a project in my art class, and everyone else was talking among themselves. Whenever I was bored or had nothing else to do at the time, I would kind of slither my way into a group and observe the conversation. I saw nothing wrong with it, but to someone else, it could be viewed as weird. This one girl thought it was so much so that she approached me and asked me why I acted like a "creeper." It stings a little bit to this day because I was still at the beginner level of learning about my Asperger's; I couldn't really find it within myself to explain it to this young lady.

A few months went by, and the same situation emerged again in a different way. I was hanging out with a group of my theater friends in the drama hall when one of my soon-to-be friends asked me, "David, why is it that you do the things that you do?" Some time had passed since the prior incident, and I had also gained more knowledge about my autism. So I sparked a discussion among the group, and I told them all about my Asperger's. That was the first time I had ever told anyone about my AS. To me, I saw it as a testament of how much I had grown: I was actually able to trust my fellow peers. It was situations like that in which I was able to start telling people about my autism. To my surprise, they were very accepting of it. They even came to appreciate me more because they finally understood why I was the way that I was. I began to take the steps necessary to overcome my biggest obstacle in order to become the person I wanted to be. With the help of Dr. Martin, I became more confident and accepting of myself—and this allowed me to clearly present my situation to my friends.

Over the course of the next few months, the spring musical auditions were coming up. I was very nervous and filled with self-doubt after not "making" the first musical when I really thought I should have. I was very uneasy this time around, so I made sure that I would be prepared; every chance I got, I worked on the dance routine. The audition was the traditional singing, dancing, and acting type that I was accustomed to, and I can confidently say that I did a great job. I didn't get a callback, so that made me quite nervous. But after a few days went by, the cast list went up and I made it!! I had reached my highest level of accomplishment (and relief)! Compared to where I was the former year, it was a complete turnaround and almost like a transformation. That moment gave me the drive to build on my successes; I would not just try my best in the arts, but I would also do the same with my schoolwork.

Between play practice and making connections with people, the months that followed were absolutely incredible. There is one particular person who has remained a big part of my life through that experience—a very special girl named Katie. To me, she was basically the perfect friend, and she was the perfect person to be around especially when you were feeling down. Not only was she physically beautiful, but it was her kind, compassionate, and genuine nature that composed an inner beauty that radiated outward. Whenever I was having a bad day, and even when I was having a good day, Katie would always be the person who I stopped in the halls to give a hug and ask about her day.

Katie was truly a one-of-a-kind girl who I met during freshman year. I grew closer to her over the course of sophomore year through the musical production. A moment showing our closeness came on the closing night. She was a senior, so it would be her last high school performance. The senior girls were all very emotional. I pulled Katie aside to tell her how much of a difference she made in my life: how she took me in, treated me like her little brother, and was really like a big sister to me. And while I was saying these words to her, she was crying. Then she hugged me and told me she loved me; ever since then, we've had that special familial bond. I will always be thankful to her entire family for their support and friendship.

Once the musical ended, I got back involved in intramural basketball and continued to be an ambassador for my school. I was even able to help one lucky guy make his dreams come true by asking a girl to go to prom with him, thanks to the help of a custom-made rap. I was thrilled with the chance to perform at the school's annual senior farewell. This meant a lot to me because many of my friends were in the senior class, and I felt honored that I got to be a part of their last days at the school. Overall, I would sum up sophomore year as a great recipe to a great deal of confidence. That year, I made drastic improvements over the year before. I had the notion that the success would continue to grow.

Lessons we learned:

- The student and caregivers must work in harmony with the school and educators to produce optimal outcomes. Form an academic "team" and work interdependently toward a common victory.

- Regardless of set curriculum templates and tracks, it might still be possible to customize choices for a better fit. If YOU (and/or your student) don't initiate the conversation to explore alternative courses, it likely will not come up.

- Encourage the student to get involved in desirable extracurricular activities as soon as possible. This will provide social opportunities, balance, and enjoyment. This is worth repeating!

- Do not base decisions solely upon the experiences of other children in the family—each child and each attended school has different priorities and traditions. Be aware of the culture.

CHAPTER TEN

High School:

JUNIOR YEAR (Lowest Low)

The school break was again utilized to improve and prepare, but ample refreshment and pleasure were also interspersed. Foremost on our minds, David needed to fulfill the state graduation testing requirements. Summer was the ideal time to concentrate on this obligation, for David was free from routine demands. A series of standardized examinations had been administered to sophomores during the spring. These needed to be passed to earn a diploma and could be retaken if initial attempts were unsuccessful. We were not surprised that David had to repeat the science portion; in fact, despite his review and careful preparation, we expected it. We were actually thrilled that this was the sole exam that required a retest. Select subjects were even conquered with above average scores, thanks to David's willingness to study review manuals and relevant class content during the preceding weeks.

I enrolled David in the public high school's summer science review course and located the study book we had initially utilized. Geared to only one test, our preparation efforts were focused and effective. On days when I worked, David reviewed predetermined sections of his high school class notes independently. We then studied basic concepts and the book when I was available to help. With the additional assistance of the formal course to reteach content and test-taking techniques, David thankfully passed by a wide margin. He could finally dismiss state mandates and simply focus on his program's requirements for his remaining high school days. What a relief!

Anticipating David's challenge with chemistry and higher-level math, I sought a jump on the fundamentals; a comfortable base of knowledge would replace his fear of the unknown with a preferred familiarity. Per my request, the high school gladly signed out a chemistry book to us, and we solicited the additional help of a dear family friend and dental student. David loved this young woman's humor and tutelage, so he was very willing to submit himself to the summer's helpful preview. We also utilized the assistance of our faithful math tutor to reprogram David's brain back into algebra mode. Coupled with the school's mandatory summer reading assignments, these efforts kept David's mind sharp; come late August, he easily transitioned back into studies with renewed confidence.

Having successfully entered the world of musical theater, David ceased the steppingstone hip-hop instruction. He continued with karate, however, until extracurricular obligations precluded time for lessons. David also unexpectedly became involved at his school: he was recruited by its spiritual leader, the incredible Mrs. Roberts. She was the guardian angel who added her support net to Tony's during latter freshman year. Throughout high school, it was her office that offered asylum and counsel as well as conversation and cheer. Mrs. Roberts provided opportunities and encouragement; she nurtured David's growth beyond academics or theater. She believed in him—and helped him believe in himself. She thus invited David to be on the school's spiritual-focused committee. Along with the team, he would undertake various responsibilities: planning the year's events and themes, assisting with retreats and orientations, and fostering the Christian spirit. Now an upperclassman, David was thrilled to take on a leadership role. He was equally happy to be involved at school throughout the summer. It was his springboard to a volunteer commitment and an opportunity to become more vested and known in nonperformance activities.

On the home front, there were the typical summer activities that we looked forward to annually. Craig came home after graduation until he began his career in his college town. He thus filled David's social void, and they enjoyed some final time living together until Craig left our home for good—something Steve had already done five years earlier.

David still enjoyed the neighborhood church festivals popular at this time of year. He continued to attend alone, which had never been a problem prior to this summer. Unfortunately, David was confronted on one excursion by a bully and sidekick who had harassed him many times before. They sandwiched him and delivered physical and emotional mistreatment. In the crowd, this went unnoticed—or ignored—by passersby.

Beyond the distress over the sporadic continuation of such antics for two years, we were concerned that they were now occurring off school grounds. Would David need to be cautious and watchful everywhere he went? Would he be nervous to go to the mall at sixteen years of age? Enough was enough.

Considering parental or legal communications in our search to put an end to this, I first talked to the school official who had encouraged our disclosure freshman year, for school had now reconvened. It soon became clear that we had never spoken about this particular student before, despite the lengthy history, so no intervention had ever actually been attempted. In all fairness, we agreed that initial measures were in order before those more extreme. It was never shared with us what transpired, but no further incidents ever occurred. It was that simple. Passing in the halls, David and this peer merely passed. That was the official end of our bully era, much to our relief. We deeply appreciate the effective intervention of this caring and committed administrator. Since then, David has appropriately dealt with negative behavior recognized as poor or annoying. Hopefully, maturity and experience will continue to bring him more clarity in defining when behavior is part of the normal—albeit undesirable—range, as opposed to when help or reporting might again be necessary in future interactions.

Summer communications regarding curriculum needs again yielded the ideal schedule for David's maximum success. Standard algebra replaced the remedial option. This placement proved to be perfect, partly due to the continued assistance of private tutoring. Our desire for remedial chemistry could not be honored, but David's teacher was so skilled in her craft that she delivered the abstract principles in ways he understood. In addition, she privately reviewed with him prior to each test to ensure his accurate processing and application of the material. She was stellar, and with my additional assistance in daily clarification and pretest preparations, David did surprisingly well.

David was finally eligible for the coveted choir class attended by his theater peers, but I learned that his participation would preclude the twice-deferred Spanish course; scheduling conflicts could not accommodate both. We needed to choose between them. Our academic leader had earlier explained to me that foreign language was not a state requirement for high school graduation, which I had assumed (school requirements may differ or change: do your updated research); however, it could impact college admittance. Although postsecondary education was still two years away, we spent the remaining summer discerning and researching David's likely future path: we needed to know now if Spanish registration was an imperative means to this end. Baccalaureate education was not even a consideration; conquering the challenges of philosophy and extensive liberal arts courses did not seem possible or necessary. David possessed no specific professional aspirations, but with his love and talent for drawing, the joint conclusion that seemed most practical and fitting was his pursuit of graphic design. Whether approaching this goal via an art school or community college, neither researched route required foreign language for entrance. So our dilemma was resolved, and further collegiate decisions were deferred. We confidently opted for choir over Spanish, knowing that our choice wouldn't hinder David's prospective plans. Building on the momentum of his improved sophomore year, we were relieved and free to pursue his fulfillment *now*. Future preparations would not overshadow or cheat his present needs.

During the college discussions just disclosed, it became evident that David was reluctant to consider his next life phase. Eventually, he confided the worry that he was not ready to leave home for a life of independence. He erroneously assumed that he would not be allowed to return if he opted for college; after all, it's what he had witnessed with Steve and Craig. I was quick to reassure him that several options were available; I explained that his brothers had moved on by choice, with readiness and opportunities—not because of any rule prohibiting their return after college. Frank and I assured David that he had a welcome home with us both during and following school. We stressed that the choices of education venue and living arrangement were two separate decisions, not necessarily simultaneous.

David was greatly relieved with this clarification. We similarly reassured him about another troubling misconception he harbored: driving was not mandatory just because a certain age was reached. David had become increasingly concerned when watching us maneuver sudden or challenging road or parking lot situations. He felt pressured that he would soon be forced to do the same, and he questioned his ability. I listed people he knew who didn't opt for licensure until their twenties, and David visibly relaxed. Frank and I assured him that he didn't need to tackle driving until he was motivated and ready. And with these two pressures off his mind, David was free to settle into the undisputed business of junior year.

David's academic performance nicely progressed with the assistance mentioned previously. Taking lecture notes became easier, for frequently, essential information was also visually presented via the utilization of PowerPoint or board notes. Patient teachers waited for the students' transcription; this alleviated the pressures of time and doubt. For David, learning was thereby reinforced by hearing, seeing, and writing the concepts. Confident that he possessed and grasped the key material, David claimed he enjoyed active participation in class discussions.

David became increasingly independent with studies at home. He quickly and thoroughly completed assignments—provided he was clear on the directions and focus. When responding in narrative form (oral or written), David made progress with answering the questions that were asked. He also improved in looking deeper than the mere regurgitation of facts. These are skills which he would continue to develop beyond his high school days.

David generally performed well on tests he could prepare for, but he continued to fall short in standardized testing. The latter required prolonged seating and concentration as well as the pressure of time constraint. Worse still was the need to recall remote information which was learned in a different manner than presented on the test. Taken without accommodations, David could not even ascertain if he properly perceived the question being asked. The state graduation tests were at least specific enough to study for; the ACT college entrance exam was quite a different story. Despite taking a review course, the material and required skills were too vast for David's adequate preparation—reflected as such in his below average scores.

I perceived the disparity between David's poor ACT marks and good class grades as a testament to just how hard he worked to master presented material; I hoped that interested institutions would deduce the same. If necessary, he could always repeat the test after applying for accommodations, for we discovered that option too late in the process to reap its benefits for that sitting. But the community college we entertained conducted its own placement evaluations, so we opted to cease consideration of further standardized testing. With no intent to pursue baccalaureate studies, we did not waste further time or energy on this matter. He had performed the baseline attempt we desired; it was on record in case it was ever required in the future.

David had obtained a speaking part in the fall nonmusical play, and he enjoyed the production and its preparations. But this was overshadowed by his sense of loss and lack of understanding in being denied admission to the esteemed show choir—an elite extracurricular group that was separate from his choral class. I shared in his confusion, for he was the only auditioning guy who didn't "make" it; with more women selected than men, some were thus left without partners. If indeed all the admitted male members had advanced dance skills, I then could accept that David just didn't meet the criteria—but that was not evident to my untrained eyes in every case. After waiting and working for two years to be part of this group, David was the singly excluded male; he was thus excluded from the surrounding social network, as well. Only worse now, he sat daily in choir class listening to talk which constantly reminded him of his peripheral existence.

Though I had watched David cope with countless disappointments over his short life, bouncing back and moving forward, it was apparent that he was stuck and struggling with acceptance this time. He didn't speak of it again, however, until the evening of the first choir concert; even then, it was only after I brought it up. It had been pushed down but not resolved. His group performed beautifully, and David's delight was obvious. But as he made his way to the audience while the elite members assembled on stage, it was evident how painful their performance was to him. Except for the outstanding, showcased moves of select male dancers, there was no choreography performed by the background male members that seemed beyond David's ability. I had hoped that the reverse would be proven to allow final realization and acceptance, but the hurt, confusion, and sense of loss merely resurfaced and were magnified. Please understand that the issue was way beyond rejection from a song and dance group—the road to social inclusion had been blocked. Nothing had ever meant more to David, though I doubt that anyone at the school realized or appreciated this. So close, but yet so far.

I must discuss David's typical response to rejection: his concern was always for the discomfort of the person turning him down, not for himself. He was quick to let this person "off the hook," good-naturedly assuring him or her that the refusal was no problem at all. He always wholeheartedly believed and accepted the reason he was given, and he moved on with no hard feelings or negative comments. I believe it was generally assumed that David would handle any denial and be fine with it—a logical assumption given his history.

I also need to stress that this was a wonderful, kind, upstanding, and Christian group of adolescents with the highest standards and achievements. I'm sure that most had no idea of David's dreams and aspirations. They were not intentionally excluding anyone, and I am confident that they were clueless to his private feelings—the plans and invitations were simply only intended for show choir members, which is the accepted norm in most social circles, clubs, or groups.

Life moved on, and David found himself thrilled to earn a speaking role in the school's spring musical—complete with a solo song and dance number. It was a comedic part and he was spectacular. It was the performance that won him universal acclaim at the school for being an all-around actor with true talent—still complimented by respected others even to this day. Finally achieving this goal, David was ecstatic, so I was shocked with the despondency that followed the play. While he had enjoyed attending cast parties and had graciously been offered cherished rides by generous peers, I later learned that he had often felt out of sync with the conversation and chemistry. In addition, it appeared that while everyone else still had show choir and the surrounding solidarity to fill their lives—David really had nothing to look forward to.

We regrouped to consider our options. David played intramural basketball to help occupy the afterschool void, and he actually enjoyed it this time around. But that was short-lived and evolved into nothing social. David had been talking about Facebook for ages; he claimed that he was out of the social loop by not participating. Frank and I had adamantly denied him access to that venue in the past, for we feared the consequences of his naivety and thought that social media might be a forum for uncontrollable abuse. He was older and more skilled now, however, and the harassment had stopped. There was a new divergent question we needed to think about: could his absence from this major mode of peer communication now be hurting him? We vowed the prior year to consider and respect David's teen culture in making decisions. In moving on with the times, we consulted our older sons regarding our concerns.

Still uncertain, we found ourselves discussing Facebook as we celebrated Easter dinner. Our niece was in company, and by the end of our visit and animated discussion, she set up said account for David—with our consent. Every possible filter was activated, and we spoke at length with David regarding the rules, consequences, and restrictions of its use. Despite our trepidation, he was launched and ecstatic. Craig immediately became his self-appointed media watch guard, monitoring his activity and appropriateness from afar. He called David on numerous occasions in the upcoming weeks (and years) to exclaim, "Get that off your wall!" David increasingly learned suitable information to share, and a new world was opened to him.

Aside from the repeated requests of one of his past bullies to "friend" him, which he was forbidden to do, David never experienced any harassing repercussions. While I was concerned that the true meaning of "friend" would become skewed, he gained comfort and support from the swift and extensive list of friends he accrued. David enjoyed the ease of communication with countless others—he felt more connected and less isolated. He also had an avenue of entertainment to fill lonely nights at home with true interactions.

On the downside, David became more acutely aware of the social gatherings and events to which he was not invited. It was this revelation that freshly opened the wounds of his real-life situation. We were aware of his disappointment, but we had no idea how deeply he ached and how hopeless he felt; he put on a relatively happy front and acted the performance of a lifetime. Once he caught up to the others on stage and in choir, David had always assumed that he would be completely integrated into their circle. He had fought through countless challenges to "arrive," but once there, it wasn't enough. With nothing left to aspire to, David despaired that he would never have the friendships he so desperately desired. With this group out of reach, he felt that there was no one left to fill that gap.

I received a couple communications from school personnel during this time period, both conveying concerns regarding David's serious disclosures to them. I talked to David and scheduled an appointment with Dr. Martin for her expert assistance. Life had seemingly been all right, so he had not seen her for quite a while.

All reached a pinnacle one Friday evening as Frank and I prepared for Saturday's planned outing. Trying to fill David's void and loss of direction, we had arranged to meet Steve and Craig in a city midway between our homes; we sought to perk David up and offer diversion. He came downstairs after spending the evening alone in his room and asked if he could talk to us about something. Startled, we noticed immediately that he had been crying. He poured out his heart, sobbing his despair, which in itself was quite frightening—for all that David had endured in the past, he had never cried or given up. This was truly a grave sign, and we were helpless to pacify him. Empty promises were just that, and no suggestion seemed viable or realistic to him at that moment. My heart broke and I felt sick. There was no denying the brink of depression and seriousness of his message. Thank God for Katie, away at college. David had called her, desperate for consolation; she offered support and a caring ear, and she finally convinced him to confide in us. We are so grateful for her wise counsel and gift of friendship. Her intervention that evening was crucial.

It so happened that a plan was already in the making. At church the previous weekend, Frank pointed out to me an announcement in the bulletin. There was a teen group that welcomed new members: it provided a weekly dinner, religious activity, and social time following a special Sunday evening church service. Current members attended several area high schools, so the potential for new friendships radiated beyond David's current boundaries. It seemed like an answer straight from the heavens. I called Beth, the youth minister and another life-changing guardian angel. We exchanged information, and I excitedly accepted her invitation for David to attend the coming Sunday's events.

Back to this sad Friday, we let David talk and cry. I explained Sunday's plan, trying to offer the hope of new potential. He was too down to see any positives, so we quietly just stayed present with love and comfort. He finally quieted in Frank's arms, and exhausted but unburdened, he slept. That made one of us.

It was a very long night. We alerted Steve and Craig very generally in the morning regarding David's delicate emotional state. David was initially very quiet at lunch, taking in the details of his brothers' seemingly exciting lives. But the visit was the medicine he needed; he soon livened up, feeling much better after going off singly with Craig to shop and talk. He had an improved outlook on the road back home and was willing to give Sunday's proposal a try.

I drove David to church and stayed for the service, sitting alone in a back pew. David introduced himself to Beth; she, in turn, introduced him to others and settled him in. There were students he recognized from school that he never really knew or associated with. There were also new, hospitable teens who welcomed him heartily into their group. Other than the priest and adult core leaders, the service was teen driven, with readings and sermon topics exclusively theirs. The predominantly adult Christian band was phenomenal. The beautiful, harmonious songs were foreign to me but well-known to the youth. Everyone participated in the most heartwarming and meaningful service I had ever attended—including, all smiles, David. My tears started flowing at the first strains of overpowering music. I felt my Dad's presence and instinctively knew that this was the answer we had been seeking—even more dramatic after Friday's events. It came just in time. My thoughts raced back to the stained-glass artwork that hung in the window of David's childhood bedroom. "Expect a Miracle" it had encouraged, and this, most certainly, was a huge one.

I left quietly at the service completion and watched David happily adjourn to the teen activities. Frank retrieved him later, and David burst through our doors, animated and excited. He loved the evening, he loved the people, and he had found the acceptance he sought.

When asked to tell the group something about himself, David had chosen to disclose his diagnosis along with other significant details. He was gratified by the positive response and was comfortable and hopeful. Lonely weekends were now filled with eagerness for Sunday evenings and additional socializing. Though he still aspired to more closely associate with his esteemed group at school, David finally realized that other options, activities, and potential friendships DID exist that could be simultaneously enjoyed. He grew in areas outside of the arts and was strengthened in his religious convictions. He found a new passion in service to others, and he attained more balance, which we knew was so critical. This modest church group had opened David's world and had saved him from despair. With renewed faith and hope, our David was back—even stronger and richer than before.

Content with his new perspective and social life, David relished the remaining school year. He enjoyed the final choir concert and came to terms with his placement, clapping and hollering as the annual award winners were announced at its completion. He, in turn, received support from peers, for he finally "lettered" in fine arts. David was more comfortable and happier among the cherished group than he had felt for a while, possibly because he had stopped trying so hard. He gained a new maturity, philosophy, and path. It had taken a while, but he completely bounced back. David anticipated senior year with renewed determination and hope, and he possessed the grit to achieve his goals. But in the interim, he would enjoy the best summer of his life to date.

After a very fulfilling sophomore year, I was nothing but hopeful that junior year would be just as successful; in many ways it was, but in others it wasn't. The bullying decreased tremendously the previous year, but that didn't mean it stopped altogether. Whenever I ran into any of my harassers off school grounds, I avoided them as much as I could and told them to stop. But there was one particular event that pushed me over the edge. I confided in my parents and school officials. Action was taken, and the bullying stopped. But then it was even more obvious to me how empty and alone my days were. All my peers had made connections with friends they had been talking to since freshman year. I saw them goofing around, going out on the weekends, and having that tight bond that didn't include me—even though I was always kind to them. What was especially hard was that I considered myself a genuine kid who was always a great friend to everyone. But I felt like no one was reciprocating my feelings. What's worse was that I started to have visions of harm coming to me; they kept flowing through my mind. I never took actions with these thoughts, nor did I conjure them up purposefully. They entered my mind at random times, uncontrollably, and even when I wasn't upset. Even with all the success I had achieved, I couldn't get these thoughts out of my head.

I think my negative emotions stemmed from feeling out of sync with everyone in my school, not "making" show choir, and feeling uninvolved with peers in drama—despite my great role in the musical and the fun that came with fame. I worked really hard to get that role so I could feel connected with my peers, yet it was not enough; I was an outsider in my own group. I feel that the main contributor to my sadness was being denied access to show choir: I was LIVID about not "making" it. I just thought that if I was qualified to get a supporting role in a musical, I had proven I could handle show choir. However, I was the only guy out of all the others who tried out and did not get in. I was confused, seeing how if I was to be included, it wouldn't have thrown off the couples since there were more girls than guys anyway.

It wasn't the rejection that put me over the edge, even though I really wanted to be in the group—it was the consequences of it. Almost every conversation during the play was about show choir, and I couldn't participate in any of that talk. More importantly, I felt that show choir was the steppingstone to developing a solid foundation with the kids in drama. In simple terms, not "making" show choir KILLED all my hopes and chances of having the social life I had worked towards throughout my high school career. I wasn't invited to their events because I wasn't in the group. It was like I arrived at my place, but the door was slammed in my face. In addition, I started to develop a routine of "wearing a mask" at that time. I smiled, but I was hurting on the inside. No one (not even my parents) knew how sad I was. Even though the bullying stopped, and even though I was becoming well-known because of the plays, I just felt deflated and hopeless. Worse than that, I lost all faith in God and in myself. I felt like God was punishing me for something I didn't know I did. It was just ultimately one of the lowest times in my life. In simple terms, I was alone!

In the spring of my junior year when I was at my lowest low, I called Katie, who was in college. I vented to her about all the pain I had been enduring that year. I was at my most desperate state. Luckily, she urged me to talk to my parents. And if you've read my mom's section, you know what happened next. We got through the weekend, and they told me about the teen group they read about in the church bulletin. I was desperate enough to try anything to get out of the funk that I was in. This is where the brightness comes in. I fell in love with it from the first day that I went, and I started going every week. I met a great group of friends; not only could they relate to me in terms of what I was going through, but they also shared the same amount of love and faith for God as I would find—and they were willing to be with me on the journey. It was also there that I met a very select group of adults who would help me grow in my faith.

Things started looking up for me. I got to know more kids and formed strong friendships. Through this experience, I realized that there was life outside of my drama friends, even though I still loved and valued that group. There were other kids that I could connect with based on different interests. It was after a mixed-up junior year that I developed the same feelings that I experienced after freshman year: next year would be completely different. But before I could think about that, I was looking forward to what was to come that summer with my church group. Summertime was finally filled with awesome activities: canoeing, going to an amusement park with friends, and doing community service.

One activity that changed everything for me was the retreat trip with these teens. I decided to go because someone dropped out last minute, so the trip was free! With the help of my dad, who was home on a vacation day, I got everything packed and got permission signed in time. More than just a great getaway, it was a chance for youth to grow closer to God and become better in touch with their faith. There was one particular night when the light bulb went on during a specific experience: it was during that time that I looked deep within myself, reflected on my life, and found myself thankful to be where I was at that moment. I remember being so happy and overjoyed because I realized that everything I had gone through in my lifetime had led to that moment. It resulted in me being thankful and hopeful for a bright and successful future. I walked away from that night as a new person who was not only confident in himself—but also in God. It was then that the true meaning of "everything happens for a reason" was revealed to me, and I took on that motto from that day forward. I developed the drive to "go" for what I wanted, not caring about the outcome as long as I tried my best. When I got home, I didn't hope that senior year would be the best year of my life—I KNEW it would be. For not only was I armed with new experiences, I was armed with my newfound faith.

Lessons we learned:

- Investigate the rationale for the teen's reluctance or nervousness regarding a situation. Fears may be unfounded, and misconceptions may require clarification (in contrast, valid basis *may* be found, with further preparation and/or help thus necessary).

- Really talk to your child at regular intervals regarding his/her feelings, happiness, and struggles—don't just take things at face value and assume that all is well if it looks that way. Sensitive issues may be hidden and missed if not sought out.

- Seek and be open to *new* potential avenues for fulfillment or socialization: one COULD be life changing!

CHAPTER ELEVEN

High School:

SENIOR YEAR (Highest High)

Summer exploded with a barrage of graduation parties. I had to admit that Facebook was the key to this social inclusion. For the first time ever, Frank and I needed to arrange *our* social lives around David's, for we provided his transportation—a concession we most happily made. He still reached saturation after one or two hours, keeping us "on call," but it worked to fill all his needs. He was honored to receive personal invitations, as well, and he enjoyed staying connected with everyone through the staggered celebration circuit that took him to August.

Outside of school-required reading, it was the first time in David's scholastic life that I exempted him from academic review or preparation over the summer. With qualifying examinations successfully behind him and math and science requirements completely fulfilled,

David was study free! With his sights on renewed senior year goals, he utilized this available time for physical conditioning. David ran and used weights to improve his endurance and strength; he aimed to increase his stamina in preparation for show choir. Unable to drive, attempts to find part-time work within walking distance were not successful.

Since a definite correlation still existed between increased free time and incidence of chit-chat, Frank and I strongly encouraged him to explore volunteer opportunities for the benefit of all involved. Since the teens' Sunday evening gatherings took a hiatus during the summer, a variety of social and volunteer activities were planned instead. David enthusiastically participated, and he began his service by performing in the teaching play at the weeklong vacation Bible school for young children. It was his first experience working with youth, and he very much enjoyed it.

As Bible camp successfully concluded, several teen members gathered in the parking lot, preparing to depart for a three-day retreat. Participants had committed to this trip prior to David joining the group, but there was a vacancy for one more attendee, so Beth invited him to come along. He excitedly asked Frank to pack his necessities, meet him at the church, and complete required forms. In record time, David was on the bus among individuals who would soon become trusted and close companions. They traveled to a religious college, and David got his first glimpse of dorm life and independent living. A weekend of growth and personal revelation ensued, and he returned happy, refreshed, and more secure in his goals and direction. Fate (or the heavens) had again intervened with providing opportunity at the time it was needed most.

Invested in this teen group, David volunteered for every solicited duty he could possibly fulfill. The dedicated youths visited an assisted living center, did chores for their church, and performed other similar worthwhile services. But aside from work, the group enjoyed a summer packed with social activities: bonfires, a white-water rafting trip, and an amusement park excursion. These adventures were infinitely more special to David because they were shared with peers—not with the family who had always anchored his social life. He conquered his fear of coasters, and he easily hung out with guys who enjoyed his company as much as he did theirs—typical teenage simplicities that David had always longed for but had never totally experienced.

It seems that David may have gotten a little too comfortable with becoming a "cool" teenager. While waiting to board the bus to the park, he ran into the sister of a past schoolmate with whom he shared a friction-filled history. In speaking with her, David flippantly called her brother a crude slang name, and that was the last they interacted that day. He had no idea that he had inadvertently caused offense—until Beth made me aware the following afternoon. As David and I seriously discussed the situation, he was immediately remorseful and was appalled to realize that he had inflicted a discomfort similar to that which he had so often received. Of his own doing, he called the girl's residence and apologized immediately via a phone message. He felt terrible and learned a huge lesson. It was an isolated incident and the lone time that I have ever been contacted for him misbehaving. But no one is perfect—and despite that indiscretion, David is still the kindest person I know. He has since used that experience to keep him cognizant of the power of his words and is selective in his expressions. He learned from a mistake and turned the situation into an opportunity for growth.

David was also involved at the high school. He assisted with the planning and preparation of upcoming programs and events, just as he had done the previous summer. A senior this year, he took a more active role and served on additional committees that provided more varied experiences. His strengths were increasingly recognized and utilized, and relationships from committee associations multiplied accordingly. David was an unofficial "poster child" for the school, entrenched in both its mission and activities. He proudly sported the letter jacket we bought him for his birthday that year. It was a nice accompaniment to his class ring and the perfect uniform for the devoted ambassador that David had become.

David embraced the year that finally commenced. Academically, he continued his art training and college prep path. In addition to a third year in choir, he was able to supplement his required courses with electives that we hoped would enhance life skills and eventual independence. Examples of the latter were web design and computer training, nutrition and fitness instruction, and a practical business class. Though the personal finance and nutrition options required my input and tutelage, David was independent with most of his studies, except for web design. Here he struggled to understand the directions and explanations of the teacher—he could not "see" what the others perceived, and he became quite nervous that he was lost. My inability to tutor him (due to my own knowledge deficit) magnified his helpless feelings.

As was my custom, I met with the teacher within the first few weeks, but I timed this meeting to be subsequent to David's own self-sought assistance. Since David continually interrupted the lessons with personal questions, it was decided that he could seek help from fellow students during class; their varied explanations, practical examples, and immediate feedback would hopefully enlighten him. Instructor clarifications would come in turn, and validation of David's work would come from both sources. This was extremely valuable, and David finally caught on, especially as resolving nervousness allowed him to better "hear" and understand explanations. He learned the foreign principles via tactics that best matched his needs: he heard, he saw, he applied, and his performance was reinforced via confirmation. Characteristic for David, he became prematurely anxious at the prospect that he might fail, but he then settled down after finding accommodations that worked. David ultimately became more independent in the class and did very well. This is a great example of the unique outcomes that can emerge from parent/teacher discussions. The issues of all parties can be illuminated, and ideas for resolution can be born and tried—often with mutual benefits.

While we attended the final "back to school night" of David's high school career, Frank and I were shocked with an inundation of complimentary, touching comments that came from both parent and staff sources. It seemed that David had been involved with a freshman welcome/ orientation where he was asked to address the class. He told his story, emphasizing how the negative behavior of some classmates had impacted him; he implored the students to treat everyone respectfully to allow dreams to be realized for all. In addition to incoming freshmen, the talk was attended by select senior peers and volunteering faculty who worked on the event. David humbly finished his presentation, not appreciating its effect or even mentioning the details at home.

Evidently, students were touched enough to share the message with their parents, many of whom knew us personally. Several attending seniors approached David afterward to express their surprise and shock at his disclosure—they had possessed no prior inkling of the loneliness and sadness he had experienced. David's risk had highly paid off; his heartfelt revelation had generated positive discussion and perhaps would prevent future incidents and pain for others. We were floored at the feedback we encountered; Frank even received an email at work from a coworker who learned that the speaker was our David. It was then that we realized how David's negatives could benefit others—and how his gifts of public speaking and Christian concern could enhance his effort. He was truly special—as we had always known. We were just thrilled that others were looking beyond his Asperger's to realize this, as well.

Choir and its related involvement were still incredibly important to David, but he now had other outlets and a healthier balance. He was more relaxed, and he was increasingly better understood. He also continued his participation within the teen church group, with several of its members overlapping David's high school social circles.

Of huge importance, David found the courage to again audition for show choir, but this time he was victorious in his efforts. Entrance won him confidence, pride, and the realization that dreams are attainable if one continues to work towards them. He was now a part of the group small talk and social gatherings, and he never took for granted the specialness of this belonging—even beyond high school graduation.

The stars seemed to be aligned in his favor, for David was also cast in his desired role as Jacob Marley in *A Christmas Carol*. It was his all-time favorite play and one he had always aspired to appear in; we found it very symbolic that this dramatic, coveted part would be the finale performance of his high school supporting roles.

It seemed that life could not get any better until a kind and talented freshman friend accepted David's homecoming invitation—without hesitation and on his first attempt. They would join the other choir couples for pictures and dinner, and they would sit with the group at the dance itself. Finally! It was David's ultimate high school experience, and it surpassed any expectation he had ever dared to consider. Sitting among the friends he cherished beyond all others, it was a dream come true. The group photo capturing his joy and acceptance is still fondly and triumphantly displayed in his bedroom at our family home.

The fall choir concert was beautiful. David was thrilled to participate in the show choir portions, and he was rightly proud of his hard-fought progression to this ultimate prize. He danced on par with the others and blended well with the group. Though nothing marred his performance talent-wise, I was distressed with a new and noticeable behavior. While in robed performance, David's quivering hands dramatically shook the music pages he held. Thankfully, his gifted memory of the words and music allowed him to eliminate the book. This resolved the immediate distraction but not the physical cause. Scrutinizing his every movement in the days that followed, there was no denying the escalation of tremors that occurred exclusively in his hands. Concerned for his prospective occupation and fearing another attention-grabbing difference, I scheduled an appointment with David's neurologist. Adjustments of his tic medication followed.

David strove to juggle rehearsal and academic demands. I became his driver and personal assistant to help him maximize and utilize free time. Healthy meals, instead of fast-food runs, were a priority we shared. I often personally delivered home-cooked dinners to the school that I timed for his break or transition between rehearsals. On other days, I retrieved David to eat, study, and "chill" at home during longer interludes between school and later practices. I did anything necessary to alleviate his stress, prevent continuous stimulation, and make it all work. We considered these to be family accommodations, and they were well worth the effort. We were thrilled with his new active life and would do anything to support it.

For David, senior year was huge developmentally as well as socially. He was finally assimilated into the high school scene and was free of crises, so I directed efforts toward working on more subtle challenges. Frank and I focused so much (and for so long) on perfecting his behavior that, in some aspects, David possessed better social skills than many "typicals" we encountered. Due to his experiences, he also developed a maturity beyond his years, incongruent to the naiveté and seeming cluelessness he often simultaneously displayed. Working to fine-tune subtle social glitches, he continued making progress to the degree that his Asperger's was becoming much less perceptible in familiar situations and with close acquaintances—and was often a surprise to those unaware of his diagnosis. In foreign circumstances and among strangers, however, differences and regressed responses were (and are) still glaringly obvious, though they diminish with repetition and familiarity.

Several tactics helped David navigate new situations, improve communication, and extend his learning beyond his actual experiences. Of great value, David and I would analyze scenarios that occurred to him or to others. We would discuss how situations were handled and dissect the effects of various word choices or actions taken. This would improve his perception of both sides. I would ask David, "What could have been done differently?" or "How do you think the person would feel if..." and so on. Applying principles from my professional education and practice, I found that asking David questions to get him actively thinking, judging, and involved seemed to yield better understanding and retention than merely talking *at* him. Concrete examples also provided more potential for novel realizations and improved learning.

A valuable forum that allowed growth and "safe" conversation practice was gathering with extended family, such as for birthday or holiday celebrations. Not having sisters, David's interactions with his cherished female cousins aided his exchanges and ease with young lady peers. Comfortable and relaxed with the familiarity and understanding of his relatives, David would socialize, and I would monitor unnoticed from afar. I could then cue him if he was inappropriate or just allow him to interact per his discretion.

When later alone, David and I would evaluate his performance. I would always begin by first saying what he did well in order to boost his confidence and openness to further comments. I would then follow with my impressions and suggestions for any problems I noticed: the topic and length of his speech, his delivery, his give and take, his tendency to interrupt, or whatever issues presented. And I would conclude with praise and reinforcement of his progress and things he did right. He accepted the negative comments better when sandwiched between positives, for it was easier on his self-esteem. He was never angered by the critique; rather, he was disappointed and brought down. He obviously self-assessed a better performance in some instances, and he was eager to attain this higher level—both for his sake and to please me and his conversers.

We expanded this exercise to a critique of socialization which occurred in any setting where I was also present: at school, at plays, at social dinners, and so on. Over time, David learned with practice and feedback, and he became more appropriate, comfortable, and skilled. He still tended to blurt out all his news in successive sentences, and this was followed by an uncomfortable silence when he was spent. He might also occasionally break into rap or performance, but this negative inclination was thankfully dwindling. He was becoming more natural among familiar individuals and was learning the art of asking as well as telling. We worked on his spatial distance, for he still stood or followed too closely at times. David made steady progress. He has become remarkably smooth with telephone business, but we continue to critique his witnessed interactions even currently, for he always strives to perfect the art of face-to-face and group conversation.

David and I often covered *potential* topics in our discussions. I tried to anticipate probable situations, and we talked about the related and desirable social behavior; David would therefore be ready and confident in his reactions, should the need arise. I aimed to prevent his inappropriate reflex responses; I instead tried to prepare him for future events. Since every scenario cannot possibly be anticipated, challenge and potential mistakes still loomed. We thus tried to amass useful strategies, rules, and positive experiences from which he could pull and apply. Importantly, I tried to help him consider the effects of his words and actions and encouraged him to think things through. I strove to develop his awareness of peoples' reactions to his behavior; this could then guide his adjustments. A very simple example of where he might practice these concepts would be in classroom discussions: David had a tendency to participate overzealously without my presence to cue his restraint.

I capitalized on the teachable moments of everyday life whenever possible, whether originating from David's experiences and questions, unplanned developments, issues of acquaintances, or current events. Taking advantage of David's piqued interest or "need to know" usually resulted in better learning. Spontaneous teaching of witnessed happenings became a standard intervention that yielded success repeatedly. In any notable incident observed, whether of social or other significance, I would explain its components and we would discuss it in detail. This was extremely valuable to expand learning beyond his narrow experiences. For example, it was an incomparable teaching tool to illustrate driving scenarios with "dos and don'ts" (when the appropriate readiness arose). David witnessed practical examples supplemented by immediate verbal explanations; this had an impact on his understanding as well as his retention.

Another tremendously useful learning tool was practice with me via role play. This gave David an edited and acceptable script, and it also improved his confidence and delivery. It was a means of safe experimentation with a trusted coach, and it provided instant feedback for improved outcomes. In critiquing his solicited verbalizations, I also taught him what not to say and why. Occasionally he would add some of these discussions and scripts to his repertoire and use them in other social encounters; I often heard our same words echoed and adapted to various situations (which was my goal). This strategy was typically utilized to help David formulate an invitation (such as for a dance) or practice a request for a self-advocated need. It has also assisted his response in awkward situations.

David often shared his problems, challenges, fears, and confusions with me. Sometimes he was eloquent and well-spoken. On other attempts, his communication was unclear; he used words incorrectly or could not express exactly what he was trying to convey. Again, applying techniques that I learned and utilized at work, I found it best to validate my interpretation of his thoughts and feelings. I would ask for his verification of my understanding by repeating back to him what I heard him say. He would then either concur or refute and retry. Once the issue was clear, we could brainstorm potential actions to take. This tactic of verification was often necessary even in regular conversation in order to correctly understand each other's messages and communicate effectively.

David was a joy, but he did possess characteristics that were unintentionally quite exasperating. He often appeared clueless regarding obvious needs. For example, when David would enter or exit the house, he might repeatedly step over the delivered newspaper that lay on the porch. Yet, it would not occur to him to bring the paper in. In another instance, as I would race around the kitchen preparing a meal, David would innocently stand in my path and block my progress. Returning with us from a vacation or grocery shopping, David would hop out of the car and into the house, never even considering the need to help carry suitcases or purchases inside. Moreover, he would allow the door to slam behind him, making it more difficult to open for juggling followers, saddled with bags. He just seemed oblivious.

Contrary to what this portrayed, David was the most caring person ever. If one would simply ask for his assistance and redirect him, he was most willing and quick to oblige – it was just that you had to ask. Unless something was made a rule or a routine task (like putting his used dishes in the dishwasher), expecting David to do it spontaneously would likely result in disappointment (or worse). It was the type of behavior that could potentially infuriate a future partner if not understood or discussed. Teaching the expectation and presenting my perspective, however, led to the desired response in later instances. As discussed in prior chapters, the behavior was not instinctively realized, but it could be successfully learned. You just had to explain or demonstrate the "obvious" expectation, and David came through—though he sometimes still required an occasional subtle prompt.

It was equally frustrating to give David directions solely in spoken form. It was, and still is, difficult to explain specifics so that he could clearly comprehend the request or expectation. He often simply had to be shown. However, if words alone were utilized, two types of instructions were the most difficult to convey. First, a verbal listing of needs would likely not be remembered or completed in full. For example, if I asked David to set the table with a variety of items, something would inevitably be missing. Second, and closely related, it was a huge challenge to describe the location of an object that David was looking to find. For instance, verbally directing him through the search details to bring me something that I needed from the basement could be quite taxing and futile.

Bolick discusses tactics geared toward aiding teens' "attention" (34-37), a couple of which I *instead* applied to improve David's ability to follow directions. First, Bolick advises waiting to present a subsequent group of instructions to the teen until after the initial group has been completed by him or her (35). This worked better for David than when he received all the information at once; it enabled him to process each detail and keep up. Accomplished incrementally, the overall request seemed more doable and less nerve-racking to him. Much like a computer, David seemed to freeze if multiple commands were piggybacked without waiting for each to be done successively.

More directed to my challenge than to David's, it was Bolick's example for a second tactic that really hit home; it enlightened me as to how *my* personal change might help David complete what I asked him to do. In that sample, Bolick discourages inquiries that disrupt the teenager's performance of a requested task, thus taking the teen off topic (35-36). Often guilty of this, though formerly unaware of the impact, I consciously tried to limit my tendency to ask or tell David things while he attempted to follow my given directions; I then realized that my disturbance might ruin his concentration and sabotage his efforts. Unless he sought clarification, keeping quiet while he worked through a request seemed to increase his success.

I found that any hint of annoyance while I directed David through a seemingly obvious quest made him anxious, and it proportionately marred his "hearing" along with the outcome. Though it was often easier and faster to give up and perform the task myself, this only resulted in wasted energy by all. David felt deflated, and I lost more than I gained—both in my efficiency and in my progress with him. Investing the required patience and time on the forefront saved us the loss of each in the long run. Once accomplished, David could easily comply with future repeat requests; I gained a ready assistant and he gained experience, independence, and self-satisfaction. I believe this initial investment is worthwhile, but it must be anticipated, understood, and patiently accepted.

In communicating with David regarding tasks and directions, requests that were too general were as problematic as rattled-off details: neither produced the desired outcomes. Asking David, "Did you clean your room?" or "Are you finished getting ready?" would often yield frustrating results, despite his resounding, "Yes!" Inevitably, old papers would be scattered about, or he would come downstairs unshaven. The problem was that he HAD done both; it was just that his idea of the necessary inclusions varied from mine. With our different perceptions and his lack of recall for the litany of tasks (despite his ability to memorize an entire script), the repeated omissions were wearisome.

To remedy this, I first explained exactly what I wanted David to do. Then, I slowly repeated the directives as per my recent discussion. That is, inspired by Bolick, I gave him one request or grouping at a time and waited until each was completed prior to continuing with the subsequent appeal (35). As an alternate method, David would proceed independently; when he announced that he was finished, I then verbally confirmed with him, item by item, that he had completed my entire mental checklist. This latter approach enabled him to immediately rectify missed tasks, and it also improved his future attempts via instant feedback, reinforcement, and practice. I sought to establish a routine that he would follow as habitually as he followed his self-set routines. Again, he was totally willing to comply, but the included essentials needed to be clearly taught—in ways that he learned best.

This system worked beautifully when I was available to coach David, but I wished to additionally prepare him for instances when he was on his own. Realizing that he responded well to written supplementation of verbal information (recall what helped him in class), I typed a list of his hygiene tasks and put it in the bathroom to facilitate his independent completion. This assisted initially, but embarrassed that the list would be obvious to visitors, David soon placed it in a drawer. Not seeking it out when needed, he was back to where he started. In later years we perfected this strategy, and I will share the details in the appropriate chapter.

Sometimes a problem is posed by abstract directions that are open to differing interpretations. For example, "turn the paper" can be done in varied ways. At other times, it is David's literal thinking that interferes. I recall one such incident while studying with him for a past biology test: I handed him the book with a portion of the Krebs cycle and asked him to copy it, for our computer printer was able to photocopy. After an inordinate amount of time, he finally returned with a pencil sketch of all the chemical reactions involved - he had indeed "copied" it.

David shared with me a classic example of the above challenges, which he totally defused with humor—the latter being an accomplishment in itself and a learned asset. Apparently, he and a drama director were together trying to maneuver a cumbersome piece of scenery. David received verbal directions for the navigation, but he didn't understand the prompts and fought the movement rather than assisting. His problem with interpretation and his challenges with coordination and common sense were quickly combining to escalate the director's frustration. In a comedic fashion, David finally exclaimed, "Well EXCUSE ME for being autistic!" So shockingly unexpected was this reality check that the director burst out laughing and commended David on his remark. I marvel at this story on several levels: David's learnt understanding and use of sarcasm, though foreign and offensive to him in his early years; the self-acceptance of his diagnosis with the higher-level ability to laugh about it; the learnt use of humor; and the smooth way in which he handled and resolved mounting frustration. Truly, David had come remarkably far - transcending, I believe, how many "typicals" would have handled this situation!

These are samples of AS characteristics and communication difficulties which require discussion, understanding, advocacy, and sometimes accommodations in order for David to attain optimal outcomes. Considering the above, imagine David's challenges in class, during a job orientation, or with a roommate or wife! (Hopefully the latter will read this book!)

Suddenly it was Christmas break. In grave contrast to David's freshman time travel, this exciting and final year was passing too quickly. Though David was busy with the extracurricular and social activities he had always longed for, he supplemented this involvement with a variety of volunteer and service activities in the school, church, and community. David attended a second overnight retreat with a new group on the other side of town; he was further strengthened in his faith and gained meaningful clarification. Navigating this experience was beneficial, for David didn't know any of the other attendants. It was different from the summer teen experience but valuable in a new dimension. David's sense of self and future came more into focus; his growing spirituality gave him strength, passion, and a new perspective regarding his life struggles. He was unwavering in his convictions and void of embarrassment or insecurity as he started to make them known.

I grew more concerned regarding David's increasing tremors, restlessness, and constant need to move, and his neurologist made medication adjustments. David exhibited a bout of extreme symptoms which prompted school personnel to notify me, but it was his shaking, screaming, and hyperventilation in class the following month that lead to another ambulance summons. There was no evident cause for this event; David denied feeling stressed and was happier than he had ever been. I wondered if the medication's potential side effects were partially to blame. I soon sought the assessment of a different neurologist to start afresh with David's tic control.

Meanwhile, the spring musical was in full swing, and David totally enjoyed his ensemble role in his last production on that treasured stage. He cherished the cast parties and received rides from peers often. I no longer frequented the school because of special-needs appointments, for those had been temporarily transcended—but I often attended as a typically involved parent. Presence and participation were incomparable for five main reasons: 1) to "be in the know" and gain information firsthand, 2) to see and hear others' impressions of David, 3) to witness (and possibly critique) David's interactions with others, 4) to cement further closeness with him, and 5) to "give back." I consequently knew the people he held dear, and we bonded in respecting each other's talents and associations. Even at his advancing age, he was proud to have me speak in his health class or work on the school auction. It increased fun and fulfillment for both of us, and I loved to personally witness his happiness and accomplishment. It was well earned.

David was fortunate to be among a group of high school guys who made an overnight retreat together (David's third retreat of the year, with each one differing greatly). He kept the proceedings confidential, but I gathered from his generalities that he was able to express private feelings and obtain closure for incidents gone by. Suffice it to say that he returned home at peace with himself and felt closer to these boys—who were suddenly men. They had grown up together over the past four years and hugely more on that very weekend. He was also more committed to his faith, and he used his life experiences to launch a marinating idea into a "pay it forward" project for his religion class.

David accepted his diagnosis and successfully conquered obstacles to reach his goals. He realized that he would always have challenges, but he was secure with who he was and where he was going. He was anxious to help other peers find the strength to rise over hardships, grow from their challenges, and treat those with differences as equals; David hence began to speak to adolescents from various schools and groups. Beth, his church group leader, contacted fellow teen leaders and neighboring school officials to find interested audiences. Subsequently, David's speaking took off via contact and referral. When all was said and done, he shared with over 500 students and extended his talks beyond the proposed end of his original class project. His faith, experiences, and gift of public speaking combined to effectively impact his audiences, and the presentations helped David to further discern his life vocation, as well.

Accompanying David to a spring orientation at the community college we had chosen, I repeatedly overheard his response to the classic question, "What's your major?" He always instantly replied that he would start out in graphic design but then hopefully transfer into education. Back in our car, I confronted him with those remarks. Typical of David, he confided that he didn't want a career in art but was afraid to disappoint us. I told him that it was his life, not ours, and I quickly reassured him that we would support him in any endeavor. I explained that we had simply tried to direct him to a practical option in a field in which he displayed talent and interest. I was then shocked to hear him proclaim that he'd like to teach junior high English: language arts had always challenged him due to processing issues related to his Asperger's. I had to admit, however, that his writing skills had greatly improved as the corresponding mechanics were increasingly learned. Correct word usage and critical analysis continued to challenge him, but the field was broad, and he delighted in other aspects of language arts. Undoubtedly, continued education and practice would further improve his weaknesses and skills. It would be vital for him to select the appropriate population to teach.

David enjoyed working with junior high students during his motivational speaking and decided to focus on this age group. He was confident that he could teach in a way that kids could respond to; he felt he would recognize the all-too-familiar signs that a student needed a different approach. David also believed he would recognize the subtle activities of bullies trying to imperceptibly antagonize others, and he longed to stop (or better yet—prevent) such activities. Though I verbalized imagined challenges and his need for flexibility, I would be the last person on earth to discourage him from trying. He had amazed us for years and had proven his ability to achieve the unexpected. Relieved and excited, he expounded on his passion as we headed home, anxious to share his enlightenment and change in plans with Frank.

Realizing that a baccalaureate degree would now be imperative, I immediately began researching potential programs. Unbelievably, a local college met and surpassed David's every need – another "expected miracle" perhaps? High school foreign language was not a prerequisite (phew!), drama and choir opportunities were available, and the college was small and Catholic. But most importantly, it possessed a unique and incredible department that supported students academically – ironically, one which Mrs. O'Neill (David's first grade teacher/guardian angel) helped launch.

David ambivalently yearned for the college campus life that his peers anticipated and his retreat's "dorm days" revealed. At this school, he could securely try independent living in a controlled dormitory setting, for safety nets and intimate class size eliminated many risks; Frank and I would also be quickly accessible if need be. Having learned our lesson regarding transitional needs, we opted for preliminary community college enrollment so that David could adapt to academic organization and study practices. The baccalaureate experience, including dorm housing, would follow two years later; this would additionally promote his independence. David was ecstatic and greatly favored this stepwise approach. He realized that he would be overwhelmed and less likely to succeed by jumping into both changes at once; furthermore, he did not feel ready to leave home and his life coach (me!) just yet. The mere plan, in and of itself, was enough for him at that time.

Unsuccessful in obtaining a prom date, David opted to attend unaccompanied. He was invited into a mixed group of couples/singles and had a wonderful time. Picked up in his friends' limo, he was ecstatic to be included in their group photo session; this was attended by all the proud and adoring parents (I was front and center!) who couldn't capture enough memories. A member of the prom committee, David was active in planning the event, so the reality which unfolded was all the more appreciated. He danced all evening with multiple partners, and despite not winning, the highlight was his nomination for Prom King—an honor which he held dear and victorious, regardless of the actual outcome. The final concert and show choir performances were spectacular. As I reminisced in the audience, I couldn't help but feel overwhelmed at David's acceptance and assimilation into this coveted group. But as life would have it, just when he finally belonged, it would soon be time for David (and everyone else) to break away and start all over. Based on the transient nature of its commuting population, I supposed that community college held little potential for bonding relationships; I looked for another interim association to fulfill David's social and performance needs. This would provide the balance in college transitioning that he so hugely lacked when starting high school.

Fortified with further training, experience, and lessons learned, David earned a wonderful part in the summer musical at the community theater where he camped and aspired as a child. Triumphantly, the same director who had once rejected Dave (albeit with valuable, constructive counseling) now embraced his potential contribution and complimented his progress. Growth and fortitude had finally equipped David for this next level of theater.

I hoped this attainment would provide him with an avenue for lifelong joy and ease his separation from his beloved high school associates.

In the days leading up to graduation, the seniors shared a final retreat day of comradeship, recollection, and closure. There were two treasured parts of this tradition: 1) the receipt of heartfelt letters from peers who chose to correspond, and 2) the review of self-set goals that were personally written and sealed during the initial freshman retreat. At that first gathering, they had all assembled as individuals and were, perhaps, strangers; now, they were bonded as the class of 2011. They had matured from young teens into young adults, and they were strengthened in love and character from shared experiences that promoted growth and wisdom. As I drove David home and he reflected on that day, he proudly marveled at his realization that he had fulfilled every single goal he had set for himself—whether superficial or deep and meaningful. Via his nonchalant response to my inquiry, I was also astounded to learn that he had written to a most unlikely peer: the guy who had caused him the most sustained and unnerving harassment. And it was NOT a letter revealing the torment experienced; instead, it was a letter of understanding and forgiveness which yielded the recipient's acknowledgement the following day. They parted on good terms, and David felt finished. How humbling is that?

The final two quarters yielded 4.0 grade point averages which were independently earned, and David graduated in the top third of his class. At the Baccalaureate Mass, he received the U.S. Presidential Award for volunteer service as well as the school's version of a similar award. But the most significant accolade was David's cherished receipt of an esteemed award for Christian living. He was one of three seniors who earned that coveted tribute. Recipients are honorable, service-oriented individuals who embody their faith and Christian principles. Amidst the thunderous and approving applause, I choked back tears as I realized that it was the same award that Tony had received in that very church three years before. (Yes, I had done a lot of crying in that church!) Talk about irony...

Contrary to the typical desire for a graduation party with peers, David requested a "Victory Dinner." His objective was not to congratulate himself; instead, he wished to honor and show appreciation to relatives and family friends who had supported his journey to triumph. We held an intimate and meaningful dinner at his favorite restaurant, and it was truly a treasured gathering that he often acknowledges though time has since passed.

David still had not mustered the courage to attempt driving, but he remained focused on mastering other challenges. To a functioning level, he had learned most of the social skills which come naturally and effortlessly to most. Nonetheless, chit-chat, a degree of cluelessness, and other differences still lingered. He desired and awaited dating, a special friendship, and independence. The power, however, was in David's positive attitude and enthusiastic optimism. Sure, we had been blessed with an early diagnosis and the time, resources, and guardian angels to maximize intervention, but it was David's grit, faith, openness to assistance, and resilience that made all the difference. He lived (and lives) his belief that there are no limits if hard work, support, and confidence prevail. Balancing out his challenges, he possessed a maturity and wisdom beyond his years.

Despite some earlier dark times, David emerged from high school feeling happy and fulfilled. He was secure in who he was—with both his strengths and weaknesses. Even if he was sometimes different, he possessed the courage and comfort to be his own person with his own style. David rejoiced in every victory, took nothing for granted, and maintained a hard-earned sense of humor. Thriving, he was excited to start his new phase of life. Frank and I were busting with pride and amazement for all that David had achieved. And we were extremely confident that he was not yet finished: neither with accomplishment—nor challenge. Regardless which of these surfaced, we were ready and happy to support our hero in any and all future endeavors.

The following is an excerpt of a rap that David wrote his senior year. I feel it captures and expresses his enlightenment, shift in direction, and cocoon emergence.

I will close this significant life era with part of his slang yet poignant reflection:

Startin out something new

No one to talk to... ...

But that's the past:

I'm movin forward from now on

It's all behind me:

All the pain and sadness

I'm done

Being treated like an outcast

But, man, that soon passed

Never realized I would come this far doin
things my way

I knew I'd see the day

When I would see the light shining with its
bright rays

You always gotta have hope lookin up at the
sky

Gotta shoot expectations oh so very high

Gotta see what the future has in store for me

Now I'm outta my shell I can break free

David's thoughts now follow:

From the beginning of my senior year, I realized that, hands down, this would be the best year of my life! During the summer, Mrs. Roberts asked me to speak in front of the entire freshman class at their retreat. She gave me the opportunity to tell the story of my life, which I had longed to tell. This is what first sparked my interest in motivational speaking. At that retreat, I talked about my hardships throughout high school and explained how I never wanted anyone in that room to go through what I went through. I encouraged everyone to treat their peers with respect and as equals, and I asked them to always be there for each other when times got hard. Through this speech, I felt like I was honoring my debt to Tony. It was because of what he did for me in MY freshman year that made me want to talk to the current freshmen. By doing this, I felt like I was reincarnating the genuine actions that were offered to me, and I wanted to be the one to offer my love and support to the new class.

After the speech, I got praise not just from the freshmen but from MY peers as well. The guys said that they had no idea of what I had gone through and that they were very touched. Some of the girls said they were even on the verge of tears from listening to my speech. I thought I did a good job, but I questioned if it really made a difference. At the end of my senior year, I was able to talk to some of the freshmen and ask them how their year had gone. They said it was a good first year of high school for them: no one was picked on, everyone got involved, and everyone was treated with respect –at least the ones I asked. I felt like I accomplished my mission.

After this great kickoff to senior year, I continued with some awesome classes and gained a fresh outlook on life in general (thanks to my recently discovered faith I talked about in the previous chapter). As the weeks went on and the schoolwork accelerated, the most anticipated moment of my high school career was just around the corner: show choir auditions! After not "making" it the prior year, my confidence was a bit off in deciding whether or not to audition. However, thanks to the summer before, I decided to go for it. As long as I tried my best, I couldn't ask for anything more. I went into the audition self-assured but also extremely nervous. I was relieved when we got to the dance audition because it was based on hip-hop style! Because of my previous hip-hop dance classes, I proudly completed the steps in a graceful way.

A few days went by, and I decided that I would ask a girl to the homecoming dance. She was a freshman with the reputation of being a phenomenally talented actress and singer, so I thought she would be a perfect fit. I saw her in the halls, I caught up to her, and based on the way my mom and I rehearsed, I asked her if she would do me the honor of going to homecoming with me as friends. And she said yes!! I kept my cool and expressed my gratitude; once she was out of sight, I broke the DL code to the extreme! I was relieved and excited all through the day.

Just when I thought things couldn't get any better, the show choir results were posted and I GOT IN!!! At that point, I was ELATED!!! When I saw that list, it was more than just a feeling of happiness. After not making show choir the previous year, I could have been like, "Well, I didn't make it last year, so why would this year be different?" But after the preceding summer, I made a promise to myself that I couldn't go wrong if I gave it my best and put my faith in God. So when I found out that I made it, I was not only proud of my accomplishment but also of staying true to myself and my faith. I walked out of school that day with a fresh outlook on life. I was also determined that senior year WAS going to be different.

After show choir auditions, fall play auditions came along. I was excited for the one selected because it was one of my all-time favorites that I had always longed to act in: "A Christmas Carol." Those who knew me well knew that I could recite the entire play from memory, so I was determined to "make" that one! The auditions were a mix of reading from the script and participating in an interview, which I felt went very well. The highlight from that day was when my director/ drama teacher told me that I had come a long way. A few days went by and the cast list was posted—I was on it!! I got the part of "Jacob Marley," which I was ecstatic about, and I was SO eager to get everything going. Once the show choir and play rehearsals started, I finally had the life that I had striven for since freshman year: I had connected with my peers, I was included in discussions, and once homecoming neared—I had my own group!

On the day of the dance, I got decked out, wore the color-coordinated tie, and got the corsage. My date arrived at my house, we took pictures with our families watching (just like Steve and Craig always did), and then we went over to our friend's house for more pictures and dinner with the group. These were not just any friends—they were the special people I had always longed to be involved with!

As the music played and I danced with my date, I reflected on how far I had come in those last few years: being there with a beautiful girl, a class who knew me for who I truly was, and at last, a group of friends who I could finally call "my friends." What I took away from that moment was that everything happens for a reason; also, everything I went through in the past made me the person I was in that moment and the person I am today writing this passage. Once the night was over, my parents asked me how it was, and I had one word in mind: magical. Every single time I think back to that night, this is the word that pops into my head.

The fall play opening night arrived, and I was determined to make my mark like the year before. My performance led to recognition and positive feedback from family, friends, and strangers. Overall, it was very successful, and I got to live my dream role. Once that was over, spring musical auditions had arrived, and surprisingly, I was very nervous. Scenarios of not making my last musical of high school were popping into my head. But I had faith, and I feel it was this faith that overpowered the demons that were inside of me. Unfortunately, we would not find out the results until during winter break, but thankfully, I had activities to occupy my time!

The last school day before vacation, I was in my choir class, and my friend handed me an invitation to the annual show choir Christmas party. I remembered it from last year and how I felt when all the kids in show choir were going – except for me. Only this time, I WAS a kid in show choir, so I was able to go!! I was pumped, excited, and basically any positive adjective that can describe how overjoyed one is about receiving a longed-for invitation. The night finally came. I met up with the gang for a lovely dinner at my friend's house, and we planned to later go Christmas caroling. When we were all together, singing and acting silly, I felt so lucky and so blessed to be in the position that I was in. I had fully accomplished the biggest goal that I could ever set for myself: I was a part of something bigger than a club—I was a part of a family! We took pictures, looked back on memories, and reflected on how fast the time had gone. I walked away from that night again feeling accomplished, relieved, and so blessed to be where I was. The next day, I found out I was cast in the spring musical! I had finished a great first semester, and it was time to move on to an even greater second and final semester!

Once school started again, rehearsals began for the musical, and I was having an ultimate blast! But I decided I would take this year to get even more in-depth with my faith, as well. My school offered an all-male retreat for three days and two nights in order to grow: not only as men, but men of God. I was really looking forward to it, for my two older brothers had gone on it at their high school and had nothing but positive feedback about the experience.

My fellow "brothers" and I left school and headed off to the unknown. I not only discovered some things about myself but also about my peers on the retreat. This was another game changer in my life because I had grown jealous of a lot of these guys over the course of my high school journey. They

*were the guys who I especially thought had the "perfect life."
But on the retreat, we all opened up, showed our vulnerable
sides, and most importantly, showed who we really were as
people. Hearing what some guys went through during their
lives and hearing the challenges that some had endured really
opened my eyes to what my envious blinders were blocking
me from. What I took away from those moments was that not
one person in this world has a perfect anything—especially
the perfect life. We all go through struggles, and it is times
like these that we should be there for one another. Whatever
hardships we are going through, though they may be different,
we are not alone. Leaving the retreat, I realized that what
we view on the outside of people doesn't always correlate
with what goes on inside. We walked away with newfound
relationships and appreciation.*

*Before I knew it, the musical had premiered. For the rest of
the seniors and me, this would be our very last performance
in a high school setting; as the days were counting down, we
started to feel the emotions rising. Throughout our school
careers, all of us drama kids became a family; it was at the
gathering prior to the closing performance that I really grasped
the reciprocal love and emotion of everyone in that room. The
musical would not only be my last performance at this school
but the last with this group of people. I remember that day
with a wide range of emotions: I was happy, sad, nervous—
and fulfilled. Prior to the opening number, our director asked
all the seniors to come forward, and he reminisced on how
far we had come. As I was hearing his words, it opened my
eyes to see that he really did love and care about every single
one of us. It helped me overlook the pain of the previous year.
Once again, his speech was a solidification of how everything
happens for a reason. What I went through, not only the
prior year but during my whole high school life, made that
particular moment SO much more special. We all enjoyed each*

other's company, on and off stage, one last time. I walked away from that experience not only an accomplished actor but a valuable member of a special group of people.

Once the emotional musical was over, prom was on the horizon. While watching everyone in school come up with extremely creative ways to ask their potential dates to prom, I decided to do my own thing and go to prom "solo"; when people asked me who I was going to prom with, I said, "The whole senior class!" Prom was already off to a great start: I was part of a fantastic group of friends, I reserved some dances with some extremely beautiful girls, AND I was a Prom King nominee!! That was icing on the cake for me; I didn't care whether I won or not because the young men who are nominated for it must have a pretty high reputation, and I was one of those young men. It was another reminder and reward for how far I'd come, and it represented that I truly made a great name for myself. So I went to prom with my group, cast my ballot for Prom King (I didn't vote for myself), danced with some incredible girls, heard the announcement of the Prom King (not me, but I was still ecstatic), and closed the night with a class tribute to the seniors. "After prom" activities concluded a memorable night. I went in with no expectations and came out surprisingly on cloud nine.

Based on a "Pay It Forward" project in my religion class, an opportunity arose for me to continue my motivational speaking, which I hadn't done since the beginning of the year. The objective of the assignment was to go out into the community and simply perform acts of kindness toward others. Everyone else was doing things like volunteering in hospitals and food banks while I decided I would make mine a little more unique. I talked to my youth minister, and she was able to set up gigs at the local Catholic grade schools, youth groups, and religion classes to help me spread my message.

The objectives I wanted to get across to the youths I talked to were the ones I mentioned in the previous "retreat" and "freshman talk" paragraphs. It started off as an assignment; however, I kept getting phone calls from other schools and youth groups asking me to come in and speak even after the project was completed. I was always happy to go. It died down by summer, but ever since then, it has developed into a true passion; it is something that I hope to incorporate into my life in the future.

Graduation was upon us. But before all that, the show choir had our very last rehearsal before the final concert. The emotions and bond we had with one another were exactly like that of the spring musical. It was set in stone that we would always be there for each other; while we would never again experience the past year's moments, they would always be with us. We would never forget the good, the bad, and the alright.

I completed my high school career with an overall 3.6 grade average. Before the actual graduation, I attended the memorable Graduation Mass/Award Ceremony. It was there that I discovered my ultimate reward. As the awards were being announced, the three Christian-based awards were presented. At my school, this is one of the biggest honors anyone can receive. The assistant principal was reading a list of positive characteristics of one of the persons to receive the award; as I was sitting there, I heard, "... and this award goes to David Petrovic." I immediately perked up, and the church was filled with applause. As I got up, people were clapping before, during, and even after I received the award. It was, hands down, one of the best feelings of my life. It was also when I felt I had finally paid my total debt to Tony, and my mission was accomplished.

As I was getting into my cap and gown, flashbacks were flowing through my head. I headed to the auditorium where I would not only graduate from high school but from an old life to a new one. As I stood on that platform and they called my name, I walked across that stage with my head held high. As I accepted my diploma, I could feel the love in the room. I also felt the love of many spiritual keepers who looked after me and kept me on the right path. And when I moved my tassel, it was then that I knew: this chapter is done; it's time to start anew.

What I hope you all get out of this are some life lessons that I have learned. The actions that we perform, positive or negative, can have huge consequences. A negative action, such as name-calling (like I had done myself), could ruin a person's day; even worse, it could push someone too far. Think about it: you don't know what that person goes through on a daily basis. You don't know what hardships are faced at home, which is something to keep in mind. But a positive action, such as saying a simple "Hey what's up?" or inviting someone over to sit at your lunch table, can have a tremendous effect on the person's self-esteem, happiness, and even faith.

We also need to understand that people's differences do not make them "inhuman." What I've been taught through my religion is that we are all made in the divine image and likeness of God, and each one of us has unique attributes and talents. Just because a person is different, that gives us no right to discriminate against him or her solely based on the differences. Not one person is greater than another, no matter what each person's talents and strengths are.

One other important thing I've learned throughout my life is that nothing is ever perfect, especially the perfect life. The perfect life is something that FAR exceeds reality. From what

I've seen, even star athletes, the wealthy "model" types, and smart people can all have their own inner demons. Like I explained before, you don't know what that person goes through daily. Since no one has the perfect life, there is no sense in longing for a different one. As humans, we all have cloaked struggles. Do not be envious of others' riches but work on becoming your own jewel.

Life has many crazy obstacles, and they're thrown everywhere we go. Here are what I think are great ways to achieve a positive mindset to get through these obstacles. When something happens to us, we all have a choice of whether to sit at home and feel sorry for ourselves or to take the obstacles that have been hurled at us and transform them into something positive. Another way to find comfort during a tough situation is to reach out to people in your community who either have experienced or have a taste of what you are going through. You never have to go through a tough situation alone. Look deep within yourself, discover your inner strength, and be thankful for the blessings you HAVE been given.

*Finally, having faith, I feel, is the biggest key to overcoming obstacles in our lives; this is what helped me greatly—it restored and even changed my life. I believe that everything happens for a reason. The people and things that are brought into our lives (and even taken away) and all the good or bad things that have happened **were** there—and **are** there—for a specific purpose. No matter what life throws at you, I feel you can get through it with faith.*

Starting high school as a young, challenged freshman, I always ran out of the school like a crazy person because I was so desperate to get out of there. I had no friends, no social life and no hope. And I always asked the question, "Why Me?!" But look at what happened in four years. I was able to finish high school always running into someone I knew everywhere I went. I graduated in the top third of a class of 221 kids. I was a Prom King nominee. After not making it the year before, I successfully "made" my school's show choir. I was a recipient of my school's treasured Christian graduation award, and I was invited to countless grad parties. Now, it doesn't mean the struggles are over—because they're not. I'm always going to have struggles, but with hard work, determination, and the support of others (as well as faith), instead of having a life I have no control over, I can have the life I've always dreamed of!

Lessons we learned:

- If not already occurring, encourage the student to begin independently self-advocating for needs. This should follow ample preparation, with the continued availability of adult input as needed. Practice and confidence while still in a familiar environment might increase the likelihood of future success when the teen advocates alone in new situations.

- Seize and utilize all opportunities for teaching – even relevant scenarios separate from personal circumstances. This can improve the teen's insight, perspective, and learning via concrete examples.

- The investment of time and energy to improve the teen's conversation and subtle social skills is well worth the cost.

- The teen's willingness to accept constructive critique and trusted coaching can greatly enhance learning and progress.

- Consider or continue parental involvement both at school and in places where your teen is active. Don't merely assume that he/she no longer needs or wants you there solely because of his/her age. Your presence speaks volumes and is a worthwhile investment.

- Do not underestimate the power of attitude and positive thinking—the same for faith and hope.

CHAPTER TWELVE

College:

Phase One

The continual barrage of graduation parties kept David socially engaged on the summer weekends, and weekday evenings were filled with rehearsals for his community theater debut. The show was wonderful, and David's contribution was very solid. He bonded with a whole new group and was thrilled to be affiliated with talented actors of all ages and backgrounds. Just as we had hoped and anticipated, this new association became his center of socialization while attending community college. For while he loved his classes and met interesting people at school, no social life emanated from his enrollment there. We expected this, however, so David was not the least bit disappointed; instead, he felt proud to be handling his academic load and the requisite study adjustments. He loved the increased opportunities for independence that this college experience provided and realized that it was a stepping stone to his dreams.

Before expounding further, let's go back to the summer's experiences and preparations.

David's tremors were minimally perceptible by the time his new neurologist performed her initial examination. David reaped the benefit of her thorough assessment, and she gained a unique perspective with her comprehensive and fresh look, noticing clues previously undetected. Anxiety and panic attacks were thought to be the underlying causes of episodes which precipitated past ambulance summons, and the doctor recommended intervention by a specializing psychologist on three fronts: training in alternate responses for tic control (to augment medicinal efforts), techniques to prevent and treat anxiety/panic, and intervention to quell David's driving phobia – as well as his worry for family members who put themselves at risk when taking the wheel.

The summer was thus filled with time-consuming visits to the same hospital that hosted David's childhood speech therapy. Because his tics and tremors were finally under optimal control at the first of these appointments, we chose not to have him learn additional therapeutic measures at that time. Rather, we preferred to use our limited number of visits to focus on driving and college transition concerns. We sought to help David adjust to anticipatory stresses and ambivalence regarding his frightening (though welcome) life stage progression.

David's attempts to gain employment within walking distance were again unsuccessful, so his biggest job remained college preparation. To minimize chit-chat and partake in constructive activities, David helped at the children's vacation Bible school for one final year, but further activities with his beloved teen group were not allowed beyond high school—as a participant, that is, but not as a junior leader! Aware of David's love and unique perspective for this association, the teen leader proposed that David fulfill requirements which would enable him to assist the core leadership group. It was a perfect solution; David could contribute young ideas and remain socially involved with peers, but he would also interact with the younger junior high population. This was an obvious asset given his newfound career path. Social opportunities remained throughout the year, but a leadership twist was added, and David could learn from the examples of trusted mentors.

Deepening his faith and leadership opportunities, David applied and was chosen for a special program at the same retreat conference that he attended the previous summer. The return commitment, however, spanned a week at the Catholic college. The ensuing personal experience and insight piqued David's interest in considering the Catholic priesthood. This was a vocation he discerned for years, and he continues to do so. I counseled him to enjoy the present and to expand life experiences that would better equip him to make such a choice. I encouraged him to allow fate to provide opportunities that would assist his decision. Eventually, David came to his own conclusions and concurred with my advice, but those are details I will leave for him to disclose. Regardless, his week away increased his confidence in his ability to live independently at college, and it provided Frank and me with a rare opportunity to jet off alone to visit Craig in Chicago, where he then resided.

Along with David's therapy to reduce his driving fears, Frank and I dangled this same Chicago carrot before him to encourage the next step in his licensure. As a combined graduation and birthday gift, Frank and I arranged for David to visit Craig for a weekend; David would travel alone and depart precisely on the eighteenth anniversary of his birth. David was ecstatic and up for the challenge. The problem was that he needed an acceptable form of identification to board the flight— and a temporary driver's permit happened to fit the requirement perfectly! (No accident here!) With fears decreasing and motivation increasing, we seized the opportunity; Frank obtained the study manual containing the essential material for the licensing exam. Since men are often interested in driving, I asked him if he would spearhead the effort to ensure David's preparation. He agreed, and I left David in Frank's capable hands, informing the former that he had half the summer to master the material. Both felt confident in the challenge assigned, so I bowed out and left them to their tactics.

Possibly one of the most significant events of the summer was my attendance at an incredible autism seminar. The sponsoring organization was well connected with specialized centers throughout our area, and they hosted many talks and activities for professionals and families alike. The keynote speaker was fantastic, and the remaining talks could be individually selected to fit every level and need. Tables were manned by sponsors of every type. Information was imparted and products were sold. Ironically, I met an accommodation center representative from the same baccalaureate college where we ultimately planned on enrolling David. When I informed the gentleman of this eventuality, he described their stellar program and urged me to consider placing David into their upcoming study skills session. I enthusiastically agreed, for this would augment the prep class offered by the community college; it would increase David's confidence as well as ease his nerves.

I fervently searched the remaining vendors in quest of the information I sought most: was there a special needs driving education program or an instructor experienced in the training of those with AS challenges? I was unsure of David's ability to make fast decisions based on judgment more than rule; I also questioned his capacity to quickly process ever-changing input. No one could address my question, but I was given the name of a state organization that I subsequently called. I was put in touch with a regional case worker, and I left my question on her voicemail, truly not expecting a response. But days later, I was surprised with a return message that informed me of an instructor who met our needs and happened to be located only twenty minutes away! Perhaps another small "expected miracle"? I filed away the information for future reference and instantly became more at ease with the prospect of David driving; he was not the only person who had harbored this fear!

The final perk of the seminar was the discovery of a wonderful book written by Michelle Garcia Winner and Pamela Crooke called *Socially Curious and Curiously Social: A Social Thinking Guidebook for Bright Teens and Young Adults*. It assisted with understanding and handling a multitude of situations that David encountered daily. Eager to be appropriate and successful on the upcoming college scene, David enthusiastically read this desirable book and gained relief, help, and insight. It was the first written work about AS that he consented to read; this willingness alone was a victory, aside from reaping the benefits of the book's vital contents. I plan on requesting that he reread it midway through college, for I've previously conveyed the learned lesson that a different life stage can lend a different perspective, making forgotten or overlooked material suddenly very pertinent. I also plan on attending additional seminars, as should David; the networking and exchange of information can prove to be as valuable as the topics presented—or better.

Preparations for David to attend the community college were underway. I utilized both formal orientation programs and informal drills. We attended campus information and tour sessions, and we met with a guidance counselor to determine the fall course load. Though David would eventually meet with his advisors independently, he was inexperienced and overwhelmed at present; my input was necessary to obtain a balanced and optimal schedule.

Before this meeting, David was tested in math and English to determine his appropriate entry level placement. Luckily, I kept his scores and the resultant class recommendations, for the counselor erroneously placed David in the most remedial sessions of each. Appropriate changes were later made based on my discovering intervention, but a trusting and less astute student would have lost at least a semester of studies in both math and English, along with the correlating tuition. From then on, I double checked every registered class against the curriculum guidelines for education majors, and I made preliminary lists of potential course options prior to us (or him) meeting with his advisors. This list was formulated based on regular preregistration phone conversations with an official at the college he hoped to attend in the future. I checked for transferability as well as the potential need for prerequisite courses. With the future college currently revising their program criteria, it was vital to make updated choices to allow David to optimize his community college preparation. I wanted him to remain in sync and on track with his classmates after he transferred.

Ultimately, it would be David's responsibility to keep track of his coursework and any ensuing curriculum revisions, not that of a guidance counselor. Blind faith could come with significant cost, and I clearly conveyed this message to David. I would eventually teach him to spearhead course selections and prepare for such meetings with the appropriate research, and I would stay peripherally involved in the preparation, if necessary. But too much was at stake to let it go completely at this point, especially if David aspired to graduate in a timely fashion. And of course, we welcomed the knowledge, input, and experience of his current advisers. Their guidance was significant regarding a choice of professors whose style best matched David's learning needs. We also appreciated their counsel on which courses should be staggered related to their degree of difficulty.

Besides general orientation requirements, David also needed acclimation into the accommodation program, which he gratefully qualified for. An assigned counselor for students with disabilities would monitor his performance and needs at regularly scheduled visits, and this same individual would assist him through the class registration process for future semesters. Accommodations would be jointly determined by David, the counselor, and me; David would then communicate them to each professor, and tutors would be available to aid with studies. Assistance was therefore in place if David chose to take advantage of it, but the responsibility rested on him to arrange it. Meetings would eventually be weaned to allow him to shoulder increasing independence. His accommodations included the option to audiotape classes as well as to take tests in a quiet, monitored environment separate from the classroom. Thus, there was support with the potential for growth.

Part of the orientation to this accommodation center included an evening class on organization and study skills. A daily planner was encouraged, and David preferred the traditional method to more modern electronic means. Daily unassigned work was discussed, and the instructor emphasized the student's need to plan studies in order to stay prepared. Note taking, exam preparation, and time management were also briefly addressed. These were skills that David had practiced all along in high school; it seemed that basically the quantity of work would increase but not so much the quality or method of study. This realization brought David much relief, for he was more prepared for college than he had anticipated.

The beginning of August brought additional study skills training via a week of morning sessions at the baccalaureate college where David planned future transfer. Utilizing an actual textbook with more topics, variations on prior themes, and in-depth discussions and practice, David further increased his confidence and comfort with readiness. Simultaneously, he met prospective classmates in addition to the support staff who would work with him regularly after transfer. He loved this school and its extracurricular offerings, and his enthusiasm soared after a campus and dormitory tour.

Based on David's eligibility, college personnel encouraged him to apply for the upcoming fall admission. Though fleetingly considered, Frank and I held strong to our decision for a tiered transition. An additional year at home would allow drivers' education and practice behind the wheel, and it would enable David to fulfill his commitments to the teen leadership group and community theater. Above all, he needed experience with college academic organization, writing papers, and taking exams before adding the burden of independent living. I realized, however, that transferring as a junior would have him entering the dorm precisely when his peers would be exiting for off-campus living; once again, David would be out of sync and less likely to bond with students his age. As a compromise, we conceded that David could transfer after one year of community college coursework instead of the planned two, pending his performance and readiness. David was ecstatic and determined to utilize the upcoming year to his greatest advantage, proving that readiness.

David and I discussed good suggestions from each of his recent study courses; we also considered successful techniques that worked for him in high school and me in college. Together, we merged these to determine daily practices which David should utilize. Hopefully, this would put him in the optimal position to learn course work and prepare for exams. Borrowing from a tool I had developed and utilized for thirty years in my own work practice, I made David his very own customized "black book": a tabbed pocket reference manual that contained important trivia he might frequently need. The first section included important persons, such as advisors or school personnel, along with their contact information, office hours, and so forth. Another section was labeled "study skills" and housed the recipe for success which we determined above. A third section, labeled "transportation," contained bus schedules and information for traveling to and from destinations. You get the idea: anything essential was organized into a quickly retrievable section to allow for maximal efficiency and independence. (This was prior to the widespread use of smart phones, and David preferred a hard copy reference.)

I continued David's informal orientation at the community college for the remaining week or two. David and I visited the bookstore; we noted how the required course materials were organized and discovered how to purchase books. We walked his class schedule and found the rooms for each varied day, and then I sat in the library while he made the run independently. We practiced finding the library, cafeteria, and tutoring center from different starting points and thus became more familiar with the campus. And finally, with black book in hand, we traveled to and from the school via the public bus. We found the various stops and determined which color-coded vehicles could be boarded. Following this exercise, David made the excursion solo on a separate day. He walked to and from the stops and cemented his comfort with preferred routes to utilize. With his preference for early morning classes, I could drop him off to guarantee his timely and stress-free arrival. But David would determine his return mode of transportation based on weather or fatigue, for a thirty-minute brisk walk was an alternate way home (and would simultaneously provide some exercise for the day).

With David's Chicago trip only weeks away, I reminded him to learn the drivers' manual material. I broke it down into sections that David should study while Frank and I were at work, and I checked frequently with my husband to see if he was reinforcing the material. I was told not to worry and that all was under control. And I assumed that it was until Frank took him for the exam; I received a text that David did NOT pass.

I was so upset! I didn't blame David; instead, I was frustrated with Frank – and with myself!! Frank's idea of "having everything under control" was purchasing some online sample tests. When David scored 100%, Frank assumed he was ready. Rather than asking David the material, he asked him if he understood it. David naturally responded in the affirmative, for he thought he did understand what he was reading. Not having been involved in David's education process, Frank had no idea what worked for him. This department had always been one of **my** designated duties in our unofficial domestic division of labor. Just when David was resolving his fear of driving, he had this huge blow to his confidence. Now he had to wait to repeat the exam—as well as learn the material—and his flight was in two weeks! With Frank present, I picked up the drivers' manual and started quizzing David; he knew very little besides the signage that he had easily memorized. After reassuring David that his score was not his fault, and after giving Frank an animated crash course on how David learned best, I relieved my husband of his duty and took over the prep myself. I should never have delegated this task in the first place. In hindsight, it was probably a classic example of how common teaching means might fall short for someone with learning differences.

For the following week, David and I spent dedicated time each day mastering the material. I would assign sections for him to read and memorize, and we would then come together to clarify, discuss, and quiz. I would ask questions and hypothetical situations that required him to assimilate and apply information; for example, "If you were at a four-way stop..." I would ask variations on all the possible scenarios of each type of issue; with paper and pen, I would draw illustrations to demonstrate and clarify the scenes so that he could comprehend. This was particularly useful in visualizing situations such as school bus rules or appropriate lanes to turn into. In memorizing speed limits and other information, we used associations and other tricks. I would have him repeat the rules and explain the information back to me to see if he truly understood. If he was a passenger in my car, I would also show him actual examples of things we were studying, and I regularly quizzed him on signs or signals we passed. We would repeat, repeat, and repeat. One week after his initial failure, David victoriously flashed me his temporary license (following Frank's humble transport)! Having just gone through the paces at the Bureau of Motor Vehicles, he was comfortable with the setting and the exam. Completely confident in his understanding of the material, David passed easily and was now actually knowledgeable enough to safely get behind the steering wheel!

Filled with both fun and milestone achievements, the summer was highly eventful, and David felt good about himself and the college challenge ahead. Hard work, therapeutic interventions, theater, and parties galore combined to fill his every need. The Chicago trip was the culmination, and I experienced more trepidation than the traveler.

Each leg of the trip was explained, and David would intermittently text us so that we could lead him through the boarding process. Frank and I hugged him our

278 | SANDY PETROVIC AND DAVID PETROVIC

goodbyes and pretended to leave; instead, we hung around the lobby and spied on the security checkpoint by peering through the conveniently located ornamental shrubbery. Sitcom material, we hoped security wouldn't notice us lurking and hiding; however, the only suspicions that rose centered on David. To our dismay, he was one of the passengers singled out for a more detailed inspection. His obvious nervousness probably raised the selector's attention, but David calmly obliged; unaware of the norm, he didn't realize he was asked to do anything extraordinary. When passed and excused, he delivered our anticipated text and proceeded to his gate. With David out of view, Frank and I headed for our car, but communication continued until our traveler was comfortably boarded. Craig was on the receiving end of the flight. He waited for David's arrival text and was willing to continue our game. Frank and I were well into a celebratory toast at a favorite restaurant when David's triumphant "with Craig!" text came. He felt accomplished and proud, and the brothers enjoyed a memorable birthday weekend. His return trip was independent and uneventful.

David's schedule was intentionally light in the first semester. He took only twelve credit hours; this gave him time to experiment with study strategies and learn to utilize syllabi to pace daily work. He had been exposed to paper writing and cumulative exam preparation in high school, but we expected increased volume and intensity at this new level. In hindsight, he could have handled an additional course since those chosen did not require extensive effort. Besides math and English, David took a speech class and a computer course. We should have replaced one of the latter with a course requiring more reading and writing to balance out the semester load. However, there is a lot to be said for experiencing initial enjoyment and success, both for confidence and engagement. And leftover time enabled David's participation in another community theater production, a campus theater group, and his teen Church commitment. He possessed the skills and balance he lacked during high school freshman year and acclimated with ease and enjoyment rather than with stress. He loved the experience and treasured his newfound independence. He now had the ability to come and go as he pleased, either on foot or via bus. He loved the freedom conferred and began to contemplate what driving could add.

To David's credit, he took advantage of every assist he was offered. He attended a library offering which explained how to find resources. He met with tutors weekly in almost every subject and self-advocated for arising needs. He utilized a master planner to stay organized and prevent omission. He taped lectures in select courses and listened to them that same evening, adding to incomplete or unclear class notes. He read in advance of classes to increase their meaningfulness, and he studied well ahead of exams. While I monitored and oversaw these behaviors initially, I turned the wheel over to him later in the year. He began to figure out what he needed to prioritize and how to balance academic deadlines with extracurricular conflicts. If David had a problem or poor test result, I began to ask him, "What do you think you should do?" This was more difficult for me than reflexively suggesting a solution, but it seemed essential to his progress with self-management.

David eventually shared his study plans, priorities, and timelines with me more to gain security than to ask my opinion. Since he was doing well, my only input became the validation of his sound thinking, for he still needed to strengthen his confidence in functioning solo. Except for my contribution to planning his course selections, I was minimally in the picture. As in the past, I continued to look ahead to the next life step to make sure we were prepared when we got there. At that time, this meant continued communications with individuals at the future school in addition to my welcomed presence at preregistration meetings with current counselors. But that became the extent of my routine involvement. I became a coach rather than a micromanager, and this was a necessary role change for the success of David's future plan to live at school.

Taking advantage of David's lighter course load and successful acclimation to school, we collectively decided that it was time to tackle driving. Summer counseling and temporary license acquisition had eased David's apprehension and boosted his confidence; moreover, his trust in a prepared instructor and his thirst for greater independence sparked his motivation. His "temps" would expire at summer's end, and training now would allow him to drive in snowy conditions while under expert guidance. Why wait? He was ready, and he had the time.

Beginning our adventure, the instructor asked that Frank and I both attend David's extensive first session. He thoroughly tested our son for the presence of skills and abilities necessary for driving. Then he assigned homework drills that David was to practice from the passenger seat while a parent drove, and the expert trained us all in these particulars. David spent a great deal of time studying road essentials; he learned to focus on significant information and filter out that which was irrelevant. The trainer confirmed David's correctness and ease with this feat before the beginner was ever asked to take the wheel. That time finally came, and after further skill assessment, the instructor declared his belief that David possessed the capability and necessary essentials to safely drive, pending instruction and practice. It was such a relief that an objective and trained individual came to this conclusion—rather than us as subjective parents with no idea what to look for.

In addition to one-on-one training on the road, we enrolled David into the standard eight group classes that were optional at his age; we felt that this added information was very relevant and valuable, and we welcomed the opportunity to further increase his knowledge. Deemed "able to drive" by his specialized evaluator, David was passed on to a regular (though hand-picked) "in car" instructor to continue in-depth training. Wonderful, patient, and calming, Mr. Oz was the perfect mentor. He reminded me of my own father and was experienced with teaching and encouraging the needier student in the most relaxed and trusted environment possible. I practiced countless additional hours with David, and I utilized the variety of tactics described in prior sections. With me as his co-pilot, David drove to almost every destination if a highway was not involved. Frank and I were thrilled with his progress and were now confident in his ability. David's rule-oriented nature was an asset, and his judgment was on par with any novice driver. We took our time to develop his skills and comfort, and I'll relay the outcome further on in this chapter.

An appointment with David's neurologist resulted in a new, additional diagnosis to accept: Tourette's disorder. A second sound-producing tic had emerged, and there was no denying the increase in habitual movements and mannerisms over the past years. As usual, David was unfazed and took it in stride. I was shocked and frustrated that yet another chronic condition had emerged to set him off as different—and one that could potentially call increasing attention to that fact. Had he not faced enough challenge already? On we plowed, working on prioritized needs one by one.

David enjoyed school and did meet interesting people, but he preferred to socialize at the community theater where his impending show had a holiday run. There were classmates he could have shared lunch with; instead, he chose to eat alone. This enabled him to recharge, prevented the work of conversing, and allowed relaxed dining without the self-consciousness of food sticking to his recently acquired braces. Contrary to his high school start, solitary dining was a conscious and restorative decision, not a disturbing last resort.

David discovered that if he was busy with activities that made him happy, he became more organized and fulfilled. He achieved balance with a full schedule; more than ever, he required and stopped for the downtime that he recognized made it all work. He found that one to two hours was his limit for *any* activity without a break, including a party or driving time. And he respected and allowed for that, not pushing his now recognizable signs. He was starting to master self-accommodation.

This year of transition was also one of introspection for David. Aware that he was at a crossroad of life, he wanted to make *all* the necessary decisions to ascertain a set path and itinerary. He anxiously sought to set up his entire future NOW. He even tried to decide if he could be a good father—of both types! He questioned *how* parents learned to parent and wondered if he would know what to do; at the same time, his contemplation regarding priesthood resurfaced. He seemed fixated on finding specific employment options (both of education and priestly vocations) to dispel his uncertainty of the unknown; his "topic of interest" became researching job opportunities that he could later potentially pursue.

While I supported David's exploration of dreams and options, I encouraged him to relax and enjoy the process. He had worked so hard to "arrive," but he wasn't basking in the pleasure and almost missed the significance. Many of his deadlines and pressures were self-imposed. Then one day, after what seemed like spontaneous enlightenment, he suddenly understood my counseling. He realized that he was farther ahead with professional aspirations than many of his peers. He also appreciated that he could change his course over time. Relieved, David found more joy in each day; he increasingly lived in the present rather than focusing on the future at the expense of current experiences. He still pondered and discussed potential choices, but he did so with healthy anticipation and inquiry rather than concern.

David did make some major life decisions that year and finally seemed more at peace. Perhaps my prior orchestration of his life had never allowed him to contemplate his options before—he had simply trusted my lead and willingly complied. This underscored his need for increased independence before actually leaving home. David was becoming more relaxed, confident, and willing to see where fate and experience took him. And Frank and I were learning to let him go.

Communication was still occasionally problematic for David. His speech was sometimes inappropriately formal for a given situation. For example, he once began a voicemail for a missed play practice by stating, "I regret to inform you that..." At other times, he misused his extensive vocabulary and chose incorrect or similar sounding words that did not convey what he meant—often with funny or embarrassing consequences. In one instance, he substituted "beneficiary" for "benefit," which substantially changed his message. Rehearsing with me via role play when still in high school, he considered asking a girl to a dance by inviting her to join him for "libations"; he erroneously thought he was referring to fun, not alcohol. These types of occurrences were quite common, still occur, and always present an opportunity for a good laugh mixed with continued learning.

David remained stiff and unsure among strangers, with his facial expressions and behavior conveying his discomfort. The transformation to a more natural, confident, and friendly guy was amazing when he was among those fond and familiar. In the latter situation, his differences were barely obvious.

David occasionally still made inappropriate comments or jokes simply to be included in a conversation in which he had nothing to offer. However, he only experienced one negative social incident that entire school year. David hung out with a regular group before class, and one of the guys blurted something like, "You're not funny and say stupid stuff." Surprised, embarrassed, and offended, David responded by quietly walking away. He thought he had progressed beyond this. Feeling badly and sent back in time, this was neutralized by a later surprise phone call from a concerned group member who was checking to see if he was okay. Her caring support helped him get past the negativity.

Despite some of these continued challenges, David had indeed become more skilled in many aspects of conversation. He learned to express his thoughts in stepwise mutual dialogue rather than blurting everything out in one intense recitation. He also improved in asking conversers more questions about *them* rather than focusing purely on self. In addition, he prepared some incredibly unique and entertaining presentations in his speech and other classes. He saw things differently, found beauty in everything, and wasn't afraid to take risks. David was (and is) the ultimate optimist and sincerely found every day to be great. He never complained, always focused on the good things that happened, and took care not to speak badly of anyone (ever since that summer incident following junior year). He often reminisced about his high school start, and he appreciated and marveled at his smooth, contrasting college start. We realized that this was not by chance; we were gratified that we learned our lessons and that our consequent efforts paid off.

The holiday season was filled with family, driving classes/practice, and theater. Chit-chat continued and escalated toward the end of the break as it commonly did with excess leisure time. David was ready for a more challenging semester since he had adjusted to the college and its demands. Further reinforcing this decision,

David had performed well enough to make the Dean's list his first term. He registered for fifteen credit hours, including a more difficult algebra course, an English writing class, and his dreaded science. He would also take a psychology class that required considerable reading and study. Thankfully, my inquiries revealed that this course was a prerequisite for the sophomore education class David would need to take next year. Successful completion of the "psych" would thus allow a lateral move to the new college without loss of time. Toward this end, David would additionally take a prerequisite (and transferrable) first-year education class this term; this would keep him on track and would have the added bonus of confirming his desire to teach middle school.

Besides increasing his academic challenge, David broadened his extracurricular involvement. He would participate in a play at a new outlying community theater, which required several practices per week. This would take him straight into rehearsals for the summer production at his beloved home community theater. David also planned to fulfill his commitment with the youth group and practice his driving. This new semester was definitely on the next transition tier; it escalated difficulty and demands, and it called for advanced study tactics. David's readiness for fall transfer would surely be tested. He was excited and welcomed the challenge.

Once again, David signed up for weekly tutoring in almost every class, so he reaped the benefits of the accommodations, guidance, and support offered. He appreciated the assistance, for it improved his outcomes and eased his stress – and this showed his maturity and intelligence. He was never embarrassed or annoyed with the extras; instead, he recognized them as a gift to help him reach his utmost potential and achieve his dreams.

I left David to independently manage his studies with the assistance of his college support team. There was much more reading, writing, and cumulative study this semester, and he kept me aware of his scheduled tests and deadlines. I monitored his advanced preparations and tactics, but David steered his own ship. At some point, he discovered that pacing while studying helped him to stay better focused; he claimed that his mind wandered less and that his tics were more controlled than if he sat still.

Things ran smoothly until David requested that I test him for his first psychology exam, which was scheduled for the following day. He handed me a self-completed study guide that was predominantly and alarmingly based on a lot of neurological anatomy and physiology. He knew his written answers well enough, but I was dismayed at the brevity and incompleteness of those responses. I feared he lacked the detail and full understanding to do well, and we began a crash course leading to his only near meltdown of the semester.

David got through the exam. Hoping to improve future preparations, we later discussed necessary study revisions in courses requiring heavy reading. He scored a wonderful 86%! In reviewing his returned test, I was shocked at its difficulty and thus even more in awe of his score. The multiple-choice questions required inference and discrimination, and David only received one point off on the essay—triumphantly and specifically answering the question that was asked. I have no doubt that my tutelage assisted his understanding, but my professional background probably had me demanding more depth from him than was necessary. We both learned from this experience. The remaining course focused more on psychology topics than on anatomy and physiology. Since David totally enjoyed and more easily absorbed this angle, we agreed that I would only quiz him on the information he requested, if at all. I would no longer teach further detail, for he had proven his ability to me. I trusted his tutors and preparation, and I realized that David's comprehension, critical analysis, and writing skills had markedly progressed over the years.

For the remaining semester, I coached as needed very generally instead of personally involving myself in specific situations. I helped David learn to independently troubleshoot difficulties, such as how to handle continued confusion in his math course. We brainstormed options, and he then advocated beautifully for himself. Unless there was a problem, he no longer needed or wanted my help. He shared less academic detail with me and trusted more in himself. On an important social note, he also appropriately adjusted his public signs of affection toward me and was more aware of others' reactions. Though he experienced the typical stress of a busy college student, David successfully juggled all his demands and again received recognition on the Dean's list.

He had earned his right to transfer, and we all felt confident that he could handle the increased responsibilities of dorm living. I believe the major components of David's community college success were planning, transitioning, coaching, tutoring, and advocacy – and a motivated, hardworking, and conscientious student. So, while some peers were transferring back home after negative experiences being away at college, David would do the opposite; he was prepared, confident, and goal driven.

Because of his light first semester load and his need for prerequisite, noncredit math, David required two summer classes in order to transfer with sophomore status. This was no surprise, however, and was part of our master plan. It was a choice that was well worth the smooth transition he experienced; it would also "keep him in the groove" over the summer. Conferring with my contact at his future college, we chose two courses that would enable David to be grandfathered into next year's sophomore class of education majors. He would thus not be subject to the curriculum changes affecting the class behind him. This was critical for preventing added semesters to his college career. One less credit hour would have put him in the revised class and program; this would have added a requirement and rendered a completed transfer course unnecessary. Doing this homework and having inside guidance had saved us time, money, and frustration.

I was so blessed to have found this caring leader to channel us through the process – even before David was officially accepted into the school! In this era of automated phone responses, how fortunate was I that the ultimate expert (knowledgeable of both his desired program and the upcoming curriculum revisions) personally picked up my initial call? Beyond this, she repeated her priceless counsel during my subsequent communications and guided us through important decisions each semester. Too much for mere coincidence, I consider this extraordinary service, continuity, and caring outreach to be another small miracle in our journey. Our hand was held and our needs were met until David finally caught up with everyone else; even then, we were funneled to another incredibly able and devoted team. We never floundered alone. The college partnered with us every step of the way and shared our aspirations for superlative outcomes.

Checking the website transfer criteria, I contacted our admissions connection to ensure that David was on course to matriculate in the fall. My communication was timely, for it turned out that essential application components were missing, with deadlines fast approaching. Within a whirlwind two weeks, David was admitted, in orientation, and on time to request and obtain one of the few single rooms in the dormitory.

It was this latter component which Frank and I knew would be essential for David's success. The initial suggestion came from a college program director in a conversation which transpired many months prior. Something I had never considered, this alternative presented the perfect and suddenly obvious solution for victorious campus living. With David's need for "chill" time to recharge, private space was critical. Managing his personal life independently would be huge enough in itself; I couldn't imagine the added stress of continual interaction with a stranger who might not understand or be compatible with David. Coordination and negotiation with another's schedule and traits were added burdens that were not desired at that time. Both academic and personal successes were dependent upon this arrangement, for David devoted many hours to study, and he planned to work in his room rather than in public areas. Conversely, David's chit-chat, tics, and other habits might be difficult for a roommate to adjust to and endure. For the current situation and all parties involved, a single room was the best and only viable option. This could not be left to chance! I had early and repeat communications with the housing department personnel, and we were ecstatic and thankful to learn that our request was honored when rooms were assigned.

The combined student and parent orientation was wonderful. David loved the small campus, the people, and the programs. He possessed some familiarity from the previous summer's study skills course, and that increased his comfort. Luckily, I brought proof of David's completed community college classes, for further revisions were necessary to the generic schedule which awaited him. We were referred to the program leaders who supported students with differences. They were devoted, gracious, flexible, and open to my participation; they trusted my input and realized my past contribution to David's education. I greatly appreciated my inclusion, unexpected at the collegiate level. I sensed, with gratitude and relief, that I could soon take a back seat as David and this specialized team took leadership. Classes would include offerings heavy in reading and writing, and these would be balanced by math and experiential courses. Under the guidance of the support staff and the earlier described curriculum expert, David would shoulder an intimidating seventeen credit hours, which was a typical load for his major. He planned extracurricular involvement and would thus be allowed to drop a class, if necessary. But I felt optimistic that he could handle it due to his past success, stepwise transition, and stellar new support team.

Seeking David's continued life balance, and desiring his immediate campus involvement, Frank and I encouraged him to explore the extracurricular displays surrounding the lunch hall. He excitedly went off in search of the performing arts representatives; before we knew it, David was auditioning unabashedly amidst the bustling crowd for the nun who directed choir. He reappeared and ecstatically announced that he was "in"!

Rather than feeling overwhelmed or anxious at the end of this packed orientation, David was energized and motivated to finish strong with his summer courses. He knew they were the final steppingstone to moving on to this family and campus that already felt like home. The chemistry was palpable. We were all exhilarated and thankful, for it was the perfect school and environment for David. All his needs could be met, including the ability to visit home for nostalgic nurturing or the family and community events he so deeply treasured. If college independence wasn't successful in this environment, it wouldn't work anywhere!

Adding to his confidence and pride, David was awarded choir, theater, and achievement scholarships. Separately, he earned an additional financial award from an outside affiliation based on criteria which included a personal essay. Gratefully recognized for his hard work and accomplishment, David was determined to continue his quest. It now carried a higher price tag than the community college education we had always assumed would be his route. We all agreed that the increased investment of time, dollars, and effort was worth it, but reaping partial scholarship for recognition of his hard-earned success was an honor beyond hope. David resolved to prove that he was worthy of the trust (and funding!) his believers placed in him.

Finishing finals strong, David turned his attention towards driving. He had almost three weeks available prior to the start of summer classes, and he aimed to utilize them to concentrate on skill attainment and license procurement. The fear was gone, class instruction had long been completed, and we had spent countless hours on the road. David was actually a very good driver, but the challenge remained in navigating backwards. He did not have an innate sense of which way to turn the wheel to get the car's rear headed in the desired direction. It was a skill that had to be actively learned. Backing out of the garage, he would analyze the task and reason aloud, "I want the back end to go left, and therefore I need to turn the wheel..." Though seemingly insurmountable, he eventually got it and could then back out smoothly and without premeditation. The maneuverability component of the driver's exam would be a monumental challenge to overcome. Re-enter Mr. Oz.

This patient, kind, and wonderful instructor had a way of explaining and demonstrating that made sense to David. We hired Mr. Oz for additional hours to work with David exclusively on maneuverability. Adjusting for David's saturation, Mr. Oz generously agreed to adapt his schedule to allow for split one-hour sessions rather than the typical two. He also gave David breaks to jog around the parking lot for physical and mental restoration. They approached the drill from both the right and left; in time, David was smooth, relaxed, and successful with the great majority of attempts. The instructor reiterated that perfection was not necessary, and he counseled David on how and when to realign himself if in doubt. David demonstrated his understanding and proclaimed comfort with the skill. He was as ready as he would ever be.

Per Mr. Oz's recommendation, an examination site was chosen in a less congested setting than the chaotic, intimidating, and bustling location that we commonly utilized. He took the time to explain to David all the expectations and steps that would occur during both the maneuverability and driving portions of the exam. And importantly, he suggested that I take David for a trial run to drive in the neighborhoods surrounding the center, which I did. This contributed a familiarity with the roads, speed limits, and testing facility. We watched as a teen tested for the maneuverability portion, so David saw the actual set up and drill. In effect, Mr. Oz and I were orienting him to increase his comfort and decrease his anxiety.

As Mr. Oz had so astutely commented, David had mastered the actual driving—instead of the skills, it was "the nerves" that could potentially get him. So we worked on calming the nerves. The morning of the scheduled test, Mr. Oz met us for a final quick practice of the maneuverability drill to reinforce David's confidence. David smoothly and efficiently succeeded on each repeated attempt. Despite the stress imposed, I had to admit that this drill was effective and central in teaching him how to navigate backwards—it achieved its intended purpose, pass or no pass. We stopped early to end on a positive note, for I preferred David to briefly "chill" at home with a relaxing TV escape. Per Mr. Oz's experienced suggestion, I drove us to the center with ample time to spare. This would allow David to relax as a passenger rather than to become stressed or unnerved while driving to the test. Surely, we had done all we could possibly do to achieve success.

I sat (or paced) inside the test site while David drove out of the lot with the official examiner sitting beside him. Shortly thereafter, they reappeared and proceeded to the maneuverability station. That meant that he had passed the driving portion – one down.

Not wishing to summon bad luck, I decided not to watch. Unable to resist any longer, I headed to the window. I was just in time to see him hit the orange cone housing the pole. Unbelievably, regardless of his skill and practice, David would not be licensed that day. "The nerves" had won.

My heart sank but not as low as David's face. All the empty reassurance in the world couldn't help this one. After our initial exchange and attempt at figuring out what went wrong, I tried to keep quiet and let him deal with his reality. We rescheduled for the following Friday, which was the soonest retest date allowed. We were both quietly aware that college classes would resume three days following the retake; the pressure was on, for time was running out. David then suffered through the promised call to Mr. Oz, who, after realizing it wasn't a joke, helped David regroup and handle the defeat.

A week later, we repeated the same test preparations, which included a practice session with Mr. Oz. With David's recent experience at the bureau to lend familiarity, we hoped that the second attempt would be easier, much like his temporary license venture. Having already aced the driving portion, he only (only!) needed to demonstrate his maneuvering skills. He was stellar in practice, and Mr. Oz repeated his game-day instructions and advice. After hugs all around, we proceeded—with one change. Frank would accompany David to the test center this time around. My nerves and heart could not take another witnessed defeat, and Frank lent a male calmness which I could not provide. We were all better off.

The call came while I frantically funneled my energy into gardening. Success! Another small miracle witnessed! A huge weight was lifted from all of us - Mr. Oz included. He was as ecstatic as we were and even called me three months later to check on David's progress. We are so indebted to him for his friendship and sincere, caring expertise. He provided David with exactly what he needed and has consequently enabled new social possibilities. Mr. Oz earned a place on the Petrovic Christmas card list and entered our Guardian Angel Hall of Fame.

David asked for the car that evening for play rehearsal, and we happily acquiesced. He joyfully called to confirm his successful arrival and ease with parking, and I was relieved to have that first solo drive under both our belts. He subsequently drove himself to school and rehearsals. After twenty-eight years of driving kids around, Frank and I were finally free to make our own plans—usually. You see, freeway driving was not a focus for licensure. And while David was comfortable driving the requisite increased speed, he remained uncomfortable and unskilled in independently merging onto the highway itself. We opted for a two-step driving process, much like we handled the college transition. Freeway mastery would follow a year of comfort and experience with local city driving. I had no problem with providing continued transportation as long as

David drove whenever possible to increase his skill and confidence, and he totally concurred.

David was a careful driver, and he was self-assured in travelling to places he had driven before. Contrary to his past fears, he now relayed that he loved driving and that it relaxed him—when on familiar turf, that is. New destinations or the need to follow directions still stressed him. He was not comfortable splitting his concentration between the actual driving and the lookout for landmarks or signage. To solve this dilemma, we would take David on trial runs; for example, if he was invited to a party, he would practice the route in advance with me or Frank as his coaching passenger. After scoping out parking options and having all his questions answered, David could then comfortably and safely proceed by himself for the actual event. He would subsequently add the new location to his growing list of independent trips. I imagine he will eventually become more adventurous and skilled; in the meantime, safety was our priority. And all of us appreciated any independence or freedom that his limited driving enabled.

Anticipating this challenge, we bought David a GPS for Christmas, but the spoken directions frequently seemed unclear and confusing to him; his literal understanding hampered him once more. I was sure he would retry the system as he gained more comfort on the road, so I tried to provide a practical orientation to better prepare him. I translated and explained its directives to David when he was a passenger (and Frank did the same); free from the responsibilities of driving, David could then safely concentrate on the language and signage. The commands eventually made more sense to him, and he became more open to the merit and eventual use of the system. (Unknown at that time, future advancements in GPS technology would render visual and pictorial improvements that indeed worked for his needs!) The ability to venture out alone to new and different places would hugely expand his world and opportunities.

As David's freshman year at college ended, we marveled at the dichotomy compared to his initial high school experience. But then again, we had learned many lessons since.

The summer before I started college was the beginning of some serious discernment: it was then that I had the opportunity to go back to the retreat college for the youth conference, but I went in a different way. Part of a special program, I had to apply and be accepted. Then, along with other chosen teens, I arrived several days before the conference to grow deeper in my faith. I didn't really know what to expect, but I was really looking forward to it. The first day I got there, I met all the involved people; it looked like we'd have a really great time. When we got deeper into our spirituality that week, I started to see my faith in a new light—and by the end, I also saw the priesthood in a new light. I always said I could never be a priest because I love women too much, but after going through the conference, it is something I am still discerning to this day. When I got back home, I became even more in touch with my faith. I was praying every day, reading a little bit of Scripture, and so on. I was also thinking a lot about the priesthood and how to deal with deciding about it. After talking to my parents and multiple others, I had concluded, considering my young age, that I needed to gain more real-life experience before I could make THAT kind of decision. And I still stay true to that.

After the excitement of the conference wore off, I got back on track with normal life: I got my temps, and I was getting ready to start school at the local community college. I decided senior year that I wanted to stay nearby for school. Not only did I want to ease into the college transition, but I had just become affiliated with a local community theater. I wanted to make myself known before I went off to college so that I'd have something waiting for me afterwards. I started school and I loved it—including the way the class schedules worked, the breaks in between, and the amount of work given over a period of time. College was definitely different from high school.

I didn't really surround myself with too many school-based extracurricular activities. I decided that this was going to be the year that I would focus on schoolwork and get ready for the four-year college. Musical theater would be my social outlet. I was a little nervous about theater because I wasn't sure how the directors who I HADN'T met were going to react to me. But it all worked out, for I "made" a musical in the winter, which kept me very busy. It also kept me on top of things with school because I had the drive to complete my studies during the day; this let me have more fun at rehearsals at night. I found that theater helped me grow socially; it was through the musical that I developed connections with some people at the theater. In addition to the community scene, I also took part in some acting at my college. There was a Christian theater troupe club, and I got the opportunity to perform in their Christmas showing of "The Ten Commandments." Both opportunities were great experiences, and I got a lot out of each of them.

Socializing at college was very successful, as well. Coming off an extremely good senior year, I gained the confidence to just walk up to anyone that seemed interesting and introduce myself, hoping to make a connection. It was because of this confidence that I established some good friendships that I keep with me to this day. Overall, the social scene was positive, except for a small mishap: one of the guys in a group that I hung out with before class just randomly blurted out, "Dude, you're not funny." It kind of caught me off guard. Not really knowing how to react, I just walked away and tried to process what just happened. I got home and I told my mom; she offered the traditional motherly support. It was a bit of a shock since I thought everyone was pretty cool with who I was, so I felt pretty down for the rest of the day. However, my friend, who was a part of the group, called me later that night; she made me feel 100% better—back to my old David self.

*I realized two things from that incident. 1) **Not everyone is going to be as accepting as others.** When you deal with people who can't appreciate you for who you are, simply step back and walk away from the uncomfortable situation; you don't need any toxic fumes contaminating your good air. 2) **A positive can always cancel out a negative.** If you ever become involved in a situation that brings you down, either turn to the ones you love OR seek a positive activity that can overcome the negativity. Not everyone's going to like you and/or accept you. And you know what? It's okay!!! You don't have to dwell on it; instead, find that group of people who DO love you and accept you for who you are. I will put this simply: out with the dwell and in with the swell!*

I was very successful academically my first year of college. It all started with the two study skills courses that I went through. While they did not provide me with much new information, they solidified the skills that had been instilled in me over the course of my school years; I then knew that I was prepared, and it increased my confidence. I would highly recommend a refresher study course prior to the start of college because, *even if you are one who **has** the study skills, it is possible you could develop new ways to approach your studies. If you don't have the skills, you gain all this knowledge that will increase your chances of success and decrease your stress.*

*What helped me become adjusted to the fresh surroundings was a special system of analysis and action. Before going to the school, my mother and I had to figure out the concept of maneuverability in my new environment. We determined the bus and class schedules, pinpointed the room locations, and established the allotted break times between classes. Then we physically role-played through my schedule; this meant that for each school day, **I knew where to go**. Not only did this help me become familiar with the school, but it eased my stress and made me comfortable. I was able to meet new people and get involved right off the bat because I was free to observe my natural surroundings. I repeated this process the next semester, but I did it alone. Once I became adjusted to the bus, I felt a great sense of independence in knowing that I had the power to leave school by myself whenever I wanted. I felt more in control and confident in my decision making.*

When school began, the community college's center for learning provided me with assistance. This center helped me in many ways, but the biggest benefit was the tutoring. The tutors solidified my understanding of the schoolwork, and they were able to make me feel comfortable asking for help. They didn't treat me any less than a "typical." In other words, they didn't talk down to me; they simply treated me like a regular college student who wanted help with his studies. Sometimes students with learning disabilities are extremely self-conscious and worried about what other people will think of them and their disability. With me, I had accepted the difficulties I had in school; I realized that in order for me to succeed, I needed help—and I wasn't ashamed to ask for it!

My skills of self-advocacy that I had learned in high school were put into everyday use from the beginning of school. It was in high school that I had grown accustomed to representing myself and my different needs or accommodations on a daily basis. I was able to approach my teachers and request clarification of misunderstood material. I was also confident in stepping up to the plate to simply ask for help or to suggest an alternative way of going about things. The accommodations team at the community college encouraged me to get that started at their campus right off the bat within the first week of school.

After the holiday break had ended, I started a new semester (after making the Dean's List the previous semester). This is when a little bit of stress started to kick in. What really got my nerves up was that this was the semester when I would apply to my college of choice, and I wanted to be sure that I got in. But again, thanks to my mom, I got over this. She calmed me down, screwed my head on straight, and basically said not to worry about it – I had this. So I continued on with school, did more shows, and made a few trips to the future college to start getting myself affiliated with the new school. As soon as I stepped on campus, I got the "just right" vibe—that feeling when you think, "Yep, this is the one for me."

After gathering transcripts, obtaining test scores, and filling out applications, I was accepted. Now, you would think that once you got into your school of choice the stress would be off. But when I got in, I got a little bit more stressed; I found out that I didn't have enough credits to transfer in as a sophomore and learned that my summer semester grades could determine my grade level. I knew I could get the work done and do well, but there were times when I let the situation get too wrapped up in my mind; I couldn't concentrate on anything else going on in my life. (It is something I still occasionally struggle with to this day.) When finals came along, that is when my stress started to peak through the roof. But it was also during that time that my parents taught me a very valuable lesson when it comes to college-level exams: worry about what you can control, and don't worry about what you can't. This means take matters into your own hands to prepare for a test, and when it's done, just let it all go from your mind. That was something I didn't grasp during spring semester finals, and I worried until I saw my grades. During summer finals, however, I took the advice to heart, and I ended up doing extremely well without causing myself extra stress. I was finally able to say that I was officially a sophomore in college!

*I learned two main lessons from my first year of college that I will carry beyond. 1) **Don't set expectations for today or the future.** If you go through life thinking about how a situation is going to be, you might be disappointed with the outcome. The thing is, every day brings a different surprise, and we don't know how we're going to deal with it. So when something is coming up, whether it might be school, an event, a date, and so forth, I don't set any expectations. As my dad would say, "Just roll with it!!" 2) **Continue to dream big and prepare, but be sure to take things one day at a time.** You can see how this correlates with number one; if not, I'll be happy to explain. Life is completely unexpected, and we don't know what the next day is going to have in store for us. So that is why the advice I have to offer can be summed up as learning from the past, living for the present, and hoping for the future. Like I said, life holds many unexpected twists and turns for us human beings; if we just take things one day at a time, not only will we be satisfied with today, but we'll be excited for what tomorrow brings, as well.*

Lessons we learned:

- Do not drop your teen like a hot potato just because he/she is eighteen and "in college"! High school supports have been pulled away. New procedures and processes are foreign and may be difficult for the teen to navigate. Your support and guidance may be needed at that time more than ever.

- Don't solely rely on the counselor/advisor to know course requirements or best choice schedules. Help the student research requirements and deadlines to save costly mistakes (both of time and money). The student should come prepared for advisor meetings and course registrations and should keep track of his/her progress and any program changes.

- Consider a study skills course for the student.

- Monitor the student's work plan. Assist the teen to look ahead and strategize for upcoming deadlines. Help him/her form good habits to increase the likelihood of success.

- Encourage the student to seek help when needed. Explore tutoring and assistance options at the school (or encourage the student to do this). Why not take advantage of what is rightfully offered to enable best outcomes?

- Try to coach but not manage. Wean the student to increase independence when he/she is ready.

- Focus on the positives.

CHAPTER THIRTEEN

College:

Phase Two

The summer was full and well utilized. Besides focusing on fun and refreshment, David continued to practice independent dorm-living skills. I reviewed domestic instructions and oversaw him in laundering clothes, changing linens, and cleaning his room and bathroom. David practiced waking to a self-set alarm and drove my car as often as possible, frequently transporting himself to summer classes. He completed a driving-safety program offered by our insurer. This necessitated additional Mom-supervised trips as well as independent excursions that focused on varied lessons and goals. The extra practice was timely in strengthening his skills and confidence, and it cemented my trust in his ability. David proudly drove himself to another round of graduation parties as high school friends two years behind him experienced their rites of passage. Just like all the other new drivers, he visibly dangled evidence of car keys from his pocket; it was a coveted and long-awaited symbol of prowess.

David's participation in a popular musical at his beloved community theater was the highlight of his summer. Not only was it a personal favorite, but it was one directed by his respected mentor. Even more exciting, the cast was rich with talent and esteemed actors, and David was overjoyed to be included among them—growing in skills and friends. It was a perfect mix of philosophy studies by day and social rehearsals by night, and he accessed them both independently.

Despite our trepidation over the abstract nature of philosophy, the course was surprisingly understandable to David due to the translation and teaching skills of the professor. With this challenge nearing conclusion, there was little left in a baccalaureate program that we felt was unobtainable with effort and assistance. Things were going great, which is why we were so shocked by the call.

Minutes before the Sunday curtain rose, with Aunt Renee and Brittany front and center, our home phone announced an incoming call from David's cell phone. Instantly alarmed with that unlikely timing, I instinctively hurried to the phone to hear a woman's voice in place of our son's. It appeared that instead of an imminent performance, David awaited the arrival of an ambulance; he had experienced another episode. I rushed to the theater, distraught and confused, for he was happier than ever and not under inordinate stress. I could not figure it out.

I climbed to a familiar spot beside David in the treatment vehicle. After assessing the situation and his condition, I was confident that the care needed was not that of an emergency room. Explaining his history and my plans for follow up, I took David home after the episode passed. The outpouring of support from the cast was overwhelming, and as widely proclaimed, the show did go on.

The plan from our neurologist included one recommendation that I had anticipated but dreaded nonetheless. After almost eight months of extraordinary effort by multiple parties to enable licensure, David's prized driving was put on hold pending tests of causality. (Are you kidding???) Furthermore, with our doctor's consent, the test was not immediately performed since it required sleep deprivation for optimal assessment. You see, David was entering the first term exam period and was starting a second overlapping accelerated course. We opted to briefly defer medical testing so that he could prepare for his final, for while we were assured that this delay would not pose a physical risk, a poor academic outcome could derail sophomore status and future program plans.

David weathered the classroom challenges without undue stress and received excellent marks, even with his continued involvement in the production. It was disheartening to revert to transporting him. But after a few weeks, the medical results were obtained, and David's driving privileges were restored. Thankfully, there was no evidence of neurological problems; by process of elimination, panic attacks were once again blamed. Acceptance of this was difficult, for no stress or trigger had existed; frankly, things could not have been better. But as we were reminded by David's neurologist, not all in science or medicine is explainable. We utilized the remaining school hiatus to focus on the prevention and management of anxiety—even if it's not always perceptible.

An addendum to the preceding summer, David attended another series of sessions with his psychology specialist. The current goal was to master relaxation breathing and associated techniques. Though these excursions necessitated my accompaniment because of freeway driving, we found the commitment worthy of the time and effort put forth. Primarily, therapy provided a tangible, controllable, and effective tool that worked for David in times of stress. And secondarily, the appointments provided an opportunity for him to navigate and independently function in a mega maze of a facility. David would exit the car as we approached the parking garage; he would find the office, check in, and attend the appointment alone. I arrived after parking the car, available by text if help was needed (though it never was). This practice reinforced his confidence, for he would shortly need to function at college without my presence on campus. He similarly attended orthodontist and other appointments, building on necessary skills.

I was thrilled that David chose to augment the above measures with a commitment to comprehensive exercise. It was a valued strategy I had encouraged in the past, but one which he had eventually abandoned. Concurrent with his health and fitness summer class, he finally embraced its worth and importance. Learning about specific components, he safely and religiously implemented a workout plan which he continued throughout college.

Motivated from within, he reaped both physical and emotional rewards.

Despite all these anxiety-reducing interventions, I was distressed to note the chronic stutter that emerged sometime in June. Though it didn't interfere with David's performance in song or theatrical productions, it challenged conversation and caused frustration. This stammering had occurred for short periods a few times in his past but had always spontaneously resolved; I hoped that this bout would pass, as well. The stutter varied in intensity along its course, but it now persisted beyond any past duration. I assumed that the undercurrent stress of his impending venture was the likely instigator, for his tics and acne had also increased. I decided to allow additional time for acclimation before embarking on yet another round of therapies. David's adolescence had certainly been fraught with its share of trials and tribulations, despite the simultaneous sprinkling of triumphs and elation; I prayed his future would be on a more even keel!

Maximizing David's two-week break between the summer and fall terms, we aimed to refresh and regroup. Trips to visit Steve and Craig in their respective cities provided mini vacations. Remaining days were spent excitedly shopping, preparing, and packing for David's dream upgrade to campus living.

David had been taking his medication independently for years, but he occasionally needed reminders if his normal routine was altered. Seeking a way to distinguish between meds which were needed versus already taken, we utilized a partitioned pill box. David prepared and replenished its contents weekly on a set day, and we began this practice prior to school's start to firmly establish the habit. Fortunately, these medications were timed to coincide with waking and bedtime personal needs, so thus linked to other tasks, they were rarely forgotten. Later in the year, when a temporary med was required at an additional unconventional time, he also utilized the alarm feature on his ever-present phone to alert him.

Speaking of personal needs, we aimed to prevent their omission; I typed reminder lists and laminated them for durability. These would be openly displayed in strategic locations once David's dorm room was evaluated; we had learned from the past that David wouldn't think to consult them if they were hidden in a drawer. Without my monitoring, performance must trump privacy. This was an added advantage of a single room; peers need not be aware of these personal checklists. Importantly, David strove for independence and valued any tool that would facilitate this goal. He was no longer embarrassed by "to do" lists; instead, he appreciated their assistance. I taped the "morning" and "evening" lists to his bathroom mirror during his final week at home. This proved their worth and ingrained their habitual utilization; with David's impeccable grooming and tidy room, I wondered why I had waited so long to institute this intervention!

Besides hygiene needs, the lists included tasks such as taking meds, making his bed, cleaning up behind him, setting his alarm, charging his phone, and so forth. I created a third list that reminded David of "leaving the room" needs: packing homework or study tools, turning off the lights or fans, checking the window, taking his key/student ID/wallet, locking the door, and so forth. Valuing organization, I purchased a wooden box that had a connected lid. David's keys, wallet, ID, and other personal items (including his pill box) were to be stored in it when not in use. This "go to" place would hopefully prevent loss and forgetfulness, and a closed lid would insure privacy and safety.

We sought creative approaches when David's hand tremors interfered with his ability to perform certain tasks. For example, his attempts to trim his nails were challenging, unsafe, and unsuccessful even with alternate tools: the closer he got, the more he trembled. We found solutions for this and other challenges. So, with practical issues resolved, we funneled our energy into the actual move.

I packed necessities in categorized plastic bins with lids. These stacked for ease of transport and provided vertical space-saving storage in the dorm. The snap lids also maintained the contents' freshness and cleanliness. Labels on each container enabled organization of separate units for office supplies, snacks, paper products, linens, toiletries, health remedies, and the like. Dave could easily find sought items and would keep track of their needed replacement. I then retained a master list of items and bins to simplify future packing and avoid duplication of effort.

As previously described, David ate the same breakfast daily. Stocked with its components, he would continue to do so in the comfort of his dorm room. This reduced his cafeteria visits, and college officials agreed to adjust the meal contract down to the next level. To prevent dirty dishes and simplify his life, David would utilize disposable paper products. Though not totally considerate of the environment (he did reuse them when able), I prioritized success, ease, and cleanliness over being "green" at that time.

To promote established routines and healthy eating, I would provide the mealtime "sides" David was accustomed to, as he likely wouldn't find them in the cafeteria. I planned to package his favorite produce items in individual portions and would replenish them as needed; we would see each other frequently enough to allow this luxury. Eventually, David could shop at the local supermarket and purchase these himself. But for now, he had other priorities to contend with.

Cooking, a bank card, and financial balancing would be deferred. We would give David a cash allowance to budget, and he would focus on his priorities: 1) cleaning up after himself and 2) meeting personal and academic needs. Despite my repeated requests for tidiness at home, David still customarily rose from a task leaving all materials just as they were when he finished. Aware that he was now solely responsible for his environment, we discussed his responsibilities and goals. I reiterated that dirty laundry would not be welcomed home. With the limited responsibilities given to him, we expected self-regulation for school needs, clean clothes, and a neat, organized environment in which to live and work.

David agreed with our philosophy and was excited to work toward these goals. There would be plenty of time and opportunity for future progress. Why overwhelm him with the full package now? Premature introduction of demands had intimidated David and hindered his success in the past. We wished to avoid setbacks that required recovery. Deference to his needs and pace, along with ample transitioning, had previously served us well. We therefore bowed to "lessons learned" as we strove for optimal success with the huge venture before us.

We philosophized that David would catch up with his peers in his twenties anyway; via our plan, he would be better adjusted with security, skill building, and options. I have frequently pondered my analogy that all children are potty trained by kindergarten. Despite societal pressure to achieve this goal very early, does anyone really care or ask, years later, when it actually occurred? I viewed David's reaching of adult milestones in much the same way. Ready, able, and maximally prepared, he will accomplish them in ample time on his own terms. Hopefully, he will thus remain motivated to continue his quest for achievement instead of feeling spent, defeated, and tempted to quit.

During the last few days of summer vacation, David reread favorite resources for strategies to 1) prevent and control anxiety and 2) improve social interactions. (Recall our "lesson learned" to revisit sources at intervals.) We discussed time management and AS disclosure. Despite his still-fresh experience with college coursework, David willingly reviewed learning tactics and recommendations from his study skills classes and little black book. His successful completion of recent exams and written papers boosted his confidence and calmed his nerves. So did his timely orientation to the center for support, which was intentionally held the day before he moved into the dorm. During this introductory gathering, he met with advisors, received his class schedule, learned how to arrange tutors, and received, in writing, customized accommodations that he would present to professors in the upcoming days. He had binders in tow that the center had previously tabbed for his optimal organization, and he planned to model these, ongoing, to continue his success. He would share the same requirements, expectations, and workload as any other college student, but with this program, he would receive the assistance necessary to accommodate for any differences which put him at a disadvantage. As we soon realized, he would also receive vital, wide-ranging support to help him thrive and achieve his potential.

As David walked through a campus alive with band and sport practice, there was nothing left but to begin. It was hugely exhilarating. Contrary to the nervousness of the prior year, he was excited and ready to confront the challenges before him; David knew that in addition to experience and improved skills, he had also acquired the confidence and support necessary to conquer and succeed. Furthermore, he could not wait to live among highly sought friends and acquaintances!

Moving into the dorm, David's tics and stutter were magnified; however, he attributed this to good stress rather than bad. We were thrilled to discover an unshared bathroom adjoining his room, for this would greatly simplify privacy. I initially fastened David's reminder lists to the inner door of his bathroom supply cupboard; they were in his clear view when he reached for toiletries. But after he missed a few evening med doses, I taped them in a more obvious location—at eye level on the mirror above his sink. This change led to better success.

The thick walls of this fortress-like building would beautifully stifle outside noise; they would simultaneously create a fortunate reverse buffer for David's chit-chat and concert showers. Frank suggested that David should tack a note to his inside hallway door to remind him of needed supplies, assignments, and appointments before he left the room. David and I took a trip to the laundry room to clarify specifics of machine use, and he recorded operating details in the laundry section of his black book. He also updated additional dorm and contact information in the appropriate sections of this reference. Scheduled classes and appointments were current in David's daily planner, and we discussed the importance of adding tutor sessions and other meetings as they arose. David was religious in his completion and perusal of this planner, and it became a key component of his organization and work scheme. Though I again suggested that he modernize to an electronic format, he was comfortable with the ease and simplicity of paper and pencil, so we kept with what worked best for him.

David hurried off to a mandatory dorm meeting, and I then washed his floor. (I couldn't help it!) Within minutes, I cringed as his rap resounded through the hall. I thought those days were gone, but he evidently fell back on trusted social ice breakers when he was placed in unfamiliar circumstances. It really wasn't worth a conversation, for I didn't want to bring him down. He was who he was, and his instinct would supersede my advice anyway; besides, he would momentarily be left to lead his life without my witness or critique. I just prayed that he had learned sufficient social grace to flourish and be happy. David later confided that this truly was his last rap, but he also related that he had serenaded several women as they looked out their dorm windows that evening. (Oh my!!)

David enjoyed a full weekend of social orientation and was determined to become well-known. Introducing himself to everyone he met and concentrating on their return information, David made his mark and certainly attained his goal; consequently, he was recognized and greeted around campus. David likely applied his own private "lesson learned": he obviously intended to prevent the social isolation of his high school debut.

David woke to his alarm clock ringing on the other side of the room; he took no chance of oversleeping for his first choir rehearsal! This arrangement was wisely utilized from then on. Ironically, he began his first full day of independent campus living on the fifteenth anniversary of my father's death. I most certainly believe that this was not a mere coincidence; I feel it was a reminder of the divine intervention that surely transpired over the years, perpetuating the string of miracles.

We were shocked that David called us only once during his first week on campus. Considering the strain of self-navigation and the deluge of information, we expected much more communication. Already in choir, he joined another ensemble and was preparing for his first theater audition, which was scheduled to occur in two weeks. I was mildly concerned with how he would juggle all those rehearsals along with a rigorous scholastic load, associated tutoring, and living needs. It appeared that excitement about extracurricular opportunities had neutralized any feeling of being academically stressed. He claimed to utilize deep breathing whenever pressured, and he repeated a new mantra to himself to maintain focus: "Just do the work. Just do the work."

Contrary to what I had anticipated, David's early calls were not instigated by stress or pleas for advice; instead, they emanated from excitement and pride.

He longed to share tales of self-advocacy and positive social interactions, and he fared much better than we expected. He repeatedly and genuinely exclaimed that he loved everything about the school, and this included keeping his room clean and being on his own. He was rightly proud and reveled in his successful start. He reported that he was up to date with all his necessary reading, and he responded, "Already done!" to all my to-do reminders. I realized that he was on a honeymoon and that lows were probable as work and responsibilities escalated, but we were still blown away at this incredible adjustment, which surpassed our wildest dreams.

David successfully completed laundry that week with only one questioning phone call, and he made rigid schedules to address all his needs. Later in the semester, school was closed on a Thursday for fall break; David was concerned with how he would do his laundry prior to coming home, for Thursday was laundry day. I asked him what he was doing on Wednesday, and surprised with this option to deviate, he soon became more flexible and independent in troubleshooting scheduling conflicts. True to the rules, his room was always presentable, and the bed was always made. In fact, he so emphatically followed the rules that I had to repeatedly persuade him to bring his dirty laundry home during finals week; I wished to provide him with extra study time, but he was reluctant because I had earlier proclaimed that I would not be washing his clothes!

Back to this first week, I contend that David was determined to be as successful and independent as he viewed his brothers. He infrequently initiated communication, claiming that he didn't want to call simply to call, for he despised small talk. It seemed he never fathomed that *I* might miss *him* or have my own information that I wished to share. After he learned my perspective, we settled into a more natural plan of exchange that was driven by need more than by schedule. Frank and I did, however, try to limit our calls to him in order to honor his desire for distance and self-management. Surprisingly (or not), his planned readiness resulted in a less needy student than other "typical" peers I learned of from friends.

David attended the first football home game on a packed Thursday at the end of a packed week. He stayed the first half but then walked alone the three miles back to his dorm. He recognized a need to chill and did not wish to push his luck (recall his history with football games). This was a victorious decision: he progressively understood himself.

Evidently, the week impacted David more than he realized or admitted. When we picked him up for the Labor Day break, he promptly fell asleep and remained so for the entire ride home, even ignoring the visiting Craig behind the wheel. He then flopped onto his bed and continued his nap until forcefully woken hours later. He decompressed over the remaining weekend, and David returned to school refreshed and recharged. Fully oriented and comfortable with his new routine, he was now ready to attack true college life.

Foremost on David's mind was the upcoming play audition. As much as he aspired to undertake romantic leads, he realized his excellence and niche in the comedic, "nerdy," or villainous character. As luck would have it, the fall production featured three such male leads, with David landing one of them. For once, he was thrilled to wear his braces, for they were the perfect accessory for his costume!

With the relief of earning a role, David turned his concentration towards intensifying academic studies. With my nudge, he signed up for additional and regular tutoring in all classes. Success on his first few quizzes confirmed his ample preparation, and he felt more confident. His Tuesdays and Thursdays were packed, occasionally leaving no time for lunch, and David began to feel the crunch as demands increased. I suggested that he rearrange some tutoring, placing the most challenging reviews in the beginning rather than end of such days—or better yet, on lighter days. Realizing that HE could control his schedule, David started to juggle and advocate for his needs.

David was balancing his schoolwork well with other demands and opportunities. I was thrilled that he joined a campus ministry group and took advantage of the college's social activities. My one nagging concern, however, was his inordinate investment of time in his special interest: theater – even if academic. He worked intensely on a Rogers and Hammerstein paper for a 1.5 credit hour class to the exclusion of other work. This occurred while he simultaneously struggled with a professor's challenging course design and teaching style in his most difficult class. More time and emphasis were needed on the latter than the former. A call to his mentor at the center for support quickly addressed my concerns and David's focus. I stayed in the background from then on, except for my research and input regarding his scheduling of classes. Having worked so hard to get him on the same track as sophomores who hadn't transferred, I intended to be peripherally involved until David was accepted into the education program and became knowledgeable enough to spearhead his own decisions.

This torch was passed the following semester after I made two final phone calls to clarify graduation needs. I requested and obtained the complete curriculum guidelines and coached David into documenting fulfilled requirements. We planned that he would review and update this checklist each semester; he could then make informed scheduling decisions with his advisor in the future, mindful of his options and needs. Though I would remain available for his solicited coaching and suggestions, David would take over his professional oversight and tracking responsibility. We outlined the pros and cons of further summer course work, minors of study, and a recommended class. Armed and prepared, he finally understood and could determine his path. With the assistance of his advisors, he would make intelligent and confident decisions best suited for his desires and plans. A degree within the four-year goal was feasible, barring any glitches or altered aspirations, and David would proudly lead the way to its fruition.

David was effective, comfortable, and skilled in self-advocating with either professors or school officials. In fact, among a team of "typical" students assigned a group project, David was who his small group relied on to seek assignment clarification. He would often take charge and troubleshoot problems.

Over time, as semester course loads and academic demands increased, it became evident that it wasn't the *quantity* of work that caused David stress; he welcomed hard work and was fast, decisive, and efficient in its completion. Instead, three bigger stressors were forced procrastination (such as with group projects beyond his control), the need to deal with difficult personalities (the emotional burden), and self-doubt over his understanding of expectations. Regarding this last issue, worry over "doing the correct thing" often prompted David's early and frequent communications with faculty to 1) clarify assignments or check ideas with them, 2) resolve problems or misconceptions separate from course work, and 3) validate his compliance with faculty stipulations. Actually, this was a reassurance that he had always sought—an accommodation of sorts—and it spared him grief when verification was simply obtained from the outset. Greater problems existed if questions were not asked! David had clearly learned to advocate for his needs.

When distressed or overwhelmed, David utilized the support center as a trusted source of assistance, direction, and stress relief. This group provided clarification, guidance, reassurance, and at times, troubleshooting. They took over my educational role and added a whole new academic dimension; services were complete with accommodations, tutoring, weekly coaching, information, opportunities to socialize, and eventually, career/interview preparation. In fact, David's class exams were administered in their very center. Immeasurably valuable, questions were often read to him, allowing his clarification of what was being asked; misinterpretation of questions rather than unknown material had been a frequent cause for David's past errors. With this variation in testing methodology, he was never led toward the answers – he was merely accommodated in his need to hear things in a different way for correct perception. David's success was partially due to his rightful accommodations and the dedicated contributions of this caring team. As a result, I was able to ease out of the picture, relieved in knowing that his needs were expertly addressed.

A private room was the second ingredient central to David's success and stability. This piece of campus was totally under his control; it provided a safe environment to unwind, recharge, and make life happen. Constant roommate interplay and compromise would have overwhelmed David and interfered with his coping strategies. Instead of a place of comfort, home base may have morphed into his utmost stress—with no escape. A future transition to shared living quarters with a compatible person(s) might be possible with the provision of private space, but this year presented enough novel challenges! We could not afford any extra risk.

Along with the above, it was predominantly David himself who enabled his success. He sought out resources and opportunities, utilized available assistance (with appreciation rather than embarrassment), and possessed incredible motivation. He was responsible, trustworthy, and hardworking. His optimism was astounding, and even with a bad day, he bounced back with his steadfast belief that everything happens for a reason. Resourceful and open, David began to use techniques on himself that he had learned from class were helpful for students with special needs. This humble self-application assisted his retention of new teaching skills while simultaneously improving his own ability to learn. Talk about getting your money's worth out of a course!

David continues to work on certain components of writing. While he can be verbally succinct and even eloquent, he still has occasional difficulty expressing his thoughts accurately in written form. There exists a loss in translation from his mind to print. When he reads his creation back to himself, he feels it is clear. But when questioned for further explanation, his verbal expounding is rich with undisclosed details or alternate meanings. Sometimes this disconnect is the result of grammatical errors, such as missing nouns or verbs. In other instances, words that have similar meaning or sound might be erroneously interchanged. The following are true examples which illustrate this problem. He has used "transfer" in place of "exchange" or has said, "I am anticipatory about..." when actually meaning, "I am apprehensive about..." A third cause for confusion is that David often glosses over his central premise or perspective as if the reader automatically knows it. His writing can therefore be incomplete or more superficial than the thinking behind it.

Specific questioning can draw the critical components out of David or illuminate the source of confusion. In reading his contributions to this very book, I often requested that he verbally respond to my query (such as, "What do you mean by..."), and I then had him immediately record his verbal elaborations or corrections. This would more precisely convey his intended meaning. Work on this book has not only deepened our understanding of ourselves and each other, but it has helped to develop David's writing skills and has motivated him to continue his study of the English language. In addition, it has highlighted his immense progress with higher-level abilities that always eluded and challenged him. His true intelligence and keen sensitivity continue to surprise me.

David dealt with stress and pressure nicely during this challenging first semester away from home. Power naps, prayer, exercise, and deep breathing were but a few of the tactics he utilized to cope with anxiety. He reached out to others he trusted in search of supportive conversation, and he turned to his love of television and theater for distraction. Often the latter was via media, but rehearsals also provided therapeutic escape.

There was only one "meltdown" the entire semester, and it was the culmination of repeated frustration. It was the night before David's last two midterms. He had prepared in advance and had done everything possible to organize studies around evening rehearsals. The only impediment was a professor who repeatedly delayed posting content and study guides beyond the dates he had promised delivery. With last minute receipt of the material, stress and crunch were unavoidable. David independently emailed this professor about his need to avoid procrastination via timely receipt of the course work (a great example of his ability to self-advocate), but as the hours ticked by and no information appeared, David's tension mounted. The prep essentials finally came, and David proceeded with abbreviated study to the best of his ability—but it was now too late to utilize the tutor he had previously arranged.

As Frank flipped channels in search of entertainment on this same evening, he paused on a popular show favored by David. We watched for a few minutes, curious as to its contents. With shock and unrest, we witnessed a girl suffering through a dramatic and uncomfortable panic attack amidst a very controversial plot line (not our idea of entertainment). The phone rang just after we resolved to discuss this show choice with David, and instinctively, I knew that the moment I feared had come. He was on the verge but still able to converse; I told David to hang tight and promised that I was leaving to pick him up. Frank questioned my sanity due to the late hour. But David had fought to prepare for those two midterms, and I would do anything for him to salvage that hard work. The hope and support of coming home would prevent a full-blown attack, for I already heard the relief in his voice. It would also enable a good night's sleep to achieve the best possible test results. I would wake him early and get him back in plenty of time. The plan was in motion.

Pulling in, I witnessed scores of students enjoying homecoming festivities. The bonfire was just outside his window, and I realized that sleep would have been a challenge for that reason alone. Part of me was saddened that he wasn't enjoying the fun like his peers, conscientious student that he was. But mostly, I just felt relief as I saw him waiting outside, crisis and ambulance averted.

Morning found David thankful and well rested. Following both exams, he felt good about his performances, and we later debriefed the incident. David explained that he had studied the best he could under the circumstances, and he had resigned his outcome to fate by midevening. He fleetingly considered going to the bonfire, but he was so spent after the day's events that he chose to "chill" quietly with TV instead. He turned, of course, to the favored show in question. It is my contention that it was the witnessed panic attack that did him in, not exam anxiety. Being so close to his bursting point, the relatable and uncomfortable scene probably pushed David to a threshold that would have been avoided otherwise. David concurred with this analysis, and he agreed to avoid such "entertainment" in the future.

During the upcoming Christmas break, David experienced two similar reactions while separately watching a movie and then a detective show. Both plots involved violence. David was fortunately able to reverse his response with deep breathing and self-talk at the theater, but I found him very clammy and close to passing out at home. Clearly, David is a peace-seeking man who cannot tolerate the onslaught of witnessing physical or emotional anguish.

David remained sensitive to select sounds, as well. On Christmas Eve, he painfully left the room in response to my young nephew's trial of a new electric guitar with an amplifier. David can discriminate between senseless, abrupt "noise" and loud melodious chords. His beloved music is on a subjective continuum, and I was reminded of his distress call two years earlier, seeking rescue from a noisy rock concert (ear plugs have since assisted concert attendance). David's additional sensitivity to certain vibrations likely contributed to both situations.

Soon after midterms, Frank began his routine of sending David an uplifting "text of the day," which Frank affectionately referred to as his "morning mantra." It was something special between them and David appreciated this effort. David handled stress well with no further extreme incidents occurring for the remainder of the semester. Even when faced with a final exam dilemma from the same professor who had complicated midterms, David simply tried his best with the minimal options he had. Though frustrated and distressed, he had faith that there was nothing left he could do, **and he coped**. Challenges were met with appropriate actions, and David planned far enough ahead to weather every controllable storm.

Halfway through the semester, during a heart-to-heart conversation at a restaurant, David revealed to me that he still didn't have a friend to hang out with. He followed that statement with, "I know it will come. I'm meeting people and have lots of acquaintances who like me." He always thought of what he had, not of what was missing. David had faith, hope, and patience; rather than wallow in self-pity, he chose to concentrate on what he was at college for: his future.

Shortly thereafter, David received an invitation to a Halloween party with a very meaningful guest list; he was thrilled to be among those included. He went, had a blast, and enjoyed about three hours without approaching "his limit" (the longest duration to date). Likewise, he received three coveted holiday invitations, each from different social circles, which would brighten his winter break. This included a gathering of treasured high school show choir alumni. And finally, he was invited to an off-campus party scheduled for the evening before his last two final exams. David was ecstatic with this offer, for it represented his acceptance by fellow classmates (athletes, no less—recall his contrasting experience as he started high school). He called me to run by the pros and cons of attending and wanted to practice a little role play on how to decline. For although appreciative, he had already made his decision based on all the right reasons. He simply called for confirmation of his thinking and to share his excitement at the invitation's prospect. So, he had progressed from asking for our advice; he was starting to make his own decisions and merely used us as a sounding board when needed. Rather than answers, he sought trusted input to validate his choices, give some direction, or practice suitable responses. It was a very healthy evolution based on sound thinking, and it is still a work in progress.

Theater remained David's "special interest" and life hobby. He was an expert on every surrounding community theater, every scheduled production, and the accomplishments of many participants. He spouted information as if reading a bio. Though performance was his passion, he was also an avid audience member. Frank and I drove him all over the region to allow his support of fellow thespians. He usually went alone but was quite comfortable with this arrangement, for he always saw people he knew. It also allowed him the freedom to stay and congratulate cast members after the shows, inevitably leading to new acquaintanceships. Recently, David also verbalized interest in working on productions in a stage crew capacity if prior obligations (or not "making" a show) precluded his participation as an actor; anything was an option in order to be involved. We are thrilled that David has this social outlet and cannot imagine his life without theater. (We again thank Mrs. O'Neill for her novel insight all those years ago!) Freeway driving will open worlds of opportunity to him, and I believe theater is just the motivator needed to overcome his fear of trying!

David's acting fervor was only equaled by his zeal for singing. Participating in three choral groups, he harbored a sudden concern that strain from overuse might injure his voice. Consistent with David's contention that everything happens for a reason, this fear had a monumental impact on a lifelong struggle. Trying to save his voice for a play, David stopped wasting it on chit-chat (which now was largely the performance of theater or song selections). Instead, he carried out the chit-chat silently in his head. He claimed this provided the same satisfaction and relief but without vocal cord tension or social negativity. Interventions to control this behavior had been ongoing for more than a decade, but David finally changed only when chit-chat's disadvantages outweighed its benefits—only when HE embraced the worth and need—and only when the solution came from within. With concern about its consequences and because he discovered an effective substitution, the audible expression decreased dramatically and occurred only when he was alone. A shocking but most welcome development, David at last controlled an enduring and obvious deviance.

I sat in the audience flanked by Frank and my mother, just as we had assembled countless times over the years. Aside from us parents, Mom was David's greatest fan and supporter. A lover of theater and song herself, she delighted in his performances and welcomed his solicitations for advice, conversation, and religious discussion.

This concert was different and transcended all others because of everything it represented. The harmonious Christmas strains evoked sacredness beyond the season. They resurrected images of that first holiday performance sixteen years earlier. Astounding us then with his mere cooperation, David now stood proudly in command of both the audience—and of himself. Though the "Rudolph" red nose was missing, my dad was still present. With thanksgiving and awe, he and I watched the miracle that had unfolded over the spanned years:

The confident tenor was impeccably dressed. He sported a flawlessly knotted tie and now possessed the dexterity to manipulate its formation himself. Symbolically, he tolerated it snug around his neck and over the closed top button of his crisply laundered shirt – a mere undershirt was now his only sensory protection from the rough, confining collar. He arrived on his own, prepared and early, despite no parental prodding. Braces now gone, he flashed his beaming smile in camaraderie among cherished peers. He held his song book in hands that were temporarily free of tremors, though the notes were unnecessary with all the material committed to memory. With a successful transition and stellar semester behind him, David's triumph and joy were obvious. Beyond simply meeting the challenge, he had risen above it. Not only would he survive, but he would uniquely contribute, impact others, and do great things. My notion was reinforced: with opportunity and acclimation, anything was possible. David was happy, and for what more could I ask?

The holiday break was like none before. It was completely balanced for David with family, social opportunities, and self-improvement. Steve and Craig both came home with their fiancées in company. It was the first Christmas we were all together simultaneously, and it was wonderful and memorable. David attended parties in addition to those previously discussed, and he relished the time to recharge and relax. Since his stutter persisted, we sought the expertise of a speech therapist whose frequent sessions eradicated the problem in about six weeks. Throughout the process, she taught David effective techniques that would enable his self-management of any potential recurrences.

David accompanied me to a Yoga class to experiment with this added means of relaxation and stress reduction. Despite no access to this practice at school, he enjoyed the evening and is open to future possibilities. Soon thereafter, I attended a professional education talk on music therapy, and I wondered if this venue could aid David, especially considering his passions. Two more tools might thus be summoned for future need. I have found that ideas and opportunities often present themselves when and where least expected, so I am always open and seeking—even when all is well.

David was thrilled to return to school with an invitation to room with three other students in an apartment-style dorm. Considering it an honor, he carefully weighed his options with our joint consultation, and it was unanimously agreed to be too extreme a transition at that time. We didn't want to jeopardize the long-range plan by taking too big a risk prematurely. We chose not to return to the days of "two steps forward and one step back." Senior year, however, might welcome an appropriate broadening of his living experience and social skill. But it was the invitation that mattered, not the outcome. Just knowing that he was accepted and desired, David was happy to choose the option that was best for him. His current living arrangement had served him well, and his junior year schedule promised to be even more demanding. He would live alone by strategy, not from exclusion.

Looking ahead, David is excited for the future. Summer promises further growth and celebration as new performance, academic, and social opportunities beckon. Highway and navigation skills are prerequisites, and David is now ready to tackle these; we hope you are free this summer, Mr. Oz! Highly anticipated, David will welcome two incredible sisters-in-law into our family. He is honored and elated to stand up for his brothers as they have always done for him, but his role will be as a groomsman in their weddings—both scheduled for the upcoming summer, three weeks apart!

Never has David been more optimistic or open to opportunities, for he has become secure in the knowledge and philosophy that life's lessons have imparted. We are realistic: we know that challenges will continue as life becomes more complex. But we are strengthened in our belief that every problem has a solution—and we are tenacious enough to find it!

It was an exciting summer filled with unexpected surprises, and one of them was huge: I got my driver's license! While still not comfortable on the freeway, I actually found driving to be very relaxing in known territory. What was so amazing was that in high school, when I had my driving phobia, the thought of driving caused me great stress. But once I became adjusted to it, I found that driving was a very great stress reliever. I loved that I was independent and in control of where I was going.

As the summer was ending, I began to prepare myself for the unknown of my second year of college and my first time living away from home. I was very excited, but at the same time, there were still those typical nerves about what could go great and what could go wrong. However, I decided to apply the lesson that I had learned over the course of my life: "Just roll with it." With that in mind, I was ready to take on college.

With TWO cars filled with all the necessities, mini fridge and all, we set out to my new college. Once all the work of setting me up in the dorm was done, my parents prepared to leave. As my father said good-bye to me, I remember telling him that I would keep it on the DL. But something that really took me aback was that he simply said, "You know what, D? Just be yourself." In that moment, I felt a sense of acceptance from my father. Now, I would be the first person to say that my dad loves me more than any other father could love a child. But what was cool was I believe he finally understood that, no matter how hard I tried, DL was just not for me—and he accepted that. That comment, within itself, was the kickoff to what I knew would be a great college career.

Once all the hugs and kisses were exchanged with my parents, I began to partake in the Welcome Weekend activities that the college set up for the freshmen and new transferring students: there were games, luncheons, contests, interactions, demonstrations, and a whole lot of other events that helped the "fresh" students get to know each other better. Recalling freshman year of high school and how introverted I was played a big part in me wanting to establish connections with my peers right off the bat. My instinct was to just be myself and try to make my way around to as many people as I possibly could. I went up to a person, some people, or even a large group, and I simply introduced myself and started conversations. I remember one incident when I was greeting people coming into the auditorium for a special presentation. I was "high fiving" guys as they came in, and one said, "I got so much respect for you!" That not only made me feel really good, but it also helped solidify how people liked me and respected me just for being me. As the weekend came to a close, every single new student knew who I was, and I felt very confident that I had kicked off my first year at my new college on the right foot.

As school started and the weeks progressed, I found myself easing into the independent life of a typical college student very well. I was making friends and getting involved in extracurricular activities like choir, theater, and campus ministry. With the help of the tutoring and the one-on-one attention for the special-needs students on the campus, I was doing well in my classes. This "academic" support program stretched beyond the boundaries of academics; it provided social interaction, stress relief, and a great community of support. Aside from being a tight-knit group of people, it also provided bigger and better opportunities to succeed.

I think that spending my first year at a community college was another key factor in my success at the current school. As I stated in the previous chapter, I feel that it would have been too much if I jumped into independent college life right out of high school. Community college helped me with organization, time management, and finals preparation, which made my first semester at my bachelor's degree school much more successful. Having a single dorm room also contributed to my success because I had the power to control my environment. I found that being involved in theater really helped me not only meet new people but also stay on top of my schoolwork—I had to prioritize getting my work done. Theater also provided me with great joy and happiness. Even with my newfound independence, I was never homesick. I came home almost every other weekend when I wanted to surround myself in familial bliss or attend social functions, such as high school events and local theater. It was the perfect balance.

In addition to being involved with the fine arts that I loved passionately, I also took this time at school to dig deeper into my faith—particularly my discernment of the priesthood. The college's campus minister became my spiritual advisor as well as good friend. He helped me organize my thoughts and, like my parents, told me to just keep my eyes, ears, and heart open to what God has in store for me. He also advised me to take this life I'm living one day at a time.

I am proud to say that throughout my whole first semester of being away from my family, I only had one incident of severe anxiety. Despite that happening, I was very proud of myself. Being away from my parents and being bombarded with schoolwork and such, I was very surprised to have had only one "episode." Before I headed off to school, I went through some therapy where I learned special techniques to help control my anxiety, such as deep breathing and guided imagery. I found both exercises to be helpful, but the one that helped me out the most was deep breathing during stressful situations. It calmed me down and prevented me from going extreme. I also incorporated daily routines into the mix, such as exercising and listening to music (Andrea Bocelli). These are tools I use to this day, and I highly recommend them to anyone experiencing any type of stress. I have also used my faith as a main stress reliever with methods such as praying daily and reading Scripture. For anyone who cannot seem to find relief in relaxation exercises, try incorporating your faith in the goal of acquiring peace.

The main reward that came out of my first semester, besides a 3.6 grade point average, was an epiphany moment I had towards the end. As I was living my life, diving deeper into my faith, and thinking about all I had accomplished, I discovered that I wasn't only living a happy life, I was living a very fulfilled life. I can confidently say that I was/am living a life that I would not trade for any dollar figure or to be any other person. I am now comfortable in my own skin. I am comfortable with who I am and confident in what I am able to do—and I desire to express it to other people. In addition to those qualities, I do not live life according to what other *people think about me. I recall, and agree with, words of wisdom from a TV movie I used to love when I was a kid, called "The Other Me" (produced by a Disney organization in the year 2000). It went something like this: "If I want to do something like dance, I dance. I don't care if people laugh at me.... Why should I? I'm not hurting anyone. I'm just being me. If people like me for that, great—if they don't, well, there are lots of other people out there that I **can** be friends with."*

Throughout my life, I've had people look at me in a weird way: you know, kind of like, "Well that kid is sort of—odd!" But like I said, I am who I am, and I love it. And if some people don't, well then, I'll still be polite, but I won't try for more. I'll admit, it's not always easy being me, but I wouldn't have it any other way. What I hope this section offers to everyone, "typicals" and "nontypicals" alike, is that we are who we are because God created us this way; we are all perfect in His eyes. In my opinion, a world where everyone is the same is a boring world. To summarize, be confident in who you are, own it, and love it!

Lessons we learned (for students):

- Your differences are part of who you are as a unique individual.

- Do not shut out your family just because you are in college.

- Do not try to go it alone; utilize every support possible, including tutoring.

- Do not use your differences as an excuse to get out of work. Find a way around challenges. Advocate for what you need to complete assignments.

- Stay organized and don't procrastinate.

- Get involved in extracurricular activities and clubs.

CHAPTER FOURTEEN

Fast-forward

So...then what happened?

L et us fill you in on the next several years of David's life. We chose alternative routes, and it took longer than for most new graduates, but David is prepared and fulfilled! He continues to self-advocate for accommodations when needed, but he also promotes and utilizes his strengths to make incredible contributions. His passions, differences, and unique approach to life have become refreshing assets; they no longer interfere— at least in relationships with people open enough to look beyond eccentricities to see the talents, potential, and beauty that David personifies.

But, as usual for us, getting to this point has been a long, arduous, and creative process—and certainly not easy. David has become adept at self-awareness and self-advocacy of his needs. However, he can't always anticipate what he might require in a situation that he has yet to experience. I continue to create and provide supports and strategies for him in his adulthood for novel situations or those which have proven troublesome. Because of these, and David's follow through, he has continued to progress and flourish. I suspect he will always require more support than is typical as he ages, especially during times of change or newness. But after his adjustment, the needed support lessens once more. David also continues to learn from past experiences and can apply strategies to similar situations. He has blossomed in his confidence and autonomy.

Along with our personal changes of the last several years, there has been a societal reconsideration in referencing autism, and it is seemingly driven by people on the spectrum themselves. Rather than the "person first" language (i.e., person with autism) that was prevalent during our previous chapters, "identity first" (i.e., autistic person) language is becoming preferred by many. "Person first" respects the notion that autism is not a person's entire identity, but many autistic people feel (and I agree) that autism is so pervasive in every aspect of their lives that it can't be separated from identities. Many people on the spectrum express pride, not offense, in being called autistic. It has taken some time and adjustment, but I have moved over to the "identity first" camp, and you will see that in the remainder of the book, though we still toggle back and forth. Referencing has now become a personal choice, and each person's wishes should be respected as to their preference.

David earned a Bachelor of Arts degree in Middle Childhood Education, with concentrations in English/ Language Arts and Social Studies. Ironically, he walked to receive his coveted diploma on Mother's Day, which seemed fitting for the journey we have travelled side by side. At age twenty-five, after several transitioning experiences, David finally taught full-time in his own classroom. He completed a graduate certificate in theology and is currently pursuing a master's degree with pastoral theology specialization, aspiring to teach religion at the high school level. Additionally, David is a national public speaker and continues to explore a vocation as a Catholic priest or deacon. He hopes to combine all three passions to make a difference in the world and touch other lives, and he is well on his way to achieving those goals.

Graduating from college was only the first hurdle in beginning a teaching career. David also needed to pass three state-required credentialing exams and then find a job. He began the application process for testing accommodations six months in advance, and David was granted extended time and a private room for testing, as was the case throughout college. This provided a distraction-free environment and enabled him to read the questions aloud, improving comprehension of what was being asked. Having had prior success with breaking down assignments into parts to avoid overwhelming David, we opted to schedule the exams one at a time, several months apart. This allowed him to focus on the study and completion of each section, making the overall task more manageable and less stressful. Though it took longer than for most students, he was still licensed in time for the springtime rush of job postings for fall positions. Employment is an extensive topic that David will address in the next chapter. To get to jobs, though, he needed transportation: driving!

David is capable and comfortable behind the wheel. He has mastered highways and even drives places an hour away that he has never been before. Theatre shows and public speaking engagements have given him plenty of practice driving solo in the dark and during inclement conditions. Focusing on the visual guides of his updated GPS to clarify the auditory instructions, David is even better at avoiding wrong turns than Frank or I. In fact, he frequently navigates and corrects the two of us when we travel together to somewhere new.

In concentrating on the driving skills, I never considered preparing David for the handling of traffic stops or accidents. Unfortunately, I realized this only after being summoned to the hospital—not for a physical injury, but for David's reactive panic attack following a collision. David was hit when another driver ran a red light. She reported a different version to the responding policeman, however, and David was overwhelmed with the stress of her dishonesty, fear of consequences, and anxiety over what to do. Thankfully, car damage and David's later account—stated calmly with Frank at his side—verified his innocence, but it brought to light a glaring omission in his driver's education.

Following this incident, I researched resources on what David should do under similar circumstances or in other emergencies. I found many autism safety products online, and I opted to purchase a movie that covered a variety of situations. He could hear it, see it, and learn from acted scenarios—all methods of teaching that we knew worked for him. We then discussed the content together. I also purchased an autism safety card that identified his diagnosis and listed common sensory, communication, and behavioral characteristics of autistic people. Thus, if David was slow to answer questions, responded in an atypical fashion, or shut down from the stress, the first responder would then realize he was not being resistant or uncooperative. I further personalized the card for his particulars, including my cell phone number. He keeps a laminated copy in his wallet with his driver's license; it is accessible in emergencies, and he can hand it to official personnel when necessary.

In addition, I recorded a short video on David's phone that calms him in situations when he is anxious and cannot reach a parent. He can then click on it when distressed and follow along with deep breathing, rational thoughts, and my familiar guidance. This will hopefully bring any future incidents into perspective and help him prevent or quell panic.

David is a careful driver who follows rules and speed limits, and I am totally comfortable with him driving. But being human and tired, he erred in judgment and committed a minor traffic violation coming home from a late-night rehearsal. As luck would have it, a policeman witnessed this indiscretion. It was the only time he was ever pulled over, but he recalled our training session from two years prior. David handed the officer his autism ID card along with the other requested documents, and while the officer went to his police cruiser to investigate, David viewed my video, stayed in control despite his anxiety, and handled the situation beautifully. Though he received a ticket, we still considered it a victory.

David aspires to soon move into his own apartment, since he has acquired savings, skills, and confidence. For the best outcome, we plan to wait until the timing is ideal and he is adequately prepared; success is more likely if the move coincides with a period when he is not adjusting to a new job and is not inundated with evening work. His initial years of full-time teaching required our support (best given under the same roof) and did not allow him the time needed for added domestic responsibilities. Next year promises greater ease of combining work, living, and social demands.

While I am nervous for this milestone, it is definitely time, though I am not sure that David appreciates how much is truly involved. I am confident in his growing ability to perform each separate task of independent living, but my concern is that putting it all together simultaneously might be overwhelming. I hope that the accumulated load, when added to job responsibilities, will not be too much. It will be a huge adjustment, but if David has mastered all the parts to function well professionally, I'm sure that he can do this personally, as well. Frank and I will continue to check in and coach him as needed and requested, but we will pull back as David devises his own system of management and reminders. I anticipate that a degree of watchfulness and advice will probably always be required, especially as new circumstances arise, but we will never know what David is capable of until he is given the opportunity to spread his wings. He just needs to do it and figure it out, and we need to let him go, as scary as that is. It will help him more than doing things for him that he can do himself. To be honest, I have had children in my home for almost 37 years, and I am looking forward to an empty nest.

I am realizing that when it comes to running a household, David's level of upkeep and priorities will not be the same as mine. I have finally accepted that I cannot hold him to my standards of cooking or housekeeping. As long as he is clean, safe, pays bills on time, juggles work responsibilities, and chooses predominantly healthy foods, I will consider it a major victory. It is as much an adjustment for me as for him. I will need to keep in mind that his priorities, needs, and life balance differ from mine, and his window of productivity has him "hitting the wall" quicker than I would. He will have to adjust tasks and options to find what works for him—and I will need to respect his choices. Home-cooked meals and ironing may not be as practical as frozen entrees, peanut butter, and the dry cleaner—though we are practicing a few simple recipes.

David plans to create and use an Excel spreadsheet to keep track of bills, payments, and budgeting. Frank and I plan to oversee this initially, and we will start this process while he is still at home, in order to ease the transition. Eventually, he will keep track of this himself with our periodic check-ins, just as he learned to reconcile his monthly bank statements.

Besides progress with employment, domestic chores, and personal finances, David continues to acquire other skills in preparation for moving out on his own. Mundane tasks taken for granted by neurotypicals often require additional planning, training, and supervision for an autistic person. Examples of such activities include paying for a restaurant meal via credit card, using an ATM, taking public transportation alone, arranging for an Uber, handling health care issues such as prescription refills and appointments, or grocery shopping alone. Although it sometimes seems easier and less anxiety-provoking to simply do the task for David, I realize that this also keeps him dependent on Frank and me. We currently seek out these learning opportunities to expand David's independence, for we realize his quality of life will be enhanced when he is safely able to do more for himself.

Public speaking has uniquely created a variety of such opportunities for David's independent growth, especially regarding professional communication and traveling. Initially, I accompanied David on all local trips and often prefaced many of his talks, but with his love of driving and GPS as his copilot, I now tag along only if the ride exceeds two hours or if I am invited to share my own perspectives as a co-presenter. National commitments have taken him to the next level of both speaking expertise and independent functioning.

On David's first trip to Las Vegas, I helped him pack to include all necessary items and to arrange or fold clothing so that wrinkles would be minimized. He learns and remembers best by watching and participating, rather than by spoken direction. Together, we packed up speaking paraphernalia and created laminated checklists so that all items returned home with him. There were lists for what to pack, what to have in his laptop bag before leaving for the presentation, what to set up and display before his talks, and what to collect following the talk (i.e., no flash drives left behind). I escorted David on this trip, explained each step ahead of time, and then followed several paces behind him as he navigated our way. At the airport, he made it through security ahead of me and found our gate. He told the cab driver our destination, checked in at the hotel, and keyed us into our room—all with me lagging behind, answering his questions before and after.

David did great, and while I was comfortable with him making this trip independently six months later—especially through the same airports—the need for a rental car and ninety-minute commute through Las Vegas traffic led me to tag along once more. I drove this time, but now that he has learned the steps, we are both confident he could handle a rental in the future. Frank or I would observe his execution of the entire process at a local agency in our familiar area just prior to his solo venture out of town; this would cement the procedure and increase his confidence.

A Las Vegas opportunity arose a third time and David journeyed this one completely alone. While I was nervous to let him go, I knew he was ready and willing to literally fly solo. Further postponement would only hinder his development. I needed to put his needs before my emotions and prove to him that I had faith in his abilities. He booked his hotel and flights online while I looked on. We added laminated lists for checking out of hotels, including last-minute bathroom, closet, and outlet inspections to assure all personal items made it back into his luggage. For that trip, and all trips since, I typed him a detailed itinerary, with timelines and addresses for each step. Included were when to leave for the venue or airport with considerations for traffic, how to figure out tipping for cab rides or meals, when to coordinate flight check-in amidst his speaking responsibilities, and so on. We procured David a credit card and his own Uber account. Frank supervised his first uses of the latter to teach and test it out, and he explained necessary safety considerations. David texted us his progress at each step of this initial trip, and he successfully brought home all essentials and receipts. He was proud, confident, and never stressed, and again

I attribute this to adequate preparation, transitioning, and readiness.

Since that inaugural trip, David travels unaccompanied, regardless of unfamiliar airports and cities. He enjoys the adventures and uses down time to recharge or work on assignments. He is quite comfortable finding a restaurant and eating alone, and he loves being in command of his own experience.

There are several accommodations we have implemented. First, a non-smoking room is imperative for David's hypersensitivity to smells. Second, we choose nonstop flights whenever possible to prevent the stress of missing a connection or finding another gate. If David *must* take two flights, we choose a combination that incorporates a time cushion for a potential flight delay, without being so excessive that it drains him. Third, David always packs his standard breakfast of fiber bars and peanut butter, eating comfortably in his hotel room. And fourth, we have found it wise for him to snack prior to leaving for the talk, even if dinner is part of the program, so that meal delays or an unappealing entrée would not pose a problem.

David's most important accommodation is that an extra day must sometimes be added to his trip if an event is scheduled in the evening. While the logistics might work out for typicals to deliver a quality same-day presentation after a hard day of travel, it is just too much for David to tolerate. Unless the journey is simple and allows time for him to chill or nap after hotel check-in, David could "hit the wall" during the same timeframe as the scheduled talk. Waking early to travel, complicated air and ground experiences, and time changes across zones may all necessitate that David arrives the evening before he speaks.

All of these opportunities, including talking and socializing with strangers, would not be afforded to him without public speaking. David has also learned so much about cultures and regions, and he has become accustomed to networking. He is comfortable seeking assistance and has become more resourceful. I never would have dreamed him to be independently capable or tolerant of all this activity. It just proves that you don't know what is possible unless you give it a chance.

Let us be clear: we are still on our journey! Despite how far David has come, I am aware that he will continually be challenged by each new opportunity and milestone of his future. I only hope that Frank and I have prepared him adequately; I do know that we did our best. I still worry about what lies ahead. Who will provide emotional support and advice for David when Frank and I are gone? I wonder if he will experience romance or a deep connection with a close friend. I am curious to see what ultimately transpires in his career, and I hope that his many talents and growing potential continue to be realized. And though challenges are inevitable, I fervently hope that the gut-wrenching experiences are behind him.

Our journey remains a trial-and-error learning experience, fraught with challenges. But isn't that true of every person's life—autism or not? I believe that two core elements remain central to David's success: 1) When doors close, we remain steadfast in our determination and success at opening windows, and 2) David turns the negative experiences into positive ones; he learns from hardships how to improve his coping skills, preparation, and performance.

It seems that David is in a better position than many of his typical peers! He knows what he wants, and he has the tenacity, skills, support, and work ethic to achieve it. He embraces his differences and has assimilated into the typical world while still staying true to his needs, desires, and self. As we described in Chapter One, David has indeed attained dual citizenship between his "typical" and autistic countries. He has blended his two worlds in order to comfortably coexist.

We surely do not have all the answers, but we are happy to raise questions and inspire contemplation.

Since I wrote the preceding chapters when I was twenty or younger, I am hoping that you will be able to detect a growth and maturity in my thinking, insight, and writing through these last two chapters. A lot of changes have taken place over the past six years—one of them being my ever-receding hairline, but that's beside the point!

Another change you might notice is the way I refer to my diagnosis. Going along with the 2013 revisions of DSM-5™, I have become comfortable with referring to myself as having autism, rather than the former label of Asperger's, though I still flip back and forth between them. Using the adjective "autistic" has also become more popular among those of us on the spectrum, and I personally prefer it over saying "person with autism." I feel as if it is more up-front and it removes the uncertainty. It's a good way for others to see that I'm comfortable with my autism and that it's not something to be dwelled upon. I am definitely more than just my autism, but at the same time, autism IS who I am. I call myself autistic, but if others want to refer to me as a person with autism, I am cool with that, too. I have gained the confidence and assurance of who I am and what I need, and I advocate for myself, but autism is not the main focus of my day, though it's always in the background. What people want to be called is a person-by-person choice.

As I age, I recognize the value of challenges. Personally, professionally, and spiritually, there have been many opportunities and victories, but there were also numerous setbacks. What I came to realize is that the hardships of life are necessary for growth. The tough times that I endured strengthened my coping skills and character. I am now equipped with a social body armor to deflect the attacks of petty battles in order to win the war of my convictions. Purpose can be discovered in every difficult instance.

In my speech and social interactions, I have adopted a true "less is more" manner, which is what my father had always wanted for me. In fact, I told him that's what I got him for his birthday this year! All jokes aside, I finally saw the personal and professional impact that simple words and gestures can have on individuals. I still second-guess myself at times, but I don't dwell on it as much. I am more comfortable in social gatherings and can better navigate social settings.

I am proud to say that I continue to control my verbal "chit-chat" after struggling with it for years. Doing it in my mind still gives me the same satisfaction. Ironically, modern advancements would now make my old habit blend in anyway. With Bluetooth, earbuds, and wireless devices, individuals often appear to be talking to themselves. If only this technology was invented a decade or two sooner, I could have been spared many questioning glances and assumptions!

Driving and traveling have given me a whole new sense of freedom. Preparing adequately beforehand in both situations makes all the difference in preventing mental or emotional anxiousness. It prevents rushing or forgetting needed materials. What were once stressors are now opportunities to refresh and reflect. I feel as if I have achieved a new level of life transition in being able to successfully organize and partake in new adventures of my own accord.

In moving out on my own, I recognize that I just have to "do it." I am more eager than nervous. Having talked about it and prepared for so long, I just want to get the ball rolling. With the proper organization that my parents have introduced to me, I am motivated to take on extra responsibilities, because my living space will be a reflection of who I want to become. When it's just me, I won't have the temptation of letting Mom or Dad get the jobs done for me. There will be no other option but for me to step up. I recognize that I will need their prompting at the beginning because I am not as experienced in certain areas as they are. It would almost go against everything I preach to refuse their suggestions—I would be doing myself a disservice. I am looking forward to moving out when the timing is right.

I had always wondered, and often worried, about what successful, relaxed dating would be like, especially after having a couple awkward experiences. I very much wished for a step-by-step plan to prevent treading the uneasy waters of what to do or say. For example, I wanted a guide for how soon to call someone after a date, how soon to be affectionate, and so on. I stressed about how to go about things in the proper way so as not to scare the girl off before she had the chance to know me. However, after being asked out on a date by a beautiful young lady, with both of us enjoying ourselves and each other's company, I gained peace in knowing that

I was capable of forming a natural and genuine connection just by being me. Nothing ever came of it from a romantic standpoint, but I am now comfortable and confident in being able to form a relationship with a well-matched young lady. Though I am seriously considering a religious vocation in my future, I'm still very much interested and open to exploring potential relationships with women in the present. I know that I need as many experiences as possible to help me make a well-rounded decision about my future path.

My years as a college upperclassman provided me with knowledge and insight that went beyond the scope of a classroom setting. As I expressed in an article in The OARacle, "I believe that people should never use their learning differences as an excuse. The reason behind sharing your learning differences with your professors and others is not to receive a 'get-out-of-jail-free pass.' It is to tailor a plan that matches up with how you learn best so that material can be presented in a way that you understand."

One of my greatest realizations in college is that a balance between work and play can absolutely be obtained. If one makes a schedule illustrating how much time one truly has to complete assignments, the time for extracurricular activities and socializing with friends will also be found. I even discovered that rewarding myself with the latter merriment motivated me to stay on top of my schoolwork, getting it all done in a timely fashion to allow time for fun.

That being said, life is going to throw curve balls, so it is important that students remain willing to reach out to their families for support. Just because a young adult is now living "the college life" doesn't mean that parents must be cast off to the side and neglected. Students shouldn't feel that they have to do it completely on their own! Family is there for love, support, and encouragement through the stressful times. In my life, home is where I was able to break free from my anxiety and be brought back down to a calmer mindset and a revitalized determination.

Biological family does not have to be the only source of help. Consider coaches, mentors, counselors, tutors, and friends. As I expressed in an article in Autism Parenting Magazine, "We are all combinations of gifts and struggles, but, no matter our functions and/or skill levels, asking for help is the smartest and the bravest thing we can possibly do in order to go above and beyond what might even be thought possible. By fully embracing all forms of help, my academic success wasn't the only thing that increased; it also increased my self-esteem, my confidence, and my desire to keep achieving more and more! I also grew out of denial and into the greatest form of self-acceptance possible" (Petrovic, 15-16).

As you have just read, the last half of college was a pivotal time of self-discovery. Senior year was a period in my life when I could have fun, go to parties (legally!), and confidently utilize and advocate for my accommodations in order to thrive in the classroom. However, around the start of the last semester, I did fall into a period of complacency. As a result, my grades suffered. It was then that I realized I could not go on autopilot! I have the skills and mindset, but unless I take it upon myself to put forth the effort to make it happen, those skills are worthless. Having received a reality check, I broke free from my mental slump and bounced back. I apply this lesson now in my professional life.

I developed new strategies to incorporate into my routines, and I continue to apply them to this day. First off, as soon as I'm asked to do something, I try to do it right away. I am aware that if I put something off with the intention of doing it later and do not have a reminder, I am very likely to forget. To remind myself, I utilize note cards that I keep in an easily accessible spot, such as my shirt pocket, so that I can remember to complete the task. Thanks to the help of the trusted and knowledgeable advisors in my college learning center, I was able to bounce back very quickly and graduate cum laude. I had officially achieved college grad status! But now the true work began: navigating the real world.

As I began to think about my ideal employment scenario, I decided that it would be extremely beneficial for me to take some online theology courses in order to gain a new credential. This would maximize my potential to be hired now, as well as increase my knowledge for possible future clergy work. Like all things in life, online schooling had its benefits, but it also had its challenges. I was able to fit it in around my working and speaking responsibilities and gain a certificate in the program I wanted, even though it was not offered locally. But, when it came to the style of these online courses, there were very few opportunities to communicate with the professors verbally. This was also the first time that I ventured into an academic setting without any form of accommodations. For the most part, I'd say I did pretty darn well.

When classes arose in which I struggled, there were two common reasons: either I didn't understand what the professors were looking for in terms of completing the assignments, or I was unable to accomplish their objectives in their desired formats. It was at those moments that I took it upon myself to reach out to the instructors via email or phone call, disclose my diagnosis of autism, and express what needed to potentially happen in order for me to succeed. Thankfully, I had very understanding professors who allowed me to adjust the means of completing the assignments. For example, in one class, I sent a video-recorded presentation instead of a typed research paper. From that point on, I excelled in my coursework and achieved my Graduate Certificate in Theology with a 3.6 GPA. I am applying these same strategies as I currently complete my master's degree.

In my pursuit of achieving balance, theatre continues to be my passion, providing social refreshment and intellectual insight. Throughout my life, theatre equipped me with the unique perspectives and values that I was not capable of attaining anywhere else. More than just the "glitz and glamour," it was the bond with human beings that I longed for when I was an adolescent. Theatre graced me with the confidence to approach fellow thespians that I had seen onstage but had never met personally; we established a camaraderie that quickly blossomed into growing friendships. I added these friends to the many others I met on multiple stages over the years. And although I still do not have a "best friend," I feel at peace to have many good friends who lift me up in different ways.

At this point in my life, I comprehend the full magnitude of how theatre brought me to a greater level of human understanding. From every song I sang, dance I danced, and character I portrayed alongside my musical theatre brothers and sisters, I was able to gain greater empathy, sympathy, compassion, and, above all, awareness. Having autism, I think my naiveté was greater than that of my fellow "typicals," but theatre shattered my black and white thinking to provide a more diverse, broad, and colorful perspective. This helped me in my conversations and understanding of others. It enhanced my open-mindedness, and as my emotional maturity evolved, so too did my willingness to be extroverted. This has helped me connect and empathize with my students, family, friends, or any stranger that I come across.

I initially tried theatre in the hope of finding friends, but at this point in my life, it has also given me a family. It is continuing to mold and shape me into the person that I strive to become. Whether I am in the audience, on stage, or even behind the scenes, my confidence has skyrocketed in being my unapologetically true self. So, if people like me and want to be around me, my arms are always open to welcome new friends and acquaintances. If people don't like me—or possibly even hate me—I'm still going to give them love, keep my spirits high, and offer up prayers and compassion. The way I see it, the world already has enough darkness without me adding dismalness to it. And I don't need to change in order to be accepted.

This positive mindset was almost nonexistent in my adolescent years because of being bullied. It has only been in my early twenties that I began to fully grasp how these earlier toxic experiences affected me. Realizing bullying's long-lasting personal impact, it became my mission to convey to youth/ young adult audiences that the words, actions, and exclusion (intentional or not) they impose on one another are not simply "short-term chuckles." In fact, they may result in long-term consequences for a HUMAN BEING who has real feelings.

I am not ashamed to admit that to this day I suffer from a PTSD of sorts. No matter what situation I find myself in (personal or professional), if someone does or says something that mirrors what my bullies said or did to me, I find myself replaying the past incident. The spirit-killing burden of not having any of my peers come to my rescue to stop what was happening made me feel like I wasn't worth anything. I questioned if everything they were saying might be true, and my scariest thought was that I was destined for a life of loneliness.

Thankfully, even though I still deal with flashbacks and the uncomfortable emotions of my past, I have grown to recognize the value of my whole self and no longer dwell on what happened. Everything that I have been through has made me genuinely appreciate the kindness, compassion, and love that people show me daily, both personally and professionally; I never take these blessings for granted. Of course, not every day is perfect when it comes to how I am treated or how smooth the path of life is, but can't that be said for everybody? On those days, I flood my mind with memories of friends who genuinely care about me, and that is what gives me the motivation and strength to endure the hard times and bounce back. It also helps to find a potential purpose that can come out of the situation. If I can learn from it, or use it to inspire and lift others up, the experience has value and is worth going through.

Some of the guys who bullied me back in high school have since contacted me and actually apologized. We each came to the mutual conclusion that our maturity level, or lack thereof, was the culprit behind our conflicts. We also acknowledged that we have become better people having learned from those experiences. We have since moved on, bearing no hostility.

Having gone through all my past ordeals, and even taking into account the emotional aftermath I still endure, I wouldn't change a thing. In fact, I would go through all of it many times over in order to have the beautiful moments I currently experience. Once lonely and hopeless, my life is now full of love and purpose.

Lessons we learned:

- If you don't try, how will you ever know what is possible?

- Find your strengths and what you do well.

- Advocate for your needs without shame.

- Maintain effort: don't go on autopilot.

- Struggles make you stronger.

- Do what you love.

- Stay true to who you are.

CHAPTER FIFTEEN

Acclimating to the Working World

Throughout both my mothering experience and my position as an instructional advisor for college students with learning differences, I have gleaned what I feel is an underlying truth. Discussed in previous chapters, but still highly relevant for evolving adult life, the following belief is still true. There is one constant in change—the need for transition.

Preparing for every novel experience has made all the difference in David's quality of life and confidence. Although he has gained competence in cognitive and personal skills, the increasing interactions and complexities of the academic and working worlds require additional planning and transitioning for optimal functioning. This chapter will focus on acclimation to the workplace.

As with everything else in David's life, we approached employment in stages. Because he didn't drive until he was twenty, and because summers were filled with academic pursuits and theatre (a priority for other reasons), David was never able to secure a part-time job while in school. Realizing the value of work, aside from the obvious financial rewards, we found volunteer opportunities to ease him into the employment culture. These experiences helped him learn how to seek clarification, cooperate with co-workers, and accept direction or criticism. Years later, in his first paid summer job, David dealt with a co-worker's unpleasant disposition. In a separate challenge, he disclosed to a trainer his need to have a machine explained differently before he could grasp its correct use. David would encounter similar occurrences in many jobs in the years ahead, so building his skill repertoire was essential.

All work experience is valuable. Whether paid or not, in a desired field or not, enjoyable or not—each opportunity teaches lessons and builds skills that can broaden exposure and be applied to future situations. David developed philosophies about the type of employee, teacher, and leader he wanted to become, and he molded all of his experiences into his work persona. He observed his colleagues, admiring and adopting some characteristics and behaviors, while rejecting others. But all these people and circumstances had value; some challenged his naiveté and coping skills, and others raised him to a new level of success. Ultimately, David is a more worldly man and teacher for having run this gamut of experience.

For David, being thrown into full-time teaching from the start of his career would have overwhelmed him.

Skills, strategies, and "street smarts" needed further honing in steps, and these staged advancements would additionally allow time for his certification testing to occur gradually, as previously explained. This evolution also enabled a partial desensitization to classroom stimuli as David gradually increased his exposure to it.

The following progression of positions was central to David's ultimate success: student teacher to volunteer aide in classrooms to teaching assistant to substitute teacher to long-term exclusive substitute to, finally, a full-time teacher in his own classroom. This sequence spanned a few years. Besides supplementing David's training and experience, it also served to provide the needed time and flexibility for graduate studies and continued public speaking.

Once David procured a full-time position, he and I went through our typical routine of acclimating him to logistics, travel specifics, and his work environment. Over the course of the summer, David reviewed the school's policies and procedures and also read a couple of books discussing the first year of teaching. We plotted potential routes to drive, since the commute would be forty-five minutes through road construction. Frank or I drove first, with David as a discerning passenger—timing and checking out his options. After settling on a route, David then drove it during the morning rush hour with me riding along. We established the ideal time to leave home, allowing adequate cushion, and we checked out the parking situation and surrounding neighborhood. The week before classes commenced, I assisted David with his bulletin boards and supplies, helping him organize his room and brainstorm workflow. He walked the halls to learn the building and met colleagues to gain familiarity. Acclimated to the environment, David thus gained comfort and confidence; he felt ready and excited to begin his professional life as a junior high teacher.

But despite all these efforts and his accumulated transitioning experiences, David was shell-shocked by the challenges of the year ahead. Though his reception along his job journey was favorable overall, it was extremely difficult to witness him enduring disrespectful behaviors from a few non-accepting staff members. It was different from the challenges of the tween and teen years, when I could meet with representatives at the schools or camps for assistance. I didn't feel appropriate becoming involved when David was in his twenties, even though the stakes were actually higher. Jobs are essential to livelihood and independence. There is the extra pressure and power of evaluations, job references, and word-of-mouth reputations—especially since David aspires to stay working within the same educational system, regardless of which school he may be at. His future hung in the balance.

Frank and I could only prepare, counsel, and support David as best we could from the sidelines. He would have to weather it alone and hopefully grow from his experiences. I often felt helpless, heart-broken, and furious that closed-minded individuals could cause him pain and years of regression when we worked so hard to build David's skills and confidence. Education about autism and its accompanying needs cannot occur unless a person is willing to listen and learn. We have come to the conclusion that a job search should be as much (or more) about David assessing the prospective workplace for the right fit as it is the potential employer interviewing him. And the fit must be for attitudes as well as skillset and potential. Advocacy, accommodations, and appropriate mentorship should assist with the acclimation for the benefit of everyone involved.

Over time, David leapt to the other side of the canyon to his present utopia, symbolized by our cover, and he is thriving at work. I'll leave the details of that story to him...

Let me start this chapter by telling you the story of my student teaching experience; it seems to have started a pattern. Strangely enough, it was divided between two completely different schools. The first go-round started with my wide-eyed expectations that everything would be like the movies I had seen. And for the first month, I did believe that things were going well. I was effective in teaching my students and developing a rapport and mutual respect with them. I even received a positive evaluation on a class I taught independently. But I soon realized that there were problems beneath the surface. On what seemed to be an ordinary school day, I was called into the principal's office and my student teaching experience was revoked, effective immediately. I was dazed and confused.

To this day, I still do not know the exact reasons for my termination, but it led me to soul search what possibly could have gone wrong. In my college classes, we were never taught how to navigate the environment, the hierarchy, and the unexpressed social skills involved in interacting with colleagues. But then again, maybe this was all common sense to the "typical" mind and required no instruction for most people. To me, however, it was not something that came naturally, and it caused confusion and stress.

My mind had been flooded with questions since the first day. I sought the answers from anyone whom I thought would help: were the questions too frequent, too basic, and/or directed to the wrong people? For example, I did not realize that the principal's role was not like that of the director of my college academic support program, to whom I relayed everything. In retrospect, I believe I may have sought out the principal far too much—some of my small concerns, sharing, and questions would likely have been more appropriate for my mentor teacher.

I was also plagued by sensory overload. Previously, I had only spent two to three hours at a time in a youth classroom in an authoritative capacity. This new full-time stimulation of teaching, responding to student needs, moderating lunch and recess, and learning how to find my place all contributed to an increase in some of my autistic quirks. I never disclosed that I had autism when my student teaching was approved by this school, and I couldn't help but wonder if my autistic behaviors had something to do with my removal.

I spent the next two weeks at home, trying to study for my upcoming certification exams. But I was distracted by overwhelming feelings of self-doubt, self-criticism, and fear. Would my college find me another student teaching placement to fulfill this course requirement? And would it happen in time to save the semester and allow me to graduate as planned? Did I just waste all this money and effort to major in a profession that I was not cut out for? And above all, was I incapable of being a GOOD teacher because of my autism?

On my deceased grandfather's birthday (who I believe is orchestrating my successes from heaven) I finally received the email I had been praying for. I had been offered an interview for a potential student teaching position (coincidence, or a miracle in the making?). After much preparation researching commonly asked interview questions, studying the school's mission, and mapping out my own educational philosophies in my mind, I was able to express myself comfortably and confidently in my meeting with the four interviewers. I chose to disclose my autism straight up, but I also shared why being autistic was a strength; I spoke of things that I did well because of it, and I explained how I could inspire my students. This group saw me as an asset and wholeheartedly took me on, then and there!

The supportive principal, who believed in me, was determined to give me the greatest chance to reach my untapped potential. She assigned me to the two incredible junior high mentor teachers who participated in my interview. They ultimately helped me navigate the ins and outs of the education world beyond what I learned in college. They taught me skills and methods to handle situations, and they remain my friends and mentors to this very day. Most valuable to me at that vulnerable time in my life, they showed me a new perspective. They shared that the mistakes I made were common among all new teachers; I wouldn't be penalized for them. This was important because I had become paranoid that if I slipped up, I would once again be let go without warning. I took comfort in their reassurance, but I still tried to learn from the mistakes of my past. I analyzed what I thought went wrong before and discovered potential solutions and accommodations that would prevent similar issues in my present situation.

Beyond educational strategies, my mentors provided me with emotional and mental comfort. For the most part, they understood me, and when they did not, they tried to clarify my thoughts and feelings. These are qualities vital for any mentor of autistic employees. It's not just about learning the labors of the job—it's about communication, interaction, and appropriate application. These two individuals not only launched my career...they saved it!

Looking back, I am actually very thankful that the first student teaching experience did not work out; I feel that I am a better teacher and person because of it. I still sometimes struggle with not knowing why I was eliminated in the first place, but I believe it keeps me on top of my game in my conduct with students, parents, and colleagues alike.

When I was in college, and even newly graduated, I was wrapped in a mindset of bright-eyed naïveté—not only about teaching, but also about finding a job. I failed to realize the difficulty in simply trying to get my foot in the door of this "professional Narnia": a world inhabited by beings with different thinking, insights, and even behaviors.

I was fairly confident that the conflicts and stories I had heard about individuals having to interview at many places before getting that one position was not going to happen to me. I believed that I had accomplished a lot compared to other young people my age. With all the qualifications listed on my resume, I thought I'd be every employer's first option. It turns out I was wrong. I applied for several positions, but none came to fruition. It wasn't so much anger or frustration that I felt; it was more a yearning to inquire what exactly took me out of the running for each position. Was it my area of certification? My experience? (Which, ironically, you can't get without experience!) My methods? My autism? And would anyone ever give me a chance?

Considering my life pattern, I shouldn't have been surprised that the atypical young man would be placed on an atypical career path. But when doors closed, I opened windows. I spent the following year substitute teaching, pursuing a graduate certificate in theology, and branching out in my motivational speaking. This expanded my skills and granted me expertise in a third subject area that I could teach. I would come back stronger in the spring and try again.

My experience has shown me that no area of employment is a waste, even if in a volunteer capacity. Every job I have ever had taught me things and gave me strategies for overcoming future obstacles. I learned about the appropriate timing for questions and about dealing with difficult personalities of other employees who didn't share my views. I also came to realize that I might have to disclose my need for accommodations if my diagnosis was preventing me from accomplishing a task, whether as an individual or as part of a team effort. I learned social skills distinctive for use during downtime e.g., when was the proper time to talk leisurely (including the appropriate subject matter) vs. when was it the time to buckle down and focus on the job at hand? Even my job as a public speaker helped to improve me as a writer, communicator, and person. I became comfortable, and even energized, with visiting new places and meeting new people, having only myself to rely on. These worldly experiences gave me more confidence to handle myself effectively in a school setting.

What most people fail to realize is that individuals on the autism spectrum possess invaluable skills that make them ideal employees and beneficial to an organization. Many of us are excellent rule followers, honest, and capable of excelling once we find our niche. We are not the kind of workers who would waste time on senseless activities such as daydreaming, goofing off, or being on our phones. Through the various positions I had held since high school, it became clear to me that not everyone held these same values or shared my approach to workplace duties. Initially it made me uncomfortable that everyone wasn't as dedicated as I was, *but I eventually learned to focus on myself and my choices rather than dwelling on others' potential consequences from not following rules. This became very important once I found myself navigating the professional world.*

By not yet starting a full-time position, I was able to gain many benefits from my substitute and teaching assistant (TA) experiences. These transitional roles actually helped me to become a better teacher than if I had obtained a full-time offer right after graduation. Subbing increased my ability to be more open and flexible. Observing other teachers and how they interacted with school children helped me determine who I was as a teacher; it helped me identify the kind of educator I wanted to be, in terms of my impact on students' lives. I was able to witness and experience various styles of teaching and disciplining. I was then able to solidify which qualities and methods I wanted to emulate, and disregard those I felt were ineffective or demeaning to students.

These positions also helped my ability to withstand all the different kinds of overload that come along with classrooms full of children and teenagers. There were times that I stepped out of the classroom as a TA to escape the sensory stimuli and tension, but I knew that I couldn't leave my class unattended when I worked as a full-time teacher. I adapted new coping skills to accommodate my needs that did not interfere with the students' supervision or learning. Sometimes I used ear plugs. For me, they eliminated the unnecessary white noise and better allowed me to zero in on what the students were actually saying. Another strategy I utilized was "listening" to Josh Groban, Andrea Bocelli, or Broadway show tunes in my head. This lessened my discomfort and helped to center me. During times that the class was wound up, I opted to use the last five minutes of the period to have my students enter into personal reflection or meditation with relaxing background music and dimmed lighting. This aided us all in achieving a calmer environment and mindset before continuing on to the next class.

April finally arrived, and it was time to repeat the application and interview process. But this time around, a couple of teaching positions were actually offered! I GOT A JOB! I thought the main obstacle had been overcome. I also thought I was prepared, but similar to the start of high school, things started to unravel within a couple of months. In fact, I was reminded of my tough times in high school. I felt a familiar discomfort, isolation, and hopelessness that I never thought I'd experience again.

*I assumed that I would learn the job with orientation and guidance, and that I would belong to their community. It never occurred to me that some people wouldn't have the willingness to accept me — or the faith and respect that I was **capable** of doing the job. Yes, I could advocate for myself and explain autism. But you cannot force a person to be open to what you are saying. You cannot assume that someone will be willing to put forth the extra time and effort into making it work, not only to help my performance, but for the sake of the whole team. After all, professionals are just people. But that is the point of this chapter and my public speaking. I strive to open minds and hearts to the idea that everyone would thrive if effort and training were offered to help others understand and meet individuals "where they are at." As my mother proposes, if employers are willing to make adjustments for groups like new mothers, such as job sharing and occasionally working from home, why can't similar creative solutions be considered for people with autism?*

Early in my experience at that first full-time school, I recognized that my teaching style and philosophy were different than some of my colleagues. I tried my hardest to acclimate to their ways of doing things. The problem was that I found myself amongst a group of individuals who did not understand how my autism affected me, and most of my team seemingly had no interest in helping me adapt to this new environment—nor, apparently, did they feel my ideas could positively contribute. The mentorship I received could be classified as minimal; there was little assistance in helping me handle professional and personal situations. The advice I was given in response to my questions was so general that it didn't go beyond what I had already considered. By November, I felt lost.

The treatment I received from a few individuals sunk me deeper than I had ever been before (including high school) in terms of my morale. I was called out in front of my students, which threatened to derail the respect and authority I had worked so hard to build. Some people continually focused on what I did wrong and didn't acknowledge my kindness or achievements—so why bother? It was hard for me to enjoy life, and I isolated myself in my bedroom at home. This suffering caused me to regress in my progress, determination, and confidence. Teaching is my vocation, so if someone beats down my teaching spirit, a good portion of my personal spirit is also affected. The reason I'd be up in my room was because their questioning of "who I am" led me to ponder the same notions.

Still, I rallied every day and finished the year, trying to keep my focus on giving the students the best I had. Due to low enrollment, my position was eliminated in June. Regardless, I never had any intention of returning and was already looking for other opportunities that spring. It wasn't until I was hired at a school staffed by compassionate, knowledgeable, and insightful colleagues that I was finally able to get the mentorship and guidance that every new employee needs in order to succeed—elements that are even more necessary for persons on the autism spectrum. I then truly realized that the prior year's problems were never all because of me. I also realized that I learned a lot from that first position, and I am actually very thankful for the experience.

In searching for a different job, I submitted several applications and received two very promising interviews that I thought I had nailed. One opportunity was at a school where I had previously substituted, made connections, and received encouragement. I was certain I would be offered the position since I felt I had already proven myself. And yet, for whatever reason, neither of these interviews resulted in a job offer. So again, I reevaluated my short-term and long-term goals. My mother and I brainstormed options for the upcoming year. Since I very much wanted to teach theology in high school and was still considering joining the Catholic clergy, we decided that completion of the remaining six courses to finish my Master's in pastoral theology would give me an advantage. If I chose to be a deacon, I would only have one more course to complete for the deacon track of graduate work. And if I decided to become a priest, it would prove my passion and ability for the coursework. More immediately, it would give me an added credential to teach high school religion the following year. Miraculously, we discovered a forgotten bank account in my name where my parents deposited gift money throughout my childhood. The balance exactly covered the cost of my tuition and books. It appeared that I was meant to finish this degree, and so I enrolled.

Simultaneously, I would substitute teach in the high school I attended, as well as assist with retreat planning and presentations. I had opportunities for public speaking, both near and far. I would work on writing additions to this book, and I would use the year to experience independent living by moving into my own apartment. It was a great plan. I would grow in areas aside from teaching, and I would become a stronger candidate for a full-time position the following year. I purchased my own health insurance and was excited about my plans. Once again, when doors closed, we smashed through windows.

In late August, I spoke at a teachers' retreat at a Catholic elementary school. I felt a great vibe immediately after walking in. At the conclusion of my presentation, the principal privately made a full-time job offer that was astounding to me and my family. I finally felt wanted, valued, and recognized for what I had to offer! I would teach junior high social studies half time and then function as an enrichment tutor for students in need. I would not have a homeroom, which would save me from dealing with the ever-changing, nonteaching details that had cluttered my mind in my last position.

What to do?! I knew I could be effective in the enrichment responsibilities due to my personal experience and teaching methods, and social studies was the second area of concentration included in my bachelor's degree. This job was perfect! But I had already paid for books and tuition for full-time graduate school that was starting in ten days. The elementary school started in six days, and students and parents would be visiting classrooms in just 48 hours! The principal was aware of the speaking engagements to which I had already committed, many during school hours, and she was in total support of their completion. She said she would do everything she could to make it work. Most importantly, she understood my needs and challenges, and she would provide the mentorship I desperately needed that was absent from my last position.

It only took ten minutes to make the decision after talking with my parents. The opportunity was just too perfect not *to accept. Expect a miracle? This truly was the biggest one of my life! My mother's first response to this turn of events takes us back to the first chapter, where she expressed her dream of sending this book to any of my future employers to share my characteristics and needs. Her dream was fulfilled! My employer heard me speak and purchased my book for each person attending. Talk about full disclosure: my life was literally an open book! The entire faculty and staff were enlightened. I felt respected, valued, and most importantly, understood. I was confident that I would be accepted and welcomed to the team.*

I revised my game plan. Weekends would be dedicated to work, but I would still make sure I maintained "balance" with breaks for social events, theatre attendance, and refuge in my topics of interest. I would reduce my graduate load during my teaching months, and I would finish my degree over the summer. Being busy has always brought about my peak organization, and this year would be filled with bountiful commitments. With all that I had going on, I would hold off moving into an apartment until next year. It was a whirlwind 48 hours: an official interview with the pastor, principal, and business manager; filling out numerous forms; security background checks; reading the school's handbook; setting up my classroom; and learning my way around the school.

At the beginning of this school year, I had a more realistic mindset than the previous August. I was hopeful, but not naïve. I also felt more prepared, considering that this was not my first year of teaching. Armed with my experiences from the previous year, I was able to develop and implement effective organizational strategies. Examples included laminating school calendars/schedules and then arranging them on top of my classroom desk for easy reference, or having blank notes available at all times to jot down spontaneous matters that

I would otherwise likely neglect. I worked on teaching plans and grading during the week, and I focused on graduate school assignments on the weekends.

Mom also purchased a weighted vest for me to use at home, which had offered me comfort in the first grade, but which she had since forgotten about. More and more, I could not tolerate light touch, and I craved compression to satisfy the tension in my chest. The vest became a source of comfort to me for these sensory afflictions, and it kept me grounded and focused as I sat working at my computer. I also utilized small stress balls both at work and home; it rechanneled my concentration to hold and squeeze an unnoticed item.

As it always seems to go with me, "first times" never run smoothly. The initial situation is difficult and stressful, but the second one always proves to be great, and I constantly remind myself of this during the tough times. Having learned from past experiences, I now seek out nothing less than "the right fit." Thankfully, this new position was exactly that. Right from the start, acceptance, camaraderie, and teamwork surrounded me. I am given the freedom to be the teacher that I knew I could be, but was previously held back from becoming. None of us teachers meddle in each other's classroom business because we respect the boundaries and have full confidence that learning is taking place. I have free rein of my classroom; I am truly mentored and not simply micromanaged. It feels good to be trusted.

I am frequently asked about my feelings on disclosure of my autism. In my private life, such as with dating and other social situations, my philosophy is not to disclose right off the bat. I first want others to get to know the person behind my autism. I find myself revealing pieces of my diagnosis as they naturally and appropriately fit into the conversation. I feel the same about disclosing a learning difference and/or the need for accommodations in the workplace or at a job interview. One should never feel the stress of being obligated to disclose, just as with a medical issue. However, it is important to recognize the instances that could make this discussion relevant. An example of this is when the person's condition is starting to cause problems with job performance or communication with colleagues. Should those moments present themselves, I believe that the individual should go straight to the person in charge (either physically or virtually), explain how the difference is affecting his or her performance, and then express the accommodations needed that would allow him or her to thrive.

Obviously, I am extremely comfortable talking about my autism—not everyone is. Whether it is with professors at school, people at work, or peers in social situations, I feel that the extent of disclosure is a personal choice that should bring comfort and peace to the individual who is disclosing. One can share differences and needs without necessarily revealing a diagnosis.

A good example of this occurred in my first summer job. I did not mention my autism initially, but when a co-worker was getting frustrated with my usage of a machine, I went to the trainer and explained how my autism affected my need for alternate instructions on how to operate the press. After a demonstration, I could then run it correctly and independently. In fact, I have been rehired there every summer for the past four years, so I must have performed to their satisfaction. I don't recall informing anyone else at that company that I was on the spectrum. In summary, there is no need to disclose randomly in the workplace until a situation arises where you, others, or the common goal could be affected.

In relation to disclosure in my teaching profession, I have a unique situation because my book, articles, and speaking experience are listed on my resume. Therefore, the fact that I have autism usually comes up in the interview, especially when the interview team asks me about my background, my strengths and weaknesses, or why I chose to become a teacher. My typical heartfelt response is that while I may struggle, I soar past these difficulties in terms of the positives that autism allows me to bring to the table for my students, my colleagues, and even the community. I do believe that a benefit of disclosing early is the ability to receive the proper mentorship and accommodations, but not everyone needs to know—and not every detail needs to be shared.

There are certain rights and accommodations to which people with disabilities are entitled, and it may benefit the reader to explore information on this topic. Here are two resources that explain the Americans with Disabilities Act (ADA): https://www.ada.gov/cguide.htm and https://www.usa.gov/disability-rights. To learn more about education laws and rights, this is another good website: https://www.wrightslaw.com.

So, what is my advice to employers and colleagues to help autistic employees successfully acclimate to the workplace? I have learned a lot about this topic through my various experiences. Some of my opinions are based on what I was given. Other views have resulted from what I lacked or yearned for—but then ultimately received. The amazing difference in my outcome after receiving accommodations proves how vital support truly is.

Below, I have arranged needs and actions into ten related points:

1. *A more extended, intense orientation will likely be needed, with a potential need to start light and increase the workload over time. I believe that the orientation process should not only be for the new employee to become comfortable in their surroundings, but also for the employer to discover the employee's strengths and where the person can best be placed/utilized so that he or she can excel. For example, if the individual is not comfortable around other people, assign them more private tasks and solo projects.*

2. *It is necessary to use clear language in explaining duties, protocols, and expectations; avoid generalities and vagueness. Be specific. For example, do not say, "Do this task any way that you want." Realize that an instruction may need to be repeated in several ways before it is comprehended; visual aids and demonstrations should be considered. Autistic individuals may need more time to process the information explained to them. There may be a lag prior to their response, so do not interrupt this processing delay. They may also want to confirm their understanding of the instructions before or after they are carried out. It is not that we are unable to understand; it is that information must be presented in a way that we CAN understand. For me, this is especially true for understanding workplace behavior and the unwritten rules that everyone else seems to automatically know. Patience is an investment; rushing or intimidating a person can hinder understanding and progress or may cause anxiety.*

3. *Assign the orientee a compassionate mentor who is able to provide uplifting feedback as well as encouraging critiques. This person must understand autism and be willing to coach, guide, develop, and empower the new employee—it should not be someone who is merely "assigned" the duty.*

The mentor should share his or her insights as well as invite the mentee to contribute his or her thoughts, ideas, and experiences. This communication should occur at regularly scheduled huddles where the autistic person's progress is discussed in an open, relaxed environment. The goal should be to encourage growth rather than to focus on flaws. Solving potential problems and relieving the mentee's concerns over confusing situations should always be the primary concern during these check-ins.

4. *Keep in mind that change is more stressful for people on the autism spectrum than for neurotypical people. It also takes a heavier toll on them, even if it is positive stress. Therefore, consider their desire to maintain their routines, and if there should be an anticipated deviation from their workplace plan, inform them immediately to help them prepare. Even if the change is good, any change is unsettling. Be ready to assist their need for adjustment to unanticipated occurrences.*

5. *Employers and coworkers should try their best to respond to emails in a timely fashion, especially regarding pressing issues. For me, every hour without a reply increases my anxiety to a greater degree.*

6. *Consider the sensory environment. This includes the emotional burden of accumulated stress. Adjustments may be needed to maximize the persons' tolerance — and therefore increase their workplace productivity. Examples include allowing the utilization of ear plugs or headphones to help block out noise, strategic placement of their work areas away from sensory distractions, or encouragement of movement or brief breaks necessary to refocus the mind and relieve overload. These and*

other simple accommodations can help the person regain equilibrium for effective functioning.

7. *Eye contact may be uncomfortable for a person on the spectrum. For me, directly looking in someone's eyes may cause distress from intensifying input such as emotion and distraction. I can concentrate and listen better without it. Please know that lack of eye contact from someone on the spectrum does not indicate a lack of respect or focus.*

8. *Don't be quick to judge! This can be especially applicable in a job interview situation. The candidate is in an unfamiliar room in a foreign environment with strangers who hold an intimidating power, not to mention the anticipated stress of attempting proper communication in order to express abilities and obtain a position. Therefore, the poorest impression is being formed under circumstances when a good impression is most important. Often, the individual's capabilities will not be evident in only one interview when so much pressure is on them. We tend to be more socially appropriate and relaxed as we become acclimated to the people and environment.*

9. *Be open to our ideas and opinions, regardless of our age or experience. Include us; we bring unique perspectives that may not be considered otherwise. We add value; we are not "slow" or "stupid."*

10. *Managers should take it upon themselves to check in often with the new employee regarding successes and setbacks. Address concerns early and continuously to promote growth and cohesiveness with others.*

These types of supportive measures need to be available for autistic people in every level of the workforce, from after-school jobs to established careers. Actually, they are needed for people with any other kind of difference, as well. Accommodations need to be offered, and employers need to be equipped with the knowledge, skills, and compassion to pass along this mindset from the top down. The investment of time and transitioning from the start will make all the difference.

Communication is also very important to the success of individuals. We, as human beings, ALL have shortcomings. So, when it comes to critiques, suggestions, and corrections, it is important that they be conveyed in a way that does not condemn the individual, but brings his or her attention to what he or she needs to work on in order to thrive. Employers should make an effort to communicate whether or not expectations are being met. That would eliminate unfounded anxiety about possible termination. I possessed these fears constantly because of past situations that heightened my insecurities. Thankfully, reassurance by understanding mentors provided me a more realistic perspective.

The ultimate goal should always be to work together as a team to lift one another up for the betterment of the company/ organization, as well as the individuals that compose it. We all have our own gifts, abilities, and weaknesses that make each one of us uniquely qualified to have a tremendous impact on the world. Employers should view people with autism and other differences as assets to their workplaces.

Lessons I learned:

- All work experience is valuable.

- Autistic employees can make unique, positive contributions.

- Mentorship is key to job acclimation. The mentor should be someone who understands and is willing to teach, guide, and help interpret "unwritten rules," protocols, and dilemmas.

- Advocate for accommodations for sensory, learning, and performance needs.

- Validate understanding.

- It should not be assumed that all negative occurrences are the autistic person's fault. (Let us not forget that neurotypicals aren't perfect either.)

- Maintain a work-life balance.

Our Concluding Thoughts:

As I reflect on our book title, I feel compelled to clarify our intent. At first glance, it might appear that we presume David's outcome is a miracle—that somehow his autism has been "fixed." But that is not the case. By now, it is probably evident that "Expect a Miracle" refers to the stained-glass piece (still displayed in our home) which motivated us daily to forge ahead with determination, faith, and a positive attitude. The title also refers to the many miracles occurring in *everyone's* lives, if they choose to see them as such. It refers to the skilled interventions and creativity of countless dedicated providers and educators who enable progress in clients and students. It refers to fateful events and opportunities. And it softly speaks volumes regarding the role of hope in tenacity.

David still has autism, and he always will. We do not view it as a disability or an undesirable circumstance. The characteristics of autism are what make David, David! Would I reduce challenges and hardships for him if I could? Of course! That's what this book and our lives have been about—learning to adjust and thrive. It's no different than any parent would do for any of their children, autistic or not. The challenges are simply unique to each person, and no one is without them.

In fact, David's autism has been a blessing to our family. David has humbled us with his attitude, accomplishments, and spirit. When I come across a child in the midst of a tantrum, I now have a different perspective rather than disapproval. When I think of the thousands of incredible people and experiences we would have missed had David been "typical," I can't imagine the loss of these riches. And we have learned so much about human nature and what truly is most important in life. Remember the poem about a redirected journey in Chapter One? "Holland" has indeed been an exhilarating and wonderful land of discovery!

I hope that what you got out of this book is more than a story about a young man with challenges. This book is not just for people with disabilities, but for those going through all kinds of hardships. I am a man who is going through the ups and downs of life. My autism brings about many struggles that often cause me great discomfort, anxiety, and sometimes even anger. I do not wake up each morning expecting that my life is going to be happy every day—it is not. But my life is blessed. My life is full of love and purpose. And my life is overflowing with hope. I no longer feel that I am a stranger in my own society. I like to think that I have achieved a balance between immersing myself in the "typical" world, while still recognizing my need to refresh with my own unique interests.

Whenever I struggle with something, I now try to see it as another opportunity to lift up the spirits of others who may be going through exactly what I'm dealing with—as well as a chance to strengthen my own coping, compassion, sympathy, and empathy. I never give up; I continue to have faith that everything happens for a reason.

When someone does me a kindness, my joy and fulfillment go beyond the superficial words or actions. My happiness comes from recognizing the person's sentiments and intentions behind the deed. I have FINALLY achieved making connections with these emotions that I never recognized were in existence years ago. I am so thankful to have gained the ability to connect with people on a deeper level.

Whoever is reading this book, know that you are loved and that you have purpose. There is a difference between "ability" and "purpose." Remember that. Whatever you are going through in life, you do not have to go through it alone. Whether I end up working as a teacher, a priest, a public speaker, or a career involving a marriage of all my passions, I now know that I don't just have a happy life...I lead a fulfilled life. I thank you all from the bottom of my heart for taking the time to read our book—and for seeing who I really am. It would be the greatest honor if you were able to take any kind of hope from our story.

In closing: ***Embrace a difference...and MAKE a difference.***

Our lives' journeys have revealed one recurring lesson learned:

- HOPE AND FAITH MUST NOT BE UNDERRATED

  - Do your research

  - Formulate your team

  - Derive strength, inspiration, and motivation from every possible source

  - Prepare and transition

  - Seek support and advocacy

  - Try-adjust-retry

Do all you can possibly do to achieve your goals, and then, as filtered sunlight through stained glass encouraged,

"Expect a Miracle."

Works Cited

American Psychiatric Association (APA). *Diagnostic and Statistical Manual of Mental Disorders, Fifth Edition.* Arlington: APA, 2013. Print.

---. *Diagnostic and Statistical Manual of Mental Disorders, Fourth Edition.* Washington, DC: APA, 1994. Print.

Attwood, Tony. *Asperger's Syndrome: A Guide for Parents and Professionals.* London and Philadelphia: Kingsley, 1998. Print

Bolick, Teresa. *Asperger Syndrome and Adolescence: Helping Preteens and Teens Get Ready for the Real World. 2nd ed.* Gloucester: Fair Winds, 2004. Print.

Faherty, Catherine. *Asperger's...What Does It Mean to Me?* Arlington: Future Horizons, 2006. Print.

Gray, Carol. "Appendix A. The Social Story Guide: The Social Story Ratio and General Guidelines." *Social Stories and Comic Strip Conversations: Unique Methods to Improve Social Understanding. A Collection of Materials to Accompany Social Stories UnLimited™ Presentations and Workshops.* Arlington: Future Horizons, 1997: 8. Print.

---. "A Close Look at Directive Sentences" (reprinted from THE MORNING NEWS, Jenison Public Schools, Summer 1995: 4-7). *Social Stories and Comic Strip Conversations: Unique Methods to Improve Social Understanding. A Collection of Materials to Accompany*

Social Stories UnLimited™ Presentations and Workshops. **Arlington: Future Horizons, 1997: 4-7. Print.**

– – –. *Social Stories and Comic Strip Conversations: Unique Methods to Improve Social Understanding.* **Arlington: Future Horizons, 1998. Video.**

Jackson, Luke. *Freaks, Geeks and Asperger Syndrome: A User Guide to Adolescence. 2002.* **Reprint, London and Philadelphia: Kingsley, 2006. Print.**

Kingsley, Emily Perl. "Welcome to Holland." Message to Sandy Petrovic. 16 Feb. 2013. E-mail.

Klin, Ami, and Fred R. Volkmar. *Asperger Syndrome: Treatment and Intervention: Some Guidelines for Parents.* **Pittsburgh: Learning Disabilities Assn., March 1996: 1-11. Print.**

McAfee, Jeanette. *Navigating the Social World: A Curriculum for Individuals with Asperger's Syndrome, High Functioning Autism and Related Disorders.* **Arlington: Future Horizons, 2002. Print.**

Petrovic, David. "Accepting Help Can Be Hard When You Have Autism, But So Important." *Autism Parenting Magazine,* **no. 81, Nov. 2018, pp. 15-16, www.autismparentingmagazine.com/issue-81-building-self-esteem-kids-with-autism/**

– – –. **"Conquering College."** *The OARacle, Newsletter of the Organization for Autism Research,* **28 Aug. 2018, www.researchautism.org/conquering-college/**

Winner, Michelle Garcia, and Pamela Crooke. *Socially Curious and Curiously Social: A Social Thinking Guidebook for Bright Teens and Young Adults.* **2009. San Jose: Think Social and Great Barrington: North River, 2011. Print.**

Made in the USA
Monee, IL
23 March 2021